OTHER A TO Z GU
THE SCARECROW

The A to Z of the Druzes

Samy Swayd

The A to Z Guide Series, No. 53

THE SCARECROW PRESS, INC.
Lanham • Toronto • Plymouth, UK
2009

Published by Scarecrow Press, Inc.
A wholly owned subsidiary of
The Rowman & Littlefield Publishing Group, Inc.
4501 Forbes Boulevard, Suite 200, Lanham, Maryland 20706
http://www.scarecrowpress.com

Estover Road, Plymouth PL6 7PY, United Kingdom

British Library Cataloguing in Publication Information Available

Library of Congress Cataloging-in-Publication Data

The hardback version of this book was cataloged by the Library of Congress as
follows:

Swayd, Samy S.
  Historical dictionary of the Druzes / Samy Swayd.
    p. cm.— (Historical dictionaries of people and cultures ; no. 3)
  Includes bibliographical references.
1. Druzes—History—Dictionaries. I. Title. II. Series.
BL1695.S93 2006
297.8'5'09—dc22   2005022963

ISBN 978-0-8108-6836-6 (pbk. : alk. paper)
ISBN 978-0-8108-7002-4 (ebook)

To
those awakened
by their humanity,
conscience;

and to
my parents and friends,
whose koans keep me awake.

Contents

Editor's Foreword

The Druzes are certainly one of the smallest groups that will appear in this series, only numbering about a million. Unlike most other groups, they are not concentrated in a given area but dispersed in rather small clusters among Lebanon, Syria, Israel, Jordan, and a continually growing diaspora. Yet they regard themselves—and are regarded by others—as a separate and rather unique community. This is due to their history and their traditions, their culture, and their religion. How they have managed to survive this long as a community is already an amazing story in its own right, showing not only uncommon fortitude but also the political sense to bend in the right direction more often than not and cooperate with the powers that be, which sometimes even involves siding with rivals. But this is just one of the mysteries. Others relate to their social organization and their religion, which is more often misconstrued—accidentally or intentionally—than correctly understood, and perhaps the Druzes share some of the blame for this since they have (often for good reason) tended to be more secretive than most.

So this *Historical Dictionary of the Druzes* has a lot of ground to cover. It must fill us in on a period of more than two millennia, from roots in Judaism, Christianity, and Islam to the sect's actual foundation in the 11th century and its subsequent history up to the present day. It has to supplement the rather sparse information about its political, social, and economic organization to say nothing of the religion. An added task is to distinguish between members of the community since there are vast differences between the initiated and uninitiated or from one important family to another. Many significant figures also have entries, including prophets and sages, sultans and caliphs, presidents and ministers, businessmen and writers. It also has something interesting to say about the role of women. The rather complex situation is first summed up in the introduction and then presented in greater detail in several hundred dictionary entries. The chronology traces a long and complicated trajectory, while an appendix provides the genealogy of the major dynasties. The bibliography is particularly important not because it is large (far from it) but because it is so hard to find sufficient reading matter.

There are not many "specialists" on the Druzes and Druzism; indeed, there are hardly any. Samy Swayd was born and raised in Piki'in/Buqai'a in Galilee, Israel. After a business career as administrator in the city of Haifa, he pursued his university education to the level of master's of art at the University of Washington, Seattle. He then received a Ph.D. in Islamic studies from the University of California, Los Angeles. His interest in the subject is manifest, having written and presented a large number of articles and conference papers on Druzism as well as an annotated bibliography on the Druzes and especially having established the Institute of Druze Studies, of which he is the acting director. Swayd is also the founder and editor of the *Journal of Druze Studies*, an occasional scholarly publication. But this historical dictionary is in many ways his biggest contribution since it provides readers with a broader view than has been available so far arranged in a manner that is particularly easy to access for outsiders and insiders, for the initiated and the uninitiated, and for serious students and those who are simply curious.

Jon Woronoff
Series Editor

Preface

Many dictionaries, encyclopedias, and other reference works still contain erroneous information in their entries on the Druzes. Inaccurate statements made by scholars, diplomats, travelers, and other observers in the past few centuries continue to be cited today by authors and public speakers. Much of this false information was likely propagated by both Druzes (for many of them are unfamiliar with their religious doctrine) and outside observers (for some of them have failed to verify and authenticate their sources).

Despite the substantial growth in publications in recent years on religious minorities around the world, the Druzes are still one of the most misunderstood communities in the Middle East and abroad. Thus, there remains much to be learned about the historical, political, religious, and cultural backgrounds of the Druzes both in the Middle East and in the diaspora. This reference work is only the first step in the right direction.

The objective of the dictionary is to provide the general reader and the specialist alike with concise, informative entries. The dictionary includes selected entries on a number of major families and a variety of individuals (writers, artists, diplomats, and leaders) who have contributed to Druze communities and to society in general. Though some other individuals and families may be equally important, they were not included as independent entries and are instead cross-referenced to provide some information about them. When exact dates are unavailable, approximated periods are indicated to distinguish "contemporary" from a particular "past century."

While this dictionary cannot claim to be comprehensive, the majority of the entries are not found in dictionaries and encyclopedias on the Middle East or Islamic and religious studies. The volume is also complemented with a chronology and a bibliography as well as several maps and genealogical tables.

Acknowledgments

I am very grateful to the Centers for Near Eastern Studies and European and Euroasian Studies of the University of California, Los Angeles (UCLA), and their directors Leonard Binder and Ivan T. Berend, respectively. The funding provided by the two centers made it possible for me to lead a seminar at UCLA on Muslim/Middle Eastern diasporas in Europe and North America during the spring of 2004. My regular presence at UCLA has enabled me to spend the necessary time in the library system there and to improve many of the entries in this dictionary.

I am also grateful to the Department of Religious Studies, San Diego State University (SDSU); its chair Linda Holler; and faculty and staff members for providing me with their ongoing support and a friendly academic atmosphere.

Many colleagues and friends have contributed to making this book possible. I am most grateful for the articles, books, citations, support, and advice provided during the past several years by Jere Bacharach, Irene A. Bierman, Anwar Dabbour, Dany Doueiri, Jonathan Friedlander, Alice and Jerry Gess, Iskandar Mansour, Isma'il Poonawala, Georges Sabagh, Yona Sabar, Fouad Sleem, Irving Alan Sparks, and Hossein Ziai. Many other unnamed individuals have provided me with access to their library collections and rich insights.

Special thanks are also due to Heidi Rutz, Hussam Timani, and Nabil Zeitoun; whenever these three invaluable friends came across an article or a book that could be of use for this dictionary or for my work on the Druzes in general, they enthusiastically informed me of their find. David Hirsch of the Charles Young Research Library at UCLA was most helpful in promptly providing the requested citations and alerting me to what and where additional material could be located. Appreciation is also due to J. Chase Langford of the UCLA Department of Geography for producing the maps.

The dedicated assistance in data entry and other research tasks of Anika Farber during the summer of 2003 is most appreciated. I would also like to thank Elisa Quinn Hedrick for her diligent attention to detail in entering the changes made on the first draft, for editing the subsequent revisions, and for her overall patience and assistance in handling research tasks and text inconsistencies. Her dedication and interest in the different aspects of this project have indeed contributed greatly to its completion.

Jon Woronoff, the editor of the Historical Dictionaries of People and Cultures series, is most appreciated for his thoughtful suggestions and insightful recommendations. Without his superb patience and professionalism, this book would have not been possible.

Finally, it goes without saying, however, that I remain responsible for all shortcomings in this work. I am also responsible for excluding potentially important entries that lacked or that were still awaiting verification at the time the manuscript was completed.

Note on Translation and Transliteration

All translations of terms, titles, and quotations in this work are approximate. The Anglicized form for large cities and towns is used throughout the book. Examples include Amman, Beirut, Cairo, Damascus, and Jerusalem instead of 'Amman, Bayrut, al-Qahirah, Dimashq, and al-Quds or Yerushalayim, respectively.

Except for the *hamza* (') and *'ayn* ('), diacritical marks for words in Arabic, Hebrew, Persian, and Ottoman Turkish are not affixed in this edition. Similarly, for the sake of simplicity, the prepositions and definite articles "li al-," "bi al-," "fi al-," and "wa al-" are rendered "lil-," "bil-," "fil-," and "wal-," as in the examples "lil-jabal," "bil-jabal," "fil-jabal," and "wal-jabal," respectively. Although some writers and readers may prefer spellings such as ad-Duruz, aj-jabal, ar-ra'is, and so on, in this work the use of al-Duruz, al-Jabal, al-Ra'is, and so on, is consistent. Terms containing the definite article "al-" are listed under the main expression and not under the letter "A"; thus, al-Duruz will be listed under "D," al-Jabal under "J," and al-Ra'is under "R."

Moreover, a single spelling of names and places is consistently used. For example, the name Jumblat, Joumblat, Joumblatt, or Junblatt and the place Hauran, Huran, or Houran are rendered Junblat and Hawran, respectively, throughout the book. Exceptions occur, however, when these names and places appear in the titles of bibliographic entries in European languages. In such cases, the authors' preferences are respected and preserved.

Acronyms and Abbreviations

ADF	American Druze Foundation
ADS	American Druze Society
ADY	American Druze Youth
AH	After Hijra, Migration of Muhammad from Mecca to Medina in 622 C.E.
AUB	American University of Beirut
B.C.E.	Before the Common Era
BDS	British Druze Society
C.E.	Common Era
COCA	Committee on Charitable Affairs
CORA	Committee on Religious Affairs (United States)
CORE	Committee on Research and Education
DFSW	Druze Foundation for Social Welfare (Lebanon)
DOCO	Druze Orphans and Charitable Organization (United States)
DRI	Druze Research Institute (Israel)
ICP	Israeli Communist Party
IDF	Israeli Defense Forces
IDS	Institute of Druze Studies (United States)
ITF	'Irfan Tawhid Foundation (Lebanon)
JDS	*Journal of Druze Studies* (United States)
LF	Lebanese Forces
LMD	*Lajnat al-Mubadarah al-Durziya* (Druze Initiative Committee)
LNM	Lebanese National Movement
LPP	Lebanese Phalanges Party
MEA	Middle East Airlines
PLO	Palestine Liberation Organization
PSP	Progressive Socialist Party (Lebanon)

UN	United Nations
U.S.	United States
YDP	Young Druze Professionals (Lebanon and diaspora)

Maps

Map 1. Druze Communities in the Middle East

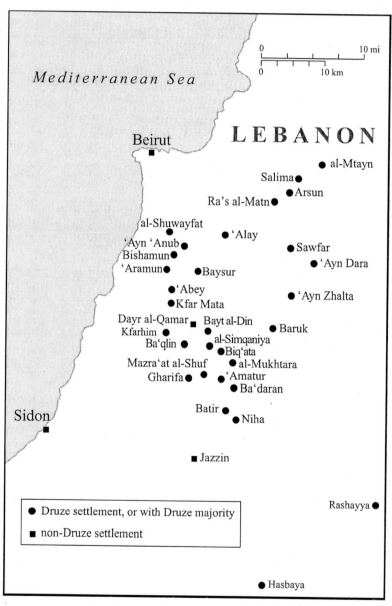

Map 2. Druze Towns and Villages in Lebanon

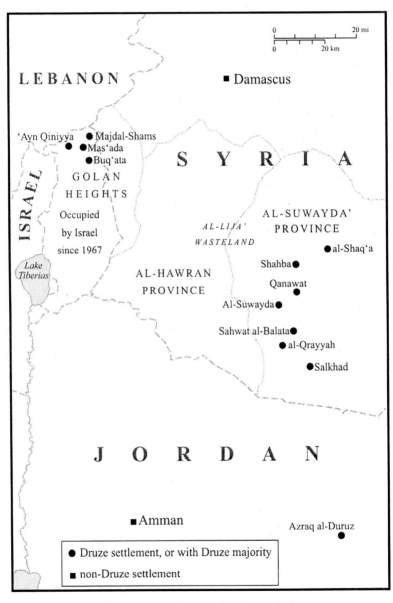

LEBANON

Damascus

'Ayn Qiniyya ● Majdal-Shams
● ●Mas'ada
●Buq'ata
GOLAN
HEIGHTS

SYRIA

Occupied
by Israel
since 1967

*AL-LIJA'
WASTELAND*

AL-SUWAYDA'
PROVINCE

● al-Shaq'a

ISRAEL

*Lake
Tiberias*

AL-HAWRAN
PROVINCE

Shahba●

Qanawat●

Al-Suwayda●

Sahwat al-Balata●

● al-Qrayyah

●Salkhad

JORDAN

■Amman

Azraq al-Duruz
●

● Druze settlement, or with Druze majority
■ non-Druze settlement

0   20 mi
0   20 km

Map 3.   Druze Towns and Villages in Syria

xxi

Map 4. Druze Towns and Villages in Israel

Chronology

2000–300 B.C.E.   The patriarchs (Abraham, Isaac, and Jacob) and the subsequent biblical prophets, some of whom are central in Druze cosmology and eschatology.

0–33   Druze ancestors are Christianized (Jesus and some of his disciples are prominent in Druze teachings).

610–632   Druze ancestors are Islamized; influential figures in Druze spirituality include Prophet Muhammad's companions Salman al-Farisi, al-Muqdad Ibn al-Aswad, and 'Ammar Ibn Yasir.

634   Battle of Ajnadayn between Muslims and Byzantines. The forefather of the Arslani-Tanukhis, 'Awn Ibn al-Mundhir Ibn al-Nu'man, dies in battle.

635   Khalid Ibn al-Walid conquers Damascus. The Arslani Mas'ud Ibn 'Awn Ibn al-Mundhir joins this Islamic army.

758   Tanukhi clans settle in Ma'arat al-Nu'man, northern Syria.

759   The 'Abbasi caliph al-Mansur sends Tanukhi families from Ma'arat al-Nu'man to Beirut to guard against the Byzantines.

763   Additional Tanukhi clans settle in Mount Lebanon.

781   Beginning of the Qaysi-Yamani conflict.

820   Spread of the Tanukhi clans in Lebanon.

831   Mas'ud Ibn Arslan Ibn Malik joins the 'Abbasi caliph al-Ma'mun in his military campaign to Egypt.

909 'Ubayd Allah founds the Fatimi caliphate in North Africa.

909–1171 Fatimi rule.

969 The Fatimi caliph Al-Mu'iz conquers Egypt and begins building Cairo and, a year later, al-Azhar.

996–1021 Reign of al-Hakim bi-Amr Allah.

996 The preparation phase of the *Tawhid Call* (*Da'wat Al-Tawhid*, hereafter, Druzism) begins secretively.

1005 Al-Hakim builds the House of Wisdom (*Dar al-Hikma*).

1015 Al-Darazi comes to Cairo.

1016 **December**: Hamza Ibn 'Ali meets missionaries in Cairo.

1017 **May**: Druzism is announced, and open propagation begins. Hamza is declared imam by al-Hakim.

1018 **May**: Hamza suspends preaching activities.

1019 **May**: Hamza and associates are attacked at the Ridan Mosque. Darazi is either killed or executed. Preaching is resumed.

1021 Al-Hakim disappears. Hamza and associates retreat to an undisclosed location, leaving Baha' al-Din as the spiritual leader.

1021–1026 Persecution of Druzes by the Fatimi regime.

1026 Propagation of Druzism is resumed by Baha' al-Din.

1027 Baha' al-Din appoints Sukayn as a missionary for Syria.

1029 Salih Ibn Mirdas is defeated by Druzes.

1034 Sukayn apostatizes; attempts to dissuade him fail.

1037 Prince Mi'dad attacks and puts an end to Sukayn's followers. Sukayn himself escapes and is later killed.

1043 Closing of Druzism; Baha' al-Din leaves Cairo.

1117 Prince Ma'n defeats crusaders near Aleppo.

1120 Ma'nis settle in Mount Lebanon.

1151   Prince Buhtur defeats crusaders in Ra's al-Tinah.

1152   Zahr al-Dawlah forces crusaders out of Beirut. The Mamluk sultan Nur al-Din grants the Tanukhis more villages.

1155   Sharaf al-Dawlah defeats crusaders in al-Damur.

1187   Saladin defeats crusaders in the battle of Hittin.

1200   The Shihabis arrive in Lebanon.

1240   Zayn al-Din defeats the Tatars in the battle of Baysan.

1257   The Mamluks give Wadi al-Taym to Sa'd al-Din.

1260   Battle of 'Ayn Jalut between the Mamluks and the Tatars. Zayn al-Din participates on behalf of the Mamluks.

1278   The Tanukhis defeat the Mamluks in Kisrawan.

1284   Druzes are defeated by crusaders in Wadi al-Taym.

1301   The crusaders kill the Tanukhi prince Fakhr al-Din and take his brother, Shams al-Din, as prisoner.

1305   Ibn Taimiyya issues a fatwa against the Druzes.

1384   Druzes win the battle of al-Na'mah against crusaders.

1386   Emir Yahya al-Tanukhi defeats crusaders outside Beirut.

1516–1918   Ottoman rule in Greater Syria.

1516–1697   Ma'ni rule.

1516   Ottomans defeat the Mamluks in Marj Dabiq and appoint Fakhr al-Din al-Ma'ni I as emir of Mount Lebanon.

1544   Assassination of Fakhr al-Din I; his son, Qurqumaz, takes over the Ma'ni principality.

1584   Emir Qurqumaz is poisoned by the Ottomans. Sayf al-Din al-Tanukhi is the acting prince of Mount Lebanon.

1588   Ottomans defeat Druzes in 'Ayn Sufer.

1590   Fakhr al-Din al-Ma'ni II is prince of Mount Lebanon.

1598   Fakhr al-Din defeats Yusef Pasha in Nahr al-Kalb.

1603   Fakhr al-Din takes control of Banyas, 'Ajlun, and Safad.

1605   Fakhr al-Din extends his influence to northern Lebanon.

1607   A treaty between 'Ali Junblat and Fakhr al-Din. 'Ali Junblat's forces are defeated by the Ottomans.

1608   Fakhr al-Din signs a treaty with the prince of Tuscany.

1613   Fakhr al-Din is attacked by Hafiz Pasha, governor of Damascus, and seeks refuge in Italy.

1617   Fakhr al-Din moves to Crete.

1618   Fakhr al-Din returns to Mount Lebanon.

1623   Fakhr al-Din defeats Mustafa Pasha in 'Anjar.

1628   Fakhr al-Din incorporates Palestine and East Jordan.

1633   Kojuk Pasha appoints 'Ali 'Alam al-Din, leader of the Yamanis, as prince of the Shuf Mountain.

1634   Ahmad Pasha attacks the Druzes. Prince 'Ali, son of Fakhr al-Din, is killed. Fakhr al-Din takes refuge in the mountain caves.

1635   Fakhr al-Din is captured with his three sons and executed in Istanbul.

1654   Emir Melhim defeats the Ottoman governor Bashir Pasha.

1665   Ahmad al-Ma'ni defeats 'Alam al-Din near Beirut.

1685   'Alam al-Din settles in Hawran, Syria.

1697   Ahmad al-Ma'ni dies, and the Ma'ni rule ends. Lebanese notables meet in Sumqaniyya and choose Bashir Shihabi as heir.

1697–1842   The Shihabis rule Lebanon.

1711   The battle of 'Ayn Dara between Yamani and Qaysi Druzes. The Yamanis are defeated and resettle in Hawran.

1795 Bashir Shihabi massacres Nakadi shaykhs in Bayt al-Din.

1810 Bashir Junblat defeats Governor Yusef Pasha.

1811 Persecution of Druzes in North Syria. Bashir Junblat invites Druzes to settle in the Shuf Mountain.

1820s Druze and Maronite peasant revolts.

1825 Bashir Shihabi II defeats Bashir Junblat in Sumqaniyya. Junblat escapes to Damascus and is later executed in Acre.

1831–1840 Egyptian occupation of Syria.

1832 Ibrahim Pasha takes Acre, Damascus, and Aleppo. Druzes are persecuted, and some Junblati, 'Imadi, and Nakadi houses are destroyed.

1837 Druzes in Hawran rebel against Ibrahim Pasha.

1839 Emir Bashir incites Maronites against Druzes.

1840 The Ottoman sultan exiles Emir Bashir to Crete and appoints Bashir III as emir of the Mountain.

1840s Druze-Maronite peasant revolt. Sectarian conflict begins.

1841 Emir Bashir III conspires against the Druze leaders.

1842 The Ottoman sultan removes Emir Bashir III, ends the Shihabi rule, and appoints Umar Pasha as governor.

1843 Europeans and Ottomans cooperate to establish governates on sectarian basis with Haidar Abi al-Lam' as the Christian governor and Ahmad Arslan as the Druze governor.

1845 Spread of the sectarian conflict in Greater Syria.

1850s Druze-Maronite peasant revolts.

1858 Rebellion of peasants led by Tanyus Shahin in Kisrawan.

1860 Fighting erupts in Mount Lebanon between Druzes and Maronites and in Damascus between Christians and Muslims. French forces arrive in Beirut.

1861 The French leave Lebanon. The *Mutassarrifiyya* as a new system of government is announced for Mount Lebanon.

1864–1914 The *Mutassarrifiyya* rule in Mount Lebanon.

1890 The *Shaykh al-Islam* in Istanbul, Ahmad Lutfi, recognizes the Druze legal system and appoints Druze judges (*qadis*).

1908 Muhammad Arslan represents Druzes in Istanbul. First Druze organization in the United States, al-Bakourat al-Durziyya, is established in Seattle, Washington.

1918 Druzes enter Damascus with the forces of King Faisal. French forces then occupy Aleppo and Damascus and divide Greater Syria into two separate states.

1920–1943 French Mandate in Syria and Lebanon.

1921 Establishment of an administratively independent state in the Druze Mountain. Fouad Junblat, father of Kamal Junblat, is assassinated. His wife, Sitt Nazirah, leads the community.

1922 A dispute erupts between Druzes and the French forces over the arrest of one Sunni rebel, Adham Khanjar, who had sought protection by Sultan al-Atrash.

1925–1927 The Great Revolt against the French occupation. Some Druzes settle in Jordan.

1928 Shaykh Tarif Muhammad Tarif dies after 40 years as the spiritual leader of Palestinian Druzes.

1940 A delegation of Syrian Druzes mediates between Druzes and Muslims in Palestine.

1942 France reunites Jabal al-Druze to the rest of Syria.

1943 Independence of Lebanon. Kamal Junblat is elected to Parliament.

1946 Independence of Syria. First convention of the American Druze Society (ADS).

1948 Independence of Israel. Druze villages in Galilee and Carmel Mountain become part of Israel.

1949 Kamal Junblat establishes the Progressive Socialist Party.

1958 Tension in Lebanon; Kamal Junblat is part of the opposition. The United States intervenes by sending 15,000 Marines.

1960 The Druze court system is established in Lebanon; first Druze women's club is opened in 'Isfiyya, Israel.

1962 The Druze court system is established in Israel and is approved by the Israeli Parliament, the Knesset.

1967 **June**: Six-Day War between Israel and the Arabs; Israel captures the Golan Heights from Syria. Golani Druzes come (and remain) under Israeli occupation.

1973 **October**: Yom Kippur War between Israel and its neighbors, Egypt and Syria.

1975 Fighting erupts in Beirut and marks the beginning of the Civil War of 1975–1990.

1976 **May**: Syrian forces enter Lebanon.

1977 **March**: Kamal Junblat is assassinated.

1978 **March**: Israeli forces invade southern Lebanon.

1980 Establishment of the Iman Hospital in 'Alay.

1981 **December**: Israel annexes the Golan Heights.

1982 Sultan al-Atrash dies. Israel invades Lebanon and reaches Beirut and the Shuf.

1983 Confrontation between the Lebanese forces and the Progressive Socialist Party leading to the War of the Mountain.

1984 Druzes and Shi'is join forces and launch an attack against the Lebanese army in West Beirut. Shaykh Halim Taqi al-Din, head of the Druze courts in Lebanon, is assassinated in his home.

1985 Israel withdraws its forces from most of Lebanon.

1987 Confrontation between Amal and the Progressive Socialist Party in West Beirut.

1989   The Ta'if Accords between Lebanese deputies.

1991   Lebanese Shaykh al-'Aql Muhammad Abu Shaqra dies; Shaykh Bahjat Ghayth replaces him.

1992   Secret talks between Syria and Israel in regard to the return of the Golan Heights to Syria in exchange for peace.

1993   Shaykh Amin Tarif, spiritual leader of the Israeli Druzes since 1928, dies. Junblati and Arslani leaders meet at Khaldeh.

1994   The Lebanese army enters Mount Lebanon. Day of Reconciliation in the Shuf attended by Ilyas Hrawi, president of Lebanon. Walid Junblat visits the pope.

1995   Sectarian reconciliation between Mazra'at al-Shuf and Bayqun in Mukhtara.

1996   Walid Junblat visits the Arslanis to discuss communal unity.

1997   Junblat meets Shaykh al-'Aql Ghayth after a lengthy period to reinforce communal unity.

1999   **June**: The first international academic conference on the Druzes is convened at the University of California, Los Angeles (UCLA).

2000   Clashes erupt in Suwayda between Druzes and Sunnis.

2001   A Druze convention held in Amman, Jordan, brings together Lebanese, Israeli, Syrian, and Jordanian Druzes.

2003   Lebanon's new cabinet is formed with three Druze members: Ghazi 'Aridi as minister of culture, Talal Arslan as minister of state, and Marwan Hamadi as minister of economy and trade. Two Knesset Druze members are elected in Israel: Ayyub Karra and Mjaleh Wahbeh.

2004   **June–July**: The 58th Annual Convention of the American Druze Society takes place in San Diego, California. **1 October**: Assassination attempt on Marwan Hamadi, former Lebanese minister of economy and trade.

Introduction

As the political telescope continues to focus on the Middle East, more attention must be given to the ethnic and religious diversity of this region. One of the most intriguing minority groups in the Middle East is now a thousand years old. It emerged in the city of Cairo; spread to what is today Lebanon, Syria, and Israel; and subsequently became known by outsiders as *Druze* (in Arabic, *Duruz*, meaning *Druzes*).

Druzes have often been misunderstood by outsiders because of their esoteric religious doctrine, the secretive nature that such a doctrine has instilled in them, and the variety of perspectives or divisions prevalent among members of the community. As a result, misconceptions have taken root, multiplied, and flourished with time.

Druzes themselves, on the other hand, have not countered misconceptions about their community; rather, they have developed or reinforced attitudes of isolationism, secrecy, and indifference. This is perhaps due to the fact that only a select few among them are initiated into the Druze religious doctrine. More important, these initiated members are often unwilling to comment on the authenticity of the Druze manuscripts and later commentaries simply because most of them are not well versed with such clandestine matters. Those who are knowledgeable, however, feel that true faith resides in the hearts of individual seekers and not in the written word. Thus, spirituality and spiritual readiness comes from within.

Unlike the early churchmen of Christianity, who were the ones to study the Bible and transmit its meaning to congregations, Druze sages have studied their scriptures and kept the spiritual knowledge to themselves; insights were shared only with one's spiritual equals. In the eyes of these sages, not all people are prepared to absorb spirituality.

Writers who have observed the Druzes closely were able to describe only the Druze manners, derive the ethical code of the community, and at times contrast it with other religious traditions. Authors who were able to access some of the Druze manuscripts were often travelers, journalists, or historians, not scholars of religion. Therefore, they read—and in most cases only heard about—such manuscripts without considering the spiritual teachings and esoteric dimensions of the Druze doctrine. In the process, many of these observers have contributed to further misunderstanding.

THE NAME "DRUZE"

Let us begin with the name of this Middle Eastern religious minority. The title *Druze*, plural *Druzes*, was given to the community, once again, by outsiders because of confusion with the name of one of the early secondary missionaries known as al-Darazi (hereafter Darazi). Outsiders perceived Darazi as the founder and leader of the new movement, and, therefore, his followers became Druzes (*Duruz*) without a close look at the place and rank of Darazi among the leading members of the movement. Darazi, allegedly of Persian or Turkish origin, came to Cairo in the year 1015 (or possibly in 1017) and joined the ranks of the new movement. He was perhaps overambitious and succeeded in using the movement for expanding his sphere of influence in Cairo and the Fatimi state in general. Nevertheless, Darazi is considered by Druzes and the Druze manuscripts to be "the first [Druze] apostate," "the deviate," and "the great heretic." The word "Darazi" remains a contemporary epithet and, when used by Druzes, implies that someone is a heretic.

Many writers believe that the title "Druze" has survived because of those who sought to defame the community by linking it with Darazi's heretical teachings. Despite the fact that the title "Druze" is, therefore, a misnomer, Druzes and non-Druzes have grudgingly accepted its usage over time. It is important to note, however, that although many books use the title "Druze" or "Druzes," such terms do *not* occur in the authentic Druze manuscripts and are still rejected or avoided by all learned members of the community.

The Druzes often refer to themselves instead as "Unitarians" (*Muwwahhidun*). This second title is found in almost all Druze manuscripts, later commentaries, and contemporary writings. In some of these sources, the title *Ahl al-Tawhid* (People of Tawhid) is also prominent.

The word *Muwwahhidun* is derived from *Tawhid*, which has frequently been translated as "strict unitarianism."

A third name, "Sons of Mercy" or "Sons of Beneficence" (*Banu Ma'ruf*), has been used in recent centuries by both Druzes and non-Druzes. Several writers have argued that Druzes are known by this name because of their "reputation for returning favors" and "enthusiastic assistance to others." In addition, the word *Ma'ruf* is also derived from the Arabic words *'arafa* (to know), *ma'rifa* (knowledge), and *'irfan* (esoteric knowledge, *gnosis*). As a result, Druzes are often mentioned in the manuscripts as *A'raf* (those who possess knowledge, the knowing), and their faith is referred to as *madhhab 'irfani* (a gnostic school).

DRUZE SOCIETY

There are approximately one million Druzes in the world today, the majority of them living in four Middle Eastern countries: Lebanon, Syria, Israel, and Jordan. In Lebanon, Druzes live principally in the 'Alayy and the Shuf regions, with smaller populations in B'abda, Marji'un, Rashaya, and al-Matn. A sizable Druze community also resides in the city of Beirut, where the judiciary and administrative center of the sect has its headquarters. The Druzes in Lebanon are approximately 7 percent of the population. Syrian Druzes live mainly in the Jabal al-Duruz; the city of Suwayda has the largest Druze population not only in Syria but in the entire Middle East as well. Additional Syrian Druzes live in the presently occupied Golan Heights and in other urban areas including Damascus and in previous centuries in Aleppo. Druzes are also a small minority in Syria, not exceeding 6 percent.

In Israel, Druzes live primarily in the Galilee and Carmel Mountain regions with smaller numbers in other parts of the nation. The Israeli Druze community is smaller than the Syrian and Lebanese communities and accounts for less than 1 percent of the Israeli citizenry. There are also a few thousand Druzes living in Jordan. Most Jordanian Druzes migrated there in the beginning of the 20th century and reside in the cities of al-Azraq, al-Zarqa, and other areas around the capital, Amman.

In addition to these larger concentrations of Druzes, smaller communities can be found in Australia, Canada, Europe, the Persian Gulf nations, the Philippines, South America, West Africa, and the United States. In all these Druze diaspora communities, members remain in close contact with their homelands and with their coreligionists in their host countries. They have established associations such as the American Druze Society in the United States, the British Druze Society in the United Kingdom, the Druze Association of Toronto in Canada, the Sydney Druze Society in Australia, and *La Druzo Brazileiri* in Brazil. To maintain their heritage, these diaspora communities invite speakers from their homelands in an effort to reinforce elements of their shared culture, history, and society. Yet, despite these strong contacts, the Druze diaspora, like other Middle Eastern migrant groups, have been affected by the cultures of their host countries, and they are slowly assimilating into the societies in which they live. Some members of the second and third generations have already lost the connection with their cultural and religious heritage.

Within Druze villages and small towns in the Middle East, the predominant occupation has always been farming. This has only in recent decades begun to change. Previously, a particular form of feudalism characterized Druze society, and the two classes of landowners and peasants dominated the Druze economic landscape. Thus, the great majority of Druzes leased land from the landowning families. But the increase in the Druze population and decrease in the amount of land available for farming forced Druzes in the past several decades, like many other Middle Easterners, to seek work in urban areas while maintaining their primary residences within the villages. Rising employment opportunities in the cities have led to a gradual improvement in the lifestyle of these Druze families, which has subsequently attracted small-scale landowners to also seek a second occupation in the city while continuing to farm in the village. Moreover, with the Gulf nations' economic boom, many Druzes have pursued jobs in these countries beginning in the late 1960s.

Rapid urbanization and modernization have not only transformed Druze village economics but also stressed the importance of education and professional training. The availability and accessibility of education in Druze society over the past 150 years have substantially improved. Elementary reading and writing skills were therefore passed informally from the few educated elders to the youth. Many students could not, however, advance beyond the third- or fourth-grade level, as schools were scarce in many small villages and family responsibilities on the farms prevented many Druzes from reaching and attending schools in more urban settings. European missionaries helped establish schools in the rural areas of the Middle East during the 19th and early 20th centuries. Many schools were also built during the French Mandate in the 1920s and 1930s.

While occupations and levels of education among the Druzes have changed substantially over the past century or so, Druze society has remained largely unchanged in its perception of the importance of the family unit and in its prioritization of the community over the individual. Extended families have often lived in close proximity to one another; brothers build their homes on adjacent land whenever possible, and decisions are often made in consultation with other members of the family. In recent decades, however, this has been changing gradually, and many Druzes find themselves seeking employment and residence in faraway locations.

DRUZE INITIATED (AND UNINITIATED)

Social and religious authority among the Druzes comes from a religious elite that has an extraordinary influence on the rest of the Druze community. Thus, it may be said that Druzism both unites Druzes into socially cohesive communities and divides them into two main classes: the initiated or wise (*'uqqal*) and the uninitiated or, literally, "ignorant" (*juhhal*).

The initiated of the community learn the precepts of their faith through discussions and readings of the sacred writings in the Druze house of prayer (*khalwa* or *majlis*) or in small groups in private homes. Only those believers who demonstrate piety and devotion and who have withstood the lengthy process of candidacy are initiated into the esoteric teachings and oral traditions of the faith. Women initiates undergo a less rigorous training since the Druze doctrine considers women to be more spiritually prepared and therefore not in need of the lengthy initiation process that men are required to undertake.

The initiated persons are easily identified by their dark clothes and white, rounded turbans. They are further subdivided on the basis of their spiritual level of advancement. Only a small group of the most devout of the initiated members are called *ajawid*, meaning the selected or, literally, "the good." In the eyes of the rest of the community, the *ajawid* serve as models for righteous behavior, truthfulness, and wisdom. They shape the conduct of the entire community. Whenever disputes arise, the opinions of the *ajawid* are both revered and followed. They not only provide exclusive authority regarding the religious doctrine but also reinforce the cultural attributes of the community, shaping its distinctive interactions within families, villages, and the rest of the world.

The uninitiated or ignorant persons make up the majority of Druze society. They may seek initiation at any age, but their acceptance is based on their character, which is assessed by the initiated ones. Although the uninitiated are indeed "ignorant" of the Druze doctrine, their behavior is expected to conform with certain prescriptions, both spiritual (e.g., fealty to God, His prophets, and His luminaries) and moral (e.g., respect for elders, honor for women, and care for children).

This communal division of Druzes into the initiated and uninitiated also has important ramifications for the political behavior of members of the community. In particular, the social structure may have facilitated the political cohesiveness and unity of Druze communities in times of peace and especially during periods of war. Thus, in this dualistic structure of Druze society, religious leadership is almost always provided by the *'uqqal*, while political leadership is exercised by the *juhhal*. Despite the power held by the political leaders, however, families continue to consult, revere, and defer to the initiated members of their own families and of the community as a whole. The initiated members exercise strong yet indirect power among the Druzes. Even though the majority of the initiated do not hold political offices, their opinions carry political weight, influencing the decisions of members of the community. The initiated individuals prescribe and model the accepted standards for the community, while the uninitiated members draw strength from as well as provide protection for the initiated and the way of life, beliefs, and values they represent. Although the majority of the *'uqqal* may be uninterested in political matters, some of them become politically involved in the affairs of the community.

In addition to the communal dualism discussed previously, a second form of dualism is replete in Druze society. There is a political force that divides all Druze communities, from the largest town to the smallest village and even within the basic unit of analysis, the family. In towns and villages, families divide themselves into two competing camps, usually joining one of the two dominant families. This is especially evident in the larger tribal alignments of the Junblat and the Arslan in today's Lebanon or their predecessors, the Yazbaki-Junblati or Qaysi-Yamani divisions. Within individual families, two separate factions often form behind brothers or cousins, each of whom is then responsible for arguing the case of one of the factions. Thus, the election of a town chief or mayor often depends on these political maneuverings of the smaller family unit. These alignments are never static; they continually change and shift, depending on how individuals or families perceive the political circumstances surrounding them.

These two types of dualism—communal and familial, religious and political—shape Druze politics. In Druze communities, large families have always occupied the positions of political leadership. Consensus building among large families (or groups of families) has been necessary to ensure peaceful governance of the community and to achieve high economic and political benefits. Many Druzes believe that familial dualism is a constructive stimulus for the lasting health of the community, providing access to more opportunities and resources than would otherwise be available. For example, throughout the history of the Druzes, central governments have had to satisfy the demands of various influential families in order to assert their own control of the region. As a result, more political positions have been granted to members of the community than would have been the case if allocation were made proportional. The familial dualism that pervades Druze society may have been the key to their power politics and their success in forging political affiliations in the countries where they live.

DRUZE DOCTRINE

Druzes do not proselytize, and their faith has been closed to new converts since 1043 C.E. Like other religious traditions, members of the Druze community consider their religious and spiritual values to be central to their daily conduct, whether they are interacting with each other or with other peoples. The Druze manuscripts describe the Druze faith as a reform movement (*harakat islah*) or sect (*madhhab*) that emerged out of the Isma'ili, Shi'i, Islamic, and Judeo-Christian traditions.

The Druze doctrine has also been described as a mystical one, for both Druzism and mysticism pursue higher levels of spirituality, promote allegorical interpretations, and underplay religious ritualism. In addition, like many mystical and esoteric traditions, the Druze doctrine advocates a system of initiation. Members of the community are required to go through an arduous process of initiation in order to become religious and advance in spirituality. Once the individual seeker joins the ranks of the religious ('*uqqal*), he must transform his lifestyle and be invested in the doctrinal teachings. If one behaves in an unacceptable manner, he is reprimanded and dismissed from the ranks of the religious or banned from attending services for a specified period of time; the period is determined by other religious members in the community. Women are also held to the same standards as men, except that they are often perceived as more inclined to spirituality; the process of their initiation is, therefore, less rigorous.

Two doctrinal categories may be outlined: *articles of faith* and *acts of worship*. The central and most important act of faith is *Tawhid*. *Tawhid* has been translated as "unitarianism," "unity," or "unification." The Druze manuscripts describe *Tawhid* as a complete conviction in the Unity of God without doubt in thought, perception, speech, or action. The sources of *Tawhid* are many and include the Hebrew Bible, the New Testament, and the Qur'an. Thus, according to these manuscripts, *Tawhid* occurred in stages, and each stage was built on the knowledge of the previous ones.

The second article of faith is veneration (*taqdis*). The Druze doctrine incorporates the teachings of seven spokesmen who preached the word of God in their respective lifetimes. These spokesmen are said to represent seven periods of history and are Adam, Noah, Abraham, Moses, Jesus, Muhammad, and Muhammad Ibn Isma'il. For each of these spokesmen, God provided a foundation (*asas*), a helper or assistant for spreading the principles of *Tawhid*; for example, Aaron was a foundation for Moses, 'Ali Ibn Abi Talib for Muhammad. Because these messengers and their helpers have come from God, Druzes revere them. In addition to a spokesman (*natiq*) and a helper in each historic period, the manuscripts tell us that there were also five main luminaries (*hudud*). Each luminary is a spiritual entity by origin and is represented in a human body. These five luminaries are the Universal Intelligence (*al-'Aql*), the Universal Soul (*al-Nafs*), the Word (*al-Kalima*), the Preceding (*al-Sabiq*), and the Following (*al-Tali*). The five colors that form the Druze flag and five-pointed star are religious symbols of the luminaries. These intermediaries of prophets, helpers, and luminaries fulfill the three levels of meaning that were essential since complete spirituality cannot be realized at once.

The third Druze article of faith is the belief in metempsychosis (*taqamus*). The concepts of "reincarnation," "transmigration of souls," and "rebirth" are more familiar terms in English usage, and all refer to the doctrine in which the soul becomes incarnate in a succession of bodies. Unlike the use of the term in the English language, however, Arabic has several words that convey different connotations. These are *naskh*, *maskh*, *faskh*, and *raskh*, meaning, respectively, the transmigration of the soul into another human body, animal, plant, or thing. Nevertheless, most Arab authors have almost always used the concept *tanasukh*, derived from *naskh*, to refer to the transmigration of the soul.

Taqamus is derived from *qamis*, meaning a shirt, which carries the implication that the body is the shirt, the material element for the soul, which is the spiritual principle. In Platonic-Aristotelian terms, the material element changes, while the spiritual or mental element remains permanent. The Druze manuscripts state that the soul is incarnated immediately without any distinction of religion, color, or race. Belief in metempsychosis has the potential of reinforcing the acceptance of people of other races and faiths among whom one might be reborn in a subsequent life. Based on their doctrine, Druzes are required to be equal in their treatment of others inside or outside their own community and maintain a constant awareness that one could become a member of that group or family in one's next life; this, however, has not always been practiced.

Worship services among Druzes take place in the worship hall (*majlis* or *khalwa*), usually on Thursday evenings, and are often structured into two sessions, open and closed. The initial, open session is very general and consists of general spiritual readings as well as common supplications and praises of God; both uninitiated (*juhhal*) and initiated (*'uqqal*) are permitted to attend. Once the open session ends, the *juhhal* leave the worship hall. Only initiated members in good standing are allowed to remain in the room during this closed session. Spiritual readings and mystical insights are then meditated on and pondered.

Druze acts of worship reflect an interpretation of the biblical teachings and commandments and the pillars of Islam. Three acts of worship may be outlined here. The first is "speaking the truth" (*sidq al-lisan*), or, in short, *truthfulness*. According to the Druze doctrine, truthfulness is the central and most important part of human conduct. The relationship of truthfulness to belief is like that of the head to the human body; neither part can function without the other.

The second act of worship is the protection of brothers and sisters (*hifz al-ikhwan*), referred to here as *brotherliness*. This second ordinance means selfless safeguarding of fellow believers. *Hifz* means protection or safeguarding, and *ikhwan*, the plural of *akh*, means friends or brothers. Thus, this principle is similar to that of the Bible: "love thy neighbor as thyself."

The third act of worship is literally that of deserting the worship of idols (*tark 'ibadat al-awthan*). It means abandonment of sin or renouncing vanities. *Tark* is the complete abandonment of something. *Awthan* (plural of *wathan*) means idols. It refers generically to sin or evil and may include many negative human qualities, such as laziness, offensiveness, and yielding to one's physical senses or desires in action or in thought.

DRUZE ORIGINS

Druzes trace their historical origins to 11th-century Fatimi Egypt. The Fatimis are Isma'ilis, and the Isma'ilis are Shi'is. The title "Shi'is" is derived from Shi'a, meaning "party," and refers to followers of 'Ali Ibn Abi Talib, cousin and son-in-law of Prophet Muhammad. The Shi'is disagreed with other Muslims over the question of succession to Muhammad. They felt (and still feel) that 'Ali was the first legitimate successor. The Fatimis commenced their rule in 909 but were overthrown in 1171 by the Ayyubi sultan, Saladin (Salah al-Din). As Isma'ilis, the Fatimis claimed that their lineage descended through Isma'il, the eldest son of the sixth Shi'i *imam*, Ja'far al-Sadiq. While this branch of Shi'ism became known as Isma'ilis or Seveners, other Shi'is recognized Musa al-Kazim, Isma'il's brother, as the seventh imam and subsequent five imams, totaling 12. Members of this second branch of Shi'ism have become known as the Twelvers (Ithna 'Ashari), Ja'faris, or Musawis. Historically, therefore, the Druzes are an Isma'ili Fatimi branch of Shi'ism.

Among the Fatimis, five caliphs (second to sixth) have special status in Druze communal history and tradition. During the reign of the first caliph, 'Ubaid Allah al-Mahdi (r. 909–934), the community was not existent, while during the last eight caliphs (r. 1021–1171), the Fatimis were either indifferent to, or at times antagonistic toward, the Druze community. Naturally, these nine Fatimi caliphs are not given any substantial attention in the Druze oral and written history and tradition.

The second caliph, al-Qa'im (r. 934–945), and the third, al-Mansur (r. 945–953), spent much of their reigns suppressing revolts against their regime and stabilizing the Fatimi base in North Africa. Under the fourth caliph, al-Mu'iz le-Din Allah (r. 953–975), Egypt was conquered, and the city of Cairo and al-Azhar University were built. The fifth caliph, al-'Aziz bi-Allah (r. 975–996), continued expanding the Fatimi state into the Arabian Peninsula and Greater Syria, where he fought both the 'Abassis and the Byzantines. In his time, the Fatimi "Call" or "Mission" (Da'wa) reached as far east as India and northern China. His successor, al-Mansur, known as al-Hakim bi-Amr Allah (the ruler according to God's order), became the sixth caliph at the age of 11. Although Druzes believe that their forefathers were followers of the second to fifth Fatimi caliphs, according to almost all historians, the Druze doctrine was either founded, approved, supervised, or simply permitted to survive by al-Hakim bi-Amr Allah (r. 996–1021), the sixth Fatimi caliph.

Druze history may be divided into three main periods: the establishment era (996–1043), the emirates era (1040s–1840s), and the modern era (1840s–present).

Establishment Era (996–1043)

Although most sources date the beginning of Druzism to 1017, here the year 996 is emphasized since al-Hakim's rule began then, and, more important, there is an indication of a 21-year period of secretive activity by leaders of the movement between 996 and 1017. Indeed, many religious movements and almost all esoteric movements begin covertly.

This period of nearly 50 years may be said to revolve around three central personages: al-Hakim bi-Amr Allah, Hamza Ibn 'Ali al-Zawzani, and Baha' al-Din al-Samuqi. They performed different historical and religious functions but left little information about their own biographies or about the motivations behind their actions.

This establishment era may be divided into two distinguishable phases: the preparation phase (996–1017) and the propagation phase (1017–1043). Once again, information is scarce and often speculative about the preparation phase since it was characterized by covert activities. It seems that during the preparation phase, the Druze sources tell us that three primary individuals, referred to as *nudhur*, were in the leadership positions, each taking turn for seven years. Subsequently, after the 21 years, the three assumed central roles but under the direction of a newly announced leader, Hamza Ibn 'Ali. In 1017, the movement was overtly declared, and the propagation phase begins. Several years later, in 1021, Hamza Ibn 'Ali retreated, and for the remainder of the propagation phase, a fourth individual, Baha' al-Din al-Samuqi, became in charge of the movement with clear direct contact with Hamza. In both phases, it is also in the sources that al-Hakim was instrumental in the establishment of Druzism as some epistles indicate.

Al-Hakim's Role

In the eyes of many historians, al-Hakim was the most controversial among Fatimi caliphs. The controversy arose mainly as a result of rumors in regard to a claim for divinity, which he apparently never made, and partly because of his early rigid or unacceptable resolutions against the social and religious practices of Sunnis, Christians, and Jews. Isma'ilis acknowledged al-Hakim as a religious leader, while the rest of society thought and declared him to be an oddity and at times insane. This perception became dominant in mainstream Islamic scholarship and later in the West as well. However, certain historians who have studied al-Hakim's actions in light of the social and religious conditions in Egyptian and, more specifically, Cairene society have come to view him as a reformer with his own style and approach.

Although al-Hakim's attitude toward the Druze faith is not fully discernible from the available sources, the Druze manuscripts regard him as the founding father of Druzism and the source of its "strict unitarianism" (*Tawhid*). Indeed, the Druzes (and the Isma'ilis) hold al-Hakim in high esteem despite the controversy surrounding his role and personality. From what little is known, it can be concluded that al-Hakim did not prevent the (Druze) missionaries from propagating this form of strict unitarianism. On the contrary, he appears to have permitted their activities, approved their writings, and protected their followers. His endorsement is confirmed in some of the Druze epistles.

The Druze sources tell of al-Hakim's role in convening the three missionaries and instructing them to begin preparing spiritually fit individuals for the new era of *Tawhid*. During the 21-year period (996–1017), the three major activists led the movement under his supervision. These activists are later referred to in the Druze tradition as luminaries (*hudud*).

In December 1016, the three activists met Hamza Ibn 'Ali for the first time in the Ridan Mosque in Cairo. Five months later, in 1017, al-Hakim passed the position of imam to Hamza Ibn 'Ali, and the three missionaries were instructed to work under Hamza.

In 1021, al-Hakim left on one of his routine trips to the hills of al-Muqattam east of Cairo but never returned, leaving fertile ground for his supporters and antagonists to speculate over his disappearance. His contemporaries became convinced that he was either assassinated by Fatimi agents, attacked by nomads who had not recognized him, or simply died of natural causes. Whatever the case, his body was never found, and historians have been unable to resolve the mystery surrounding the caliph's life and disappearance. The connection between al-Hakim and Druzes can be further illuminated through the writings and teachings of Hamza Ibn Ali, the main author behind the authentic Druze manuscripts.

Hamza's Function

Hamza Ibn 'Ali is the central authority behind Druze teachings and as such is considered by some writers to be the actual founder of Druzism. This Persian from Zawzan or Zozan in today's eastern Iran came to Cairo in December 1016 to begin teaching in Dar al-Hikmah, organize followers, send missionaries, and write a religious doctrine. Although al-Hakim was said to have regularly invited scholars to Cairo, there is no apparent evidence of contact between Hamza and al-Hakim before 1016.

In May 1017, once again, al-Hakim officially conferred the title of imam on Hamza, announcing that Hamza and his associates could begin publicly preaching their doctrine. This can be considered the beginning of Hamza's actual leadership and the first year that the movement became public. It is also the beginning of what can be called the "propagation phase," during which the *Muwwahhidun*, who had previously been practicing their faith clandestinely, were allowed to proclaim their beliefs without fear of persecution or harassment. Druze sources confirm that Hamza Ibn 'Ali sent missionaries in every direction of the earth with a document (*mithaq* or *'ahd*) by which prospective converts could commit themselves and pledge their loyalty to the new and final cycle (*dawr*) of unitarianism (*Tawhid*).

Although preaching began openly, it was once again forced to move underground as a result of the animosity of the general public, which posed a danger for missionaries and adherents alike. For example, Hamza Ibn 'Ali sent 20 of his followers to the supreme Muslim judge, Ahmad Ibn al-'Awam, asking him not to adjudicate cases relating to members of the new movement. Hamza's action was perhaps intended to stress the difference between Islamic practices of the time and the reform movement he was leading. Among other things, for example, the new reform movement prohibited polygamy and the remarriage of one's divorcée, practices that were (and still are) banned among Druzes.

During this external resistance to the new movement, an internal rivalry arose between Hamza and one of the secondary missionaries, Darazi. Darazi held an important position in the production of the state coinage and therefore attracted many followers. Although Hamza was technically Darazi's superior in the movement, he feared creating a situation in which Darazi's teachings would become more visible to the general public. Therefore, Hamza decided to stop his own activity in an attempt to prevent any confusion in the ranks of new and prospective believers.

Thus, Darazi continued his activity alone, and between 1017 and 1018 he not only deviated from the essence of the *Tawhid* message but also began to falsify the writings and teachings of Hamza in order to present al-Hakim as divine. This was done apparently in the hopes that al-Hakim would favor him over Hamza. Instead, al-Hakim withdrew his support from Darazi, and as a result, public opposition to Darazi's corrupted teachings increased. As his defeat neared, Darazi redirected the public's attack by declaring that he had acted on Hamza's instructions. Hamza's previous withdrawal from public preaching now worked against him by reinforcing Darazi's assertion that he was, indeed, following Hamza's directives. Consequently, instead of attacking Darazi, the crowd turned against Hamza's Ridan Mosque on 8 May 1017. Unable to infiltrate the gates, which housed only Hamza and a few of his followers, the attackers retreated after suffering a few casualties.

Although Darazi was eventually killed and his teachings repudiated, some writers thereafter attributed his corrupted doctrine to the followers of Hamza. In doing so, they referred to such adherents as "Druzes" after Darazi's name and portrayed Darazi as the founder of Druzism. Numerous early and later non-Druze sources do not mention Hamza at all. Ironically, Darazi's name is ubiquitous.

In the same year of al-Hakim's disappearance (1021), Hamza and his close associates went into retreat, announcing that a period of testing and trial of the believers had begun. During this period, the *Muwwahhidun* were to experience hardship (*mihnah*) and persecution. Before he withdrew from public activity, Hamza delegated the affairs of the community to one of his close associates, Baha' al-Din al-Samuqi.

Baha' al-Din's Leadership

Baha' al-Din assumed leadership of the movement in 1021. He had earlier been al-Hakim's governor in northern Syria (1015–1016), during which he conquered the city of Aleppo and implemented many of al-Hakim's missions. The first years of his leadership were marked by a period of hardship and persecution of the community that lasted five and a half years. During this time, al-Hakim's successor, the seventh Fatimi caliph al-Zahir, demanded allegiance from the *Muwwahhidun*, who recognized him as caliph, but they did not confer on him the same spiritual position of imam, which they had assigned al-Hakim. This phase was considered to be a test of the believers' ability to withstand the persecution inflicted by al-Zahir and his governors, especially in Syria and Palestine. It was at this time that the Druzes either practiced dissimulation (*taqiyya*) or began to flee to remote territories, away from the reach of the Fatimi regime and its loyalists.

After the hardship years of 1021–1026, Baha' al-Din continued public preaching with the approval of Hamza, who was in an undisclosed location known only to Baha' al-Din and close associates. He wrote epistles to both prospective converts in new destinations and to those followers who had deviated or departed from the teachings of the movement. He also sent missionaries to strengthen the believers and to give them further spiritual direction. Baha' al-Din continued his activity until the closing of the Druze *Tawhid Da'wa* in 1043. From that year to the present, no one has been permitted to join the Druze movement.

In 1043, Hamza Ibn 'Ali, Baha' al-Din, and the other luminaries left Egypt. Druzes believe that these individuals will return on the Day of Judgment. One-fourth of the world's population is said to have accepted the strict unitarian message in one form or another, under one name or another. Some are Druzes, but the majority is non-Druze. Most Druzes are convinced that the question of who is a "true believer" in Unitarianism is beyond the responsibility of individual Druzes and the Druze community at large.

Emirates Era (1040s–1840s)

While the establishment era of Druze history spans only a short period of time, this second era extends over eight centuries and is represented in three consecutive principalities: the Buhturis, the Ma'nis, and the Shihabis. The three played important roles in providing leadership to the Druze masses.

The three principalities also provided leadership and protection to other non-Druze communities in the region. These centuries were not of course devoid of tribal rivalries. On the contrary, factions and divisions existed and were more unapparent in times when the region faced external threats. When external threats diminished, factionalism resurfaced.

At times, prominent Druze families turned against each other and solicited support from their non-Druze constituencies. The Druze principle of "brotherliness" and the Christian motto "love thy neighbor as thyself" were indeed ideals visible among the devout few only.

The Buhturi Emirate (1040s–1507)

The Buhturis are a branch of the large tribe known as Sons of Tanukh (*Banu Tanukh*), hereafter Tanukhis. The Tanukhis migrated from Arabia to Iraq in the sixth century, moved to northern Syria, and settled in the Lebanese Mountains beginning in the middle of the eighth century. The central Islamic government, initially the Ummayas (661–750) and then the 'Abbasis (750–1258), encouraged and supported these early settlements because they served as a buffer zone against the Byzantines. In the first half of the 11th century, some of the Tanukhi princes and their followers joined the (Druze) movement and rose in the ranks as missionaries. One of these princes, Mi'dad al-Fawarisi, who ruled over Mount Lebanon and the city of Beirut at the time, is well known also in the Druze manuscripts and oral traditions as a defender of the *Tawhid* faith. It is because of this Mi'dad that the Tanukhi-Buhturi Emirate is traced to the 11th century.

Beginning in 1096, crusaders captured the major cities of the region, including Jerusalem, Haifa, and Beirut. In response—and in order to strengthen the northern Islamic front—the Muslim central government ordered additional Tanukhi tribes, such as the Nakad and 'Abdallah, to migrate to the region and assist in guarding it. Within the 'Abdallah family, the literature refers to the prince 'Ali Ibn Husain (d. 1157) and his son, Buhtur. Because of their location in the area, the Buhturis were referred to as the Western (Gharb) Emirate.

Some non-Druze inhabitants of these areas, such as Abu al-Jaysh, were Druze antagonists who used the battles against the crusaders, including those of Damascus (1148) and Ra's al-Tinah (1151), as an opportunity to defame the Druzes. Some Muslim rulers, however, understood the local tribal competition and rivalry and therefore did not take this at face value. For example, the Seljuks, who conquered the region during the rule of Prince Zahr al-Dawlah, acknowledged the Buhturi Emirate, thereby expanding it to include Qunaitarah and other small towns in the valley. Another such example is that of Saladin, who conquered Beirut, recognized the Druze prince Haji, and supported his struggle against the crusaders.

After the crusaders returned and reconquered Beirut in 1229, a power struggle began between the Mamluks and the Ayyubis that lasted for several decades. They fought not only each other but also the Mongols, who were moving into the area, as well as the Byzantines, who had continually persecuted the inhabitants of the region. Both the Ayyubis and the Mamluks made an effort to acknowledge the Buhturis, whose cautious policy toward the two triggered a suspicion on both sides that the Druzes were cooperating with the opponents. The Mamluks, who won the famous battle of 'Ayn Jalut against the Mongols in 1260 and ruled the region for the following 300 years, remained suspicious of the Druzes and finally withdrew their support and recognition of the Druze emirs.

At the turn of the 13th century, the Mongols reinvaded Syria and Lebanon. The Druzes, as well as Shi'is, Maronites, and 'Alawis, cooperated with the invaders. The Mamluk sultan Nasr al-Din sent an army of 50,000 to punish them. These local groups defended themselves with an army of 10,000 led by the Druze prince Abu al-Lam'. The Mamluk army quickly suppressed the combined forces and pursued some Druze troops who had fled.

The famous Muslim theologian Ahmad Ibn Taimiyya (d. 1328) accompanied the invading Mamluk army and issued a religious ruling (*fatwa*) declaring this invasion to be a holy war (*jihad*) against the Druzes and 'Alawis. In his *fatwa*, Ibn Taimiyya declared both communities apostates and instructed that they be fought and defeated. Because of this politically motivated *fatwa*, the Druzes became—and still are—viewed as heretics in the eyes of many Muslims.

Despite the destruction that this Mamluk invasion brought on the Druzes, the relationship between the Druzes and the Mamluks essentially stabilized. The Buhturis remained in charge of protecting the Lebanese coastal areas and reported to the Mamluks any infiltration by the crusaders. Moreover, by renewing their recognition of Mamluk dominance, the Buhturis managed to maintain their control over the western region of Lebanon. This persisted until the takeover of the Arab lands in 1516 by the Ottoman sultan Selim (r. 1512–1520), who is said to have been supported by the Druze Ma'ni prince Fakhr al-Din I. The latter had established his influence a few years earlier in 1507.

The Ma'ni Emirate (1507–1697)

Although the Buhturis were the prominent force in the region, they did not rule over all the Druze lands or assert their power over all Druze families. One of the emerging branches of the Tanukhi tribe was that of the House of Ma'n, who had become known during the struggle against the Byzantines in the early 12th century. With the help of the Buhturis, Ma'n and his supporters relocated to the Shuf in 1120 and established several towns there, including B'aqlin and Dayr al-Qamar. This Ma'ni clan remained relatively insignificant until the emergence of their prince, Fakhr al-Din I (r. 1507–1544). Although he was asked to support the Mamluks, Fakhr al-Din instead supported the Ottoman forces of Sultan Selim, whose army defeated the Mamluks in 1516 in the decisive battle of Marj Dabiq.

The Ottomans allowed the Ma'nis to have independent political control within the region, provided that taxes reached Istanbul promptly. Although the Ottoman caliphate in Istanbul remained supportive of the Ma'nis, local Ottoman representatives, including the governors in Damascus, showed antagonism toward the Druzes and occasionally subjected them to attacks like those of 1523 and 1524, when Druze leaders were executed, their religious manuscripts confiscated, and some women taken hostage.

Although Fakhr al-Din I remained loyal to the Ottomans, his son Qurqumaz (r. 1544–1585), with the support of both Druzes and Christians, rebelled against Ottoman rule. This young prince hired a Christian Maronite secretary in order to guarantee the alliance with the two religious communities against outside rulers and other antagonists. Toward the end of Qurqumaz's reign, however, the Egyptian commander Ibrahim Pasha I and his army marched through Lebanon and destroyed many Druze villages. Druze sources are emphatic about the property destruction and the tens of thousands of Druze casualties. The wife and two sons of Qurqumaz, Fakhr al-Din and Yonis, fled to Kisrawan and stayed there until 1590. The boys' uncles, of the Arslani clan, managed their estates during their absence and later assisted the return.

With the support of the Ottomans, the elder prince, who became known as Fakhr al-Din II (r. 1585–1635), extended the Ma'ni principality north to the Syrian city of Palmyra and south to the Sinai Peninsula. Fakhr al-Din II is known to have encouraged migration into the Ma'ni-controlled regions and to have adopted a policy that asserted religious freedom and civil equality. Although he initially reestablished good relations with the Ottoman Empire, he also signed commercial treaties with some European nobility, opponents of the Ottomans, including the grand duke of Tuscany (1606–1608). As a result, the Ottomans became gradually displeased with Fakhr al-Din II's overt ambition, and therefore they mobilized their forces against him and defeated his army at

Hasbaya in 1635. He was subsequently executed with his two sons in Istanbul.

The Ma'ni emirs, however, were permitted to continue their rule until 1697 with the Ottoman government deciding which member in the family to recognize as a prince. This policy persisted throughout the following reign, that of the Shihabi.

The Shihabi Emirate (1697–1840s)

With the transfer of power from the Ma'nis to the Shihabis, the Druzes as a whole continued to enjoy a relatively high degree of autonomy. Several leading lords joined together to support a chief overlord who was in turn recognized by both the Ottoman central government and its local representatives. During the Shihabi rule, northern Lebanon and a larger number of Maronites were incorporated into the princedom.

Intracommunal Druze feuds in Mount Lebanon have also contributed to the change in demographics. With the absence of an external threat as an impetus for unity, Druzes became divided and eventually turned against each other. Two Druze factions fought at the battle of 'Ayn Dara in 1711: the Qaysis of northern Arabian origin, among them the Ma'nis and the Buhturis, and the Yamanis of southern Arabian origin, among them the Arslanis and the 'Alam al-Dins. The decisive victory of the Qaysis forced many of the Yamanis to desert their farms and flee to the Hawran region in Syria. The consequent increase in farming jobs led Maronites to migrate from the north to the Druze areas.

The principality was gradually reduced during the Shihabi reign, and areas that the Ma'nis had incorporated earlier were lost. As a result, the region slowly fell under the political and military influence, if not control, of external rulers. The regular contact among Druze communities in the Mount Lebanon, Hawran, Galilee, and Carmel Mountains was also reduced to some degree. Sectarianism began to take root, influencing the local leadership and in turn being influenced by it. Consequently, sectarian membership was politicized, and religious consciousness began to rise. Moreover, in the 18th century, the Shihabis converted to Christianity and further reduced the Druze influence throughout the region.

In 1775, during the second half of the Shihabi rule, the Ottomans appointed Ahmad Pasha al-Jazzar of Acre to the pashalik of Sidon. Al-Jazzar emerged as an oppressive tyrant whose rule lasted three decades, during which he succeeded in using the Lebanese emirs to benefit the Turkish authorities. The Shihabi princes held only symbolic power and were often ineffective. The reign of the last of the Shihabi emirs, Emir Bashir II (1788–1840), reinforced a strong central authority exercised over Mount Lebanon and the areas adjacent to it. However, Emir Bashir II was manipulated by the Egyptian rulers, who eventually brought about his fall, the end of the Shihabi Emirate, and the beginning of internal civil strife in the early 1840s.

Modern Era (1840s–Present)

The first substantial Lebanese civil turmoil came in the wake of a decade of Egyptian occupation, during which Mount Lebanon had been subjected to extreme centralized control and, in the view of many Druze writers, to a dark era in their history. The Egyptian Ibrahim Pasha I requested that the Shihabi emir Bashir II conscript Druzes to serve for the regular 15-year term in the army. Druzes resisted the conscription, and Pasha mobilized his Egyptian army to punish the Druzes. The conflict ultimately resulted in the destruction of several Druze holy shrines, the mutilation of religious manuscripts, and the devastation of homes and farms. Such recurrent incidents of harsh measures throughout the history of the sect have no doubt found their lasting impact on the Druze psyche and collective memory.

The departure of the Egyptian army in 1840 left a power vacuum, causing violence to spread to different parts of the region. Sectarian sentiments were on the rise. In 1843, European foreign powers convinced the Ottoman sultan to pacify the area as well as to relinquish affairs in the north to the French-supported Maronites and in the south to the British-backed Druzes. For over a decade, uneasiness in the Lebanese Mountains grew and finally exploded into open confrontation, beginning with the Maronite peasants' uprising against their Maronite landlords in 1858 and then against their Druze landlords in 1860. The Ottomans, who promoted intersectarian rivalry in order to dispel any unified broad national revolt against their regime, indirectly encouraged the violence. A French expeditionary force, supported by Austria, Great Britain, Prussia, and Russia, intervened in 1860. The bloody events of that year ended in the special autonomous administration of Mount Lebanon within the Ottoman Empire.

Thus, the collapse of the Shihabi Emirate marked the beginning of two decades of social and political unrest and the establishment of a brief governing system that was safeguarded by the great European powers. This arrangement quickly failed, however, and was replaced in the early 1860s by a political regime known as *Mutassarrifiyya*, headed by a *mutassarrif* (governor). It imposed a ruler from outside Lebanon who was a subject of the Ottoman sultan. In addition, a council based on religious confessional representation was appointed, ensuring the participation of all religious groups in the decision-making process. This system of government in Mount Lebanon lasted several decades. In 1918, the French Mandate replaced the *Mutassarrifiyya*.

While the Druzes in the Syrian-Lebanese provinces were under the French Mandate, the Druzes in Palestine and Jordan came under the British Mandate. Lebanon and Syria became independent in 1943 and 1944, respectively, while Israel attained statehood in 1948 and Jordan in 1946.

The Syrian Druzes have participated in Syrian politics mostly through the well-known families there, including the prominent Atrash family. For example, they led the 1890s revolt against the Ottomans. Sultan al-Atrash is known for his rebellion against the French forces in the 1920s. He is considered the central figure of what became known as the Great Revolt of 1925–1927. Being an Arab nationalist symbol, Sultan al-Atrash continued influencing local and national politics in Syria and Lebanon, especially in regard to Druzes, until his death in 1982. In the 1967 war between Israel and its neighboring Arab states, Israel conquered vast lands, including the Syrian Golan Heights, and its Druze villages came under Israeli occupation. In the early years of the occupation, the Druze community in the Golan Heights with its leader Kamal Abu Salih Kanj managed to play the politics while remaining loyal to Syria and avoiding threats of communal displacement. Israeli attempts to annex the territory and grant Israeli citizenship to the Druzes on the Golan Heights have not succeeded because of the determination of the Golani Druzes to remain Syrian and eventually reunite with their relatives in Syria.

The Druzes in Palestine in the 1930s and 1940s were a part of the Arab Legion forces, and some of them fought against the Zionist migration to Palestine. But in 1947–1948, a split took place among Palestinian Druzes, leading to the acceptance of a neutral position vis-à-vis the announcement of the Israeli state. Some Druzes accepted enlistment in the Israeli army on a voluntary basis immediately after the establishment of the state. In 1956, Israel passed a law requiring military service of three years for all Druze males. A unit of minorities in the Israeli Defense Forces was created to include Druzes, Circassians, and in smaller numbers volunteers from other Sunni and Christian communities. Being drafted into the Israeli army, Druzes became entitled to equal privileges and rights like Jewish citizens. Gradually, the position of Druzes improved with each passing decade since the 1960s, but members of the community argue that though they have better treatment than the Israeli-Arab citizens, they are still unequal to Jewish citizens.

Through the two major factions of Junblatis and Arslanis, the Druzes in Lebanon have played major roles in the politics of the country since its independence in 1943. In 1958, the Lebanese government was challenged by an opposition party, the Lebanese National Movement (LNM), which represented a coalition of mostly non-Christian groups. Kamal Junblat played a major role and was mobilizing his forces through his Progressive Socialist Party, which he had established in 1949, to advocate political and social reforms for all sects. His rival, Prime Minister Camille Chamoun, sought help from the United States. The deployment of U.S. Marines in Lebanon for seven months enabled the national government to maintain control over its police and military forces and to restore the peace. Two decades later, however, Lebanon faced a military confrontation that erupted into a full-scale civil war in the spring of 1975. In the beginning of the war, the Druzes were a part of a loose coalition of Sunnis, Shi'is, and Greek Orthodox Christians that fought the Maronite Christian militias. Kamal Junblat was assassinated in 1977. His son Walid Junblat took his place and in 1980 was elected to lead the LNM.

When the Israeli Defense Forces invaded Lebanon in 1982, they confronted the Palestinians in Beirut. Later, they reached Shuf Mountain. Initially, they intended to enable the Phalangist militia forces to take control of the Druze areas. The War of the Mountain (1983–1985) was the biggest challenge for Druzes, not only in Lebanon itself but also elsewhere in the region as well as abroad. In short, Walid Junblat's forces regained lost towns, established his control over the area, and emerged victorious in the eyes of the community. In the war, many Christians were displaced, and arrangements were subsequently made for their return.

In the past decade, since 1994, the two Druze factions in Lebanon, through their leaders Walid Junblat and Talal Arslan, have been in a state of relative communal harmony. One may conclude that the Lebanese Civil War of 1975–1990 has forced Druzes in Lebanon and perhaps elsewhere to put aside their dualist politics and to focus on the needs of their community as a whole. The postwar era can be characterized as a period of intracommunal cooperation on both the social and the leadership levels. Furthermore, the civil war, combined with other developments in the Middle East, has also promoted interactions between the Lebanese, Syrian, Israeli, Jordanian, and diaspora Druze communities. Druzes are likely to continue playing their communal and national politics in their own respective countries while protecting their local and regional communities.

The Dictionary

– A –

'ABBASI, 'ABBASIS (r. 750–1258). A ruling dynasty that overthrew the **Umayyas** (r. 661–750), moved the central **Islamic** caliphate from **Syria** to Iraq, and founded the city of Baghdad as their capital in 754. During the 'Abbasi period, many states were established in different parts of the Islamic lands. One of these states was that of the **Fatimis**, under whose rule the Druze **movement** emerged. Some 'Abbasi **caliphs**, such as al-Mansur (r. 754–775), al-Mahdi (r. 775–785), Harun al-Rashid (r. 786–809), and al-Ma'mun (r. 813–833), supported the Druze forefathers, the **Tanukhi** tribes, in their struggle against the recurrent **Byzantine** infiltration of the Lebanese coastal areas. *See also* ARSLAN; SAWWAF.

'ABBOUD, MAROUN (1886–1962). A well-known Lebanese Christian educator and literary figure who studied in **Beirut** but spent most of his life in **'Alay**. He lived and worked among Druzes for 40 years, closely observing their religious traditions and social customs while educating many of their young people. He wrote about Druze manners in verse and prose. His poems are frequently recited, for they are rich with descriptions of Druze characteristics, including loyalty, **truthfulness**, and **brotherliness**. *See also* LITERATURE.

'ABD AL-MALIK, ABU 'ALI. A 17th-century devout **shaykh** from the region of **Aleppo**. He visited **al-Shaykh al-Fadil** (d. 1640) for spiritual guidance and became his disciple and companion until al-Fadil's death. Shaykh Abu 'Ali is known for having collected and documented his master's stories and poems. *See also* AJAWID; LITERATURE; MANUSCRIPTS.

1

'ABD AL-RAHIM IBN ILYAS IBN AHMAD. An 11th-century **Fatimi** figure and heir designate (**waliyy al-'Ahd**) to the sixth Fatimi **caliph al-Hakim bi-Amr Allah**. He was also the governor of **Damascus** until he was captured, brought to **Cairo**, imprisoned, and executed. 'Abd al-Rahim is known in the Druze **manuscripts** as one of the enemies of their **movement**; he had pursued and persecuted their coreligionists and assisted their opponents. *See also* PEOPLE OF APOSTASY.

'ABD AL-RAHMAN, SHUJA' AL-DIN (?–1343). A Druze prince of the **Buhturis** and son of Jamal al-Din Haji II. He is known for having memorized the **Qur'an** and mastered the Quranic sciences. Many have praised him for his **asceticism**, piety, and mystical **poetry.** *See also* AJAWID; LITERATURE.

'ABD AL-SAMAD. A large **family** from '**Amattur** in the **Shuf, Lebanon.** They are said to have migrated from **Ma'arrat al-Nu'man** in northern **Syria** to **Hawran** and then to the Shuf region. When the **Qaysi-Yamani** conflict ended with the **'Ayn Dara** battle (1711), a local conflict surfaced between the Samads and the **Abu Shaqras.** Later, the Samads joined the **Yazbakis** in their competition against the **Junblatis.**

'ABD AL-SAMAD, MUHAMMAD IBN QASIM (1866–1954). A devout **shaykh** from '**Amattur**. He became a *shaykh al-'aql* in 1946 after his predecessor, Shaykh **Husayn Hamady**, died.

'ABD AL-SAMAD, YUSEF. A contemporary Lebanese Druze poet who lives in the **United States** and has been widely recognized by the U.S. **Arab** and Druze communities. He is often invited to recite his **poetry** in social and educational gatherings. *See also* AMERICAN DRUZE SOCIETY (ADS); LITERATURE.

'ABD AL-SATIR. *See* ZAYTUNA.

'ABEY. A largely Druze town in the district of **'Alay, Lebanon.** The first to have settled there is the **Tanukhi emir Jamal al-Din Haji** (d. 1222). 'Abey was also the hometown of the prominent 15th-century

Druze sage **Al-Sayyid al-Tanukhi** (d. 1479), whose tomb has become a **sacred site** that is still visited by Druzes today. The town has also produced many important pious **shaykhs**, such as **Ahmad Amin al-Din** (d. 1809) and **Abu Husayn Mahmoud Faraj** (d. 1953); both have **visitation sites** there. An **orphanage** and a home for the aged are among the Druze establishments in 'Abey that serve the entire area. 'Abey was also a center of American Protestant missionary activity in the 19th century.

ABI AL-KHAYR SALAMAH, SHAYKH. *See* IBN JANDAL, ABI AL-KHAYR SALAMAH IBN HASM.

ABI AL-MA'ALI, SHAYKH. *See* SIBAT, MUHAMMAD IBN IBRAHIM.

ABI YA'LA, SHAYKH. *See* DAMASCUS.

ABKARYUS, ISKANDER YA'KUB (?–1885). A Christian Armenian writer who was educated in the National College of **'Alay** and the **American University of Beirut (AUB).** He lived in **Mount Lebanon** during the 1840–1860 civil turmoil between Druzes and **Maronites** and wrote an important eyewitness account chronicling the events of that period.

ABO HAMZY, WILLIAM. *See* HAMZY, WILLIAM.

ABRAHAM (18th–16th c. B.C.E.). The patriarch of the three monotheist religions: Judaism, Christianity, and **Islam.** In **Druzism,** Abraham is considered the third spokesman (*natiq*) after **Adam** and **Noah.** Druzes believe that Abraham and the other spokesmen helped transmit the initial and **exoteric** teachings of Unitarianism (*Tawhid*).

ABRAHAMIC TRADITIONS. *See* JUDEO-CHRISTIAN–ISLAMIC TRADITIONS.

ABU 'ABDALLAH. *See* 'ISFIYA.

ABU 'ALWAN, MUHAMMAD IBN NAJM (?–1375). *See* BARAKI, AL-.

ABU AL-DAHIR, ABU MUHAMMAD JAMIL (1886–1969). A **shaykh** from the **Shuf** region, **Lebanon**. He excelled as a mediator in many conflicts, not only among Druzes but also in other parts of that country. As a farmer, he also drew public attention to a hospitality stand that he established on the nearby highway and offered travelers free refreshments, vegetables, and fruits.

ABU DHUR. *See* ABU SHAQRA, 'ARIF IBN YUSEF.

ABU AL-FADL, ZAYN AL-DIN JUBRA'IL (?–1513). Disciple and assistant to the famous Druze sage Emir **al-Sayyid al-Tanukhi**. He gained special status both during the life of al-Sayyid and after al-Sayyid died in 1479 since he continued serving his successor, Sayf al-Din al-Tanukhi. **Shaykh Zayn al-Din** was buried next to his master, **al-Amir al-Sayyid**. His ancestors remain obscure, as some writers say he is of the **Sawwafs**, while others say he is of the Ridans.

ABU FAKHR. One of the two leading Druze **families** in **Hawran** at the beginning of the 19th century, the other being **Hamdan**. In the second half of the 19th century, other families rose to prominence, such as **al-Atrash** and Hneidi.

ABU GHANIM, FUAD IBN SULAYMAN (1892–1975). A Lebanese Druze educator from Kafr Nabrakh. He was known in the 1940s and 1950s as a poet and novelist. Among several collections of **poetry** and short stories is *George Warenstein*, a novel based on a true story that took place in the 1930s in the city of Sidon. He was given the title "the **Shuf** Poet" and wrote poetry both in classical and colloquial **Arabic**. *See also* LITERATURE.

ABU HAMDAN. A Druze **family** from **Lebanon** and **Syria**. Today, some members also live in **Jordan**, and others have migrated to the Americas. It is often said that the Abu Hamdans moved from Jisr al-Qadi to **Dayr al-Qamar** in 1835 and, later, that several members relocated to the district of **Hasbaya**.

ABU HAMZEH. One of the **Tanukhi** tribes that moved to **Lebanon** from northern **Syria** in the ninth century. Some branches of Abu

Hamzeh include Hamadeh in **B'aqlin**, Harmush in **Simqaniyya**, and **'Abd al-Malik** in Btater.

ABU HAMZEH, ISMA'IL IBN SA'B (?–1798). A *shaykh al-'aql* appointed in 1778. He was selected for the spiritual **leadership** of the community based on the initiative of Yusef al-**Shihabi** and the agreement of **'Ali Junblat**. He dedicated much of his time to improving the relations between the **Yazbakis** and **Junblatis** and succeeded to arrange the signing of a treaty in 1793 between the leaders of the two factions. He built a community **worship** center (*majlis*) in al-**Khraibeh**.

ABU HILAL, MUHAMMAD. *See* SHAYKH AL-FADIL, AL-.

ABU AL-HUSN. A large **family** with roots in northern **Syria**. Some branches moved (perhaps in the 16th century) to different parts of present-day **Lebanon**. Many members of the Abu al-Husn family have also migrated to North and South America as well as to **Australia**. Families related to Abu al-Husn include the al-Sghayyar, 'Izziddin, and Hassun.

ABU AL-HUSN, SALIH 'AMMAR. A 20th-century poet who lived during the **Great Revolt of 1925–1927** and became known for documenting the events of the time in verse describing Druze bravery, hospitality, nationalism, and mannerism. Druzes often recite his **poetry** in memorials and other gatherings. *See also* LITERATURE.

ABU IBRAHIM. *See* TAMIMI, ISMA'IL IBN MUHAMMAD AL-.

ABU ISMA'IL, NAJM AL-'ABBAS. An early 20th-century poet who documented Druze battles against the Ottoman and the French forces during the 1890s–1920s. Some of his accounts also address the conflicts of Druzes with **Bedouins** in the **Hawran** region of **Syria**. *See also* LITERATURE.

ABU ISMA'IL, SALIM IBN MELHIM (1891–1953). A Lebanese Druze who migrated to **Argentina** in 1915 and established an **Arab** newspaper there titled *al-Arjantin*. His publications on the Druzes gained attention among the first and second generations of the Druze **diaspora**. Ten years later, he returned to **Lebanon** and became a lawyer and then a judge. *See also* COURT SYSTEM.

ABU IZZIDDIN, HUSAYN IBN NAJM (1885–1927). A Lebanese Druze who migrated to Latin America and settled in **Uruguay**. He was elected member of parliament in Uruguay and later returned to **Lebanon** as an honorable consul for Uruguay. The French authorities, however, limited his activities, and he therefore departed again to Uruguay, the place of his death.

ABU IZZIDDIN, MUHAMMAD (1867–1917). A Lebanese Druze lawyer who was born in al-'Ibadiyya and graduated in 1887 from the **American University of Beirut (AUB)**. He was appointed head of the **court system** in the **Shuf** region in 1903 and subsequently served on a number of committees to inspect other court systems in the region. Muhammad is also known for his numerous articles in *al-Muqtataf* and *al-Safa'* as well as for his translations from English and French. He died prematurely as a result of illness, and his public service was acknowledged in several receptions, including one at the AUB, where the university's president, Howard Bless, was among the speakers.

ABU IZZIDDIN, MUSTAFA (1878–1949). A Lebanese Druze who was born in 'Ibadiyya and received his medical degree in 1902. A year later, he moved to **Egypt** to serve in the Egyptian army and then to Sudan to become the head of the Khartoum Hospital. After his retirement, he traveled to Paris to specialize in eye diseases and, in 1930, returned to **Lebanon** and opened a private practice. He is also known for his scientific studies and translations.

ABU IZZIDDIN, QASIM IBN HASAN (1854–1928). A Lebanese medical doctor from 'Ibadiyya. After receiving his medical degree, he worked at the Haydar Hospital in Istanbul and then became a professor of medicine at Istanbul University. In 1889, he was selected to study contagious diseases and to develop preventive measures among the pilgrims to Mecca. Abu Izziddin was successful in reducing incidents of disease from 30,336 in 1893 to 178 in 1896. He published many studies on cholera and general health in several languages, including Turkish, French, and **Arabic.**

ABU IZZIDDIN, SULAYMAN IBN AMIN (1871–1933). A writer and activist who lived and worked in **Egypt.** He formed the Syrian-Lebanese association in Alexandria and at some point also worked for the Egyptian government. Among his publications is a book on **Ibrahim Pasha**'s invasion and occupation of **Syria** in the 1830s.

ABU KHAYYAL, NAJIB. A contemporary **shaykh** poet from **Jabal al-Duruz, Syria.** He is invited to recite his **poetry** in many public forums, including occasions where prominent political or religious figures visit the Jabal. *See also* LITERATURE.

ABU KHUZAM. A **family** that originated in Yemen, migrated to Iraq, and then settled in **Ma'arat al-Nu'man** in the 11th century, when they joined the Druze **movement.** Some branches of the Abu Khuzam family, however, are Copts, **Sunnis**, and **Shi'is.**

ABU KHUZAM, MAHMOUD (1896–1973). A military commander who served for 34 years (1915–1949) in the **Lebanese army.** After he retired, he served in a few roles, such as administrative consultant for the Palestinian refugees between 1959 and 1966 and as the head of the Druze endowments (*waqf*) beginning in 1966. For his dedicated service, he received many awards (some sources say 17), including the **Cedars of Lebanon.**

ABU AL-LAM'. An ancient tribe with a branch that joined the Druze **movement** in the early 11th century. Later, however, Abu al-Lam' converted to Christianity in the middle of the 18th century. They acquired the title **emir** from the **Shihabi** emir Haidar after the battle of **'Ayn Dara** (1711).

ABU AL-LAM', ZAHR (?–1807). A wealthy, devout woman and daughter of Prince Mansur Ibn Murad from the town of Salima. Her father was instrumental in mediating between the Abu Lam's and the **Shihabis.** Princess Zahr became distinguished for her piety, wit, wisdom, and generosity. Despite the objection and threats of her **family**

members, she bequeathed her wealth to the Druze community. Her brother's attempt to kill her resulted in his own death, as he fell and died in front of her two-story palace. There is a community center and worship place (*majlis*) today in this palace.

ABU LATIF. A clan of the ancient Lakhmi tribe. They settled mostly in **'Ayha,** and later some moved to the **Hasbaya** district. They are also known as the first Druzes to settle in **Jabal al-Duruz** in 1685. Relatives of the Abu Latif are the Sa'ids in Hasbaya; the Abi Latif in al-Azraq, **Jordan**; the Fahd and Rashid in Jabal al-Duruz; the Mahmoud in the **Golan Heights**; and others.

ABU LATIF, KAMAL (1930–1985). A Lebanese Druze lawyer from **'Ayha** who later was elected mayor of that city. He was a close friend of **Kamal Junblat**. Along with his relative, **Kamal Kanj** of the **Golan Heights**, Abu Latif became the topic of discussion in uncovering a secret Israeli plan after the **Six-Day War** (June 1967). **Israel** planned to establish two states, one Druze and the other **Maronite**, as a buffer zone between Israel and its northern neighbors, **Syria** and **Lebanon**. The plan became public as Abu Latif conveyed the story to Junblat, who, in turn, revealed it to the Syrian and **Egyptian** leaders, **Hafiz al-Asad** and **Jamal 'Abd al-Naser**, respectively.

ABU AL-LAYL, RAFI'. *See* 'IZZ AL-DAWLAH, RAFI' ABI AL-LAYL.

ABU MILH, SHAYKH SALIH. *See* 'AMER, SHAYKH SALIH.

ABU MUSLIH, FARID IBN IBRAHIM. *See* MASSEY, FRED.

ABU NAKAD. *See* NAKAD.

ABU SALIH KANJ, KAMAL. *See* KANJ, KAMAL ABU SALIH.

ABU AL-SARAYA, GHANA'IM IBN MUHAMMAD. An 11th-century **shaykh** who became prominent during the emergence of the Druze **movement**. He was active in spreading the Druze doctrine in his region. Abu al-Saraya lived in Yarka and has a **visitation site**

(*mazar*) nearby the city of **Acre, Israel.** *See also* AJAWID; GALI-LEE; TURAB.

ABU SHAQRA. A large influential **family** from **Lebanon.** After the battle of **'Ayn Dara** (1711) and the end of the **Qaysi-Yamani** conflict, the Abu Shaqra competed with the **'Abd al-Samad** family until the emergence of the Junblati-Yazbaki conflict. Abu Shaqras then became **Junblati** and 'Abd al-Samads, Yazbaki. Several Abu Shaqra **shaykhs** became *shaykh al-'aqls,* including **Muhammad Abu Shaqra, Nasif Abu Shaqra**, and **Yusef Abu Shaqra.** *See also* DU-ALISM.

ABU SHAQRA, 'ABBAS IBN MAHMUD (1880–1943). A journalist who moved to **Egypt** in 1900 and worked for the *al-Muqattam* newspaper until 1904, during which time he befriended major Egyptian statesmen and literary figures such as **Sa'd Zaghlul, Ahmad Shawqi**, and Hafiz Ibrahim. In 1907, he migrated to the **United States** and worked as a reporter for a variety of newspapers, including *al-Huda, al-Bayan*, and *Nahdat al-'Arab.* In 1920, he established the paper *al-Burhan* in cooperation with Rashid Taqi al-Din.

ABU SHAQRA, 'ARIF IBN YUSEF (1899–1958). Educator, poet, and journalist from **'Amattur** in the **Shuf, Lebanon.** In addition to participating in the publication of a number of newspapers, including *al-Badiya* (1928–1929) and *al-Amali* (1939–1941), he wrote hundreds of articles in many other newspapers, at times under the pseudonym Abu Dhur. He also authored several books on Druze history, doctrine, and tradition, some of which are still unpublished. His **poetry** is mostly **Arab nationalist**, ranging from praise for **Sultan al-Atrash** and **Jamal 'Abd al-Naser** to appeal to **Palestinians** to be patient in their struggle in Palestine.

ABU SHAQRA, MUHAMMAD (1910–1991). A former Lebanese *shaykh al-'aql.* Born in **'Amattur**, in the **Shuf, Lebanon,** he lived in **Damascus** and **Suwayda** up to the 1940s. Shaykh Abu Shaqra was named *shakyh al-'aql* in 1949 and, with the support of **Kamal Junblat**, was able to unite the Lebanese Druze community under one *shaykh al-'aql* instead of two (as was the practice before his reign).

Shaykh Muhammad remained in his position until his death. He was responsible for the construction of the Lebanese Druze Community Center (*Dar al-Ta'ifa al-Durziyyah*) in **Beirut** and instrumental in the establishment of the Druze Health Institute 'Ayn wa-Zayn. Shaykh Abu Shaqra took part in the **Great Revolt of 1925–1927**, although he was only 16 years old.

ABU SHAQRA, NASIF IBN 'ALI IBN IBRAHIM (?–1750). A Lebanese *shaykh al-'aql* who lived during the time of the famous Druze leader **'Ali Junblat**. Junblat is said to have sought the **shaykh**'s advice regularly. Shaykh Nasif served the community for 15 years as the spiritual leader; he was buried in **'Amattur** and has a *majlis* there.

ABU SHAQRA, YUSEF IBN AHMAD (?–1785). Known also as *Shaykh* Abu Zayn al-Din. A *shaykh al-'aql* who challenged the **Shihabi** regime and protested the tax policies of Emir Yusef Shihabi. Emir Shihabi poisoned the shaykh along with his relative Khattar Najm Abu Shaqra in 1785.

ABU TURABAH, SHAYKH. *See* SHAYKH AL-SAFI, AL-.

ABU YAHYA, MAHMUD (1888–1941). One of the heroes of the **Great Revolt of 1925–1927** against the French forces. He also participated in the **Arab Revolt of 1936** against Jewish **migration** to **Palestine**. Abu Yahya later died in battle.

ABU AL-YAQZAN. *See* MAGHRIBI, 'AMMAR AL-.

ACRE (*'Akka* in Arabic or *'Akko* in Hebrew). An ancient Mediterranean coastal town in present-day **Israel**. Acre has served Druze farmers and traders in nearby towns and villages throughout the centuries as a commercial center for buying, selling, or exchanging goods. The 1,000-year-old tomb of Shaykh **Abu al-Saraya** is nearby the city of Acre.

ADAM. Based on the biblical account in Genesis 2–3, he is the first man created by God. In the Druze **faith**, Adam is the first spokesman (*natiq*) to advocate monotheist teachings. Like some other **esoteric** and mystical traditions, the Druze doctrine asserts that there were two Adams; one is that of the biblical tradition, and the other is referred to as the Primordial Adam (*Adam Kadmun*) in the **Kabbalah** or the Pure Adam (*Adam al-Safa*) in some **Sufi** traditions.

'ADAWIYYA, RABI'A AL-. *See* RABI'A OF BASRA.

ADHAM, THE INCIDENT OF (Hadithat Adham). *See* KHANJAR, ADHAM.

ADVERSARY (Didd). *See* SATAN.

'AHD (pl. *'uhud*). *See* MITHAQ.

AJAWID (sing. *jwaied*, the diminutive form of *jayyid*, meaning "good"). A term used to refer to the advanced in spirituality among the initiated (*'uqqal*) Druzes. Because they are the most knowledgeable in spiritual matters, the *ajawid* are the most revered and listened to in Druze society. In each Druze community, there are only a small number of *ajawid*, but they play a major role in the social and often political affairs of the community. Many of the *ajawid* lead **ascetic** lifestyles, and some become hermits. *See also* SUFISM; VISITATION SITES.

AJNADAYN, BATTLE OF. A battle fought in 634 between the **Arab-Muslim** army and the forces of the **Byzantine Empire**. Led by the prestigious commander Khalid Ibn al-Walid (d. 642), the Arab-Muslim army won the battle and subsequently facilitated the Islamization of the region. Based on early chronicles, the Druze forefathers, the **Tanukhis**, participated in this battle.

AKHNOKH. *See* HERMES.

'ALA' AL-DIN. *See* ZUHAYRI.

'ALAM AL-DIN. A **family** of **emirs** and prominent figures up to 1776, when many 'Alam al-Dins were murdered by Haidar al-**Shihabi**.

Survivors moved to **B'aqlin**, and from there, some moved to **Hasbaya**. Other survivors resettled in **Suwayda** at the end of the 18th century. There are also 'Alam al-Dins who live today in Europe and the Americas, while others are in **Jordan.**

'ALAM AL-DIN, 'ALI IBN MUZAFFAR (?–1660). A prince and leader of the **Yamani** faction. He was granted the title **emir** after **Fakhr al-Din al-Ma'ni II** was captured by the Ottomans. Prince 'Ali took control of the **Ma'ni** estates and killed some of them in 1634. He then marched to **'Abey** with his followers, murdered four emirs of his own **Tanukhi** relatives (Emirs **Yahya**, Mahmud, Nasir al-Din, and Sayf al-Din), and ordered the killing of their children so that no Tanukhi prince survived. It is said that this action was taken because these emirs had supported his Ma'ni opponents. He fought the **Qaysis** incessantly and died in **Syria** as a result of an infection from a wound in the battle of **Wadi al-Qarn** in 1650. *See also* DUALISM; QAYSI-YAMANI.

'ALAM AL-DIN, IBRAHIM (1900–1972). A medical doctor who participated in the **Great Revolt of 1925–1927** and served on dangerous missions. Later, he lived in Jerusalem until 1948, when he moved to Amman. Although he retired in 1969, he was appointed deputy minister of health in **Jordan.** Ibrahim returned to **Lebanon** but eventually moved back to Amman, the place of his death.

'ALAM AL-DIN, 'IZZIDDIN JAWAD (1305–1356). A calligrapher who excelled in inscribing scriptural passages on small objects, such as the Quranic 50-word verse of *The Throne* on a grain of rice. He received a land grant from the ruler al-Nasir Muhammad Ibn Qalawun in recognition of his artistic genius. *See also* CALLIGRAPHY; MAKAREM, NASIB.

'ALAM AL-DIN, MUHAMMAD IBN 'ALI. A 17th-century Lebanese prince and son of the **Yamani** faction leader **'Ali 'Alam al-Din**. When the **Ma'nis** did not pay the second installment of taxes to Muhammad Pasha, the governor of **Syria**, Muhammad 'Alam al-Din and his brother joined Muhammad Pasha's forces and entered the **Shuf** and **al-Matn** regions. As a result, the Yamani faction prevailed. In

1662, Muhammad Pasha killed the Ma'ni prince, Qurqumaz, in 'Ayn Mazbud and transferred the Ma'ni principality to Muhammad 'Alam al-Din. However, Prince Ahmad al-Ma'ni, who was injured in 'Ayn Mazbud, regained control over the area soon after.

'ALAM AL-DIN, MUZZAFAR. An early 17th-century leader of the **Yamani** faction. He lived in **'Ayn Dara** and is therefore often known as **'Indanri**. Muzzafar fought Prince Yunis, brother of **Fakhr al-Din II**, but was defeated. The Ottoman governor then entered al-Barouk and **Dayr al-Qamar** and burned the **Ma'ni** seat of power there, enabling the Yamani faction and its leader, Muzzafar, to take more control over the Ma'ni territories. Later, Emir Fakhr al-Din II defeated the Yamanis and their supporters, and, in 1618, Fakhr al-Din II forgave Muzzafar and granted him the area of al-Jurd. In 1622, he responded to Fakhr al-Din's invitation and, with his followers, joined the Ma'ni forces in the **Bekáa** War. He fought there under Fakhr al-Din II in the battle of **'Anjar** in 1623 against the Ottoman governor in **Syria**, Mustafa Pasha.

'ALAM AL-DIN, NAJIB (1909–1996). General manager (1952–1956) and chairman of the board (1956–1977) of **Lebanon**'s official airline, Middle East Airlines (MEA). He was born in **B'aqlin** and educated at the **American University of Beirut (AUB)** and later at the University College of Southwest of England, where he earned his engineering degree. Earlier in his life, he also served in the **Jordanian** government as secretary general in 1940. In Lebanon, he also held the position of minister of tourism in the 1960s. From 1977 to his death, he lived in London and, among other things, wrote the autobiographical books *The Flying Sheikh* (1987) and *Turmoil* (1993).

'ALAWI, 'ALAWIS. An **Islamic** sect that emerged in the ninth century. Because of their major concentrations in the Nusayriyya Mountains in northwestern **Syria** and at that time being followers of Abu Shu'ayb Muhammad Ibn Nusayr (d. 880), they are often referred to as Nusayris, especially in earlier centuries. In addition to Syria, 'Alawis live in other parts of the Middle East, including **Lebanon** and, in larger numbers, Turkey. In Turkey, they are known as Alevis.
    In the 11th century, a correspondence between the leaders of the

Druze **movement** and the Nusayri **leadership** took place, but the existing **manuscripts** are not sufficient to elucidate the nature and content of that correspondence.

The 'Alawis gained political power in the early 1970s with the rise to Syrian leadership of **Hafiz al-Asad** and the **Ba'th Party**. During these past decades, 'Alawi officers in the Syrian army have allied themselves with Druze officers on many occasions in order to maintain the balance of power in the military as well as in the political and professional arenas.

'ALAY. An old settlement on the lower slopes of **Mount Lebanon** and a resort town, especially since 1885. Many Druze establishments are found in 'Alay, including one of the five Lebanese Druze courts and the Iman Druze Association and hospital. Among the many prominent figures from 'Alay is the historian **Hamza Ibn Sibat** (d. 1520).

There is a shrine in 'Alay for **Baha' al-Din al-Samuqi**, known also as "the Shrine of the Noble" and "the Shrine of Shamleikh." 'Alay is the traditional residence of many **Arslanis**.

ALEPPO (Halab). A city in northern **Syria** with a large Druze presence during the early centuries of the Druze **movement**. Halabi, which means "someone from Aleppo," is a common Druze **family** name throughout the Middle East. In recent centuries, most Druzes of Aleppo relocated, and many resettled in **Mount Lebanon**. Among important figures from the region of Aleppo is Shaykh **Jabir al-Halabi** (d. 1640), who became *shaykh al-Islam*. *See also* HALABI-YYA, MASHAYIKH AL-.

ALEVIS. *See* 'ALAWI, 'ALAWIS.

'ALEY. *See* 'ALAY.

'ALI IBN ABI TALIB (598–661). A cousin of Prophet **Muhammad**, the first **Shi'i imam**, and the fourth Rightly Guided **caliph** of Islam (r. 656–661). He was assassinated in Kufa by one of the seceders, al-Khawarij, who had initially supported him but objected to the arbitration with Mu'awiyya and therefore defected. The **Fatimis** claim to have descended from **Fatima** ('Ali's wife and daughter of Prophet

Muhammad). The Druzes emerged out of the Fatimis. Some scholars have erroneously claimed that Druzes deify 'Ali. Instead, **Druzism** considers 'Ali as the foundation (*asas*) for Muhammad, who is the spokesman (*natiq*) of that era. As his foundation, 'Ali assisted Muhammad in teaching and spreading **Islam.**

ALLAH (Arabic for "God"). See TAWHID.

'AMAMAH (pl. *'ama'im*). Head cover for men. Known also among Druzes as *laffah*, a turban or tarboosh wrapped with a white scarf encompassing its sides. This type of headgear came to the Middle East with its diverse shapes from the East. The turban-shaped one is for the majority of the **initiated**, but the one with the special rounded design (*mukalwas*) is for those few who are most advanced in spirituality and have distinguished themselves in wisdom and religious **leadership**. The process of acquiring this high rank is incumbent on the spiritually advanced among the community. *See also* AJAWID; SHAYKH AL-'AQL; 'UQQAL.

'AMAMAH, AL-. A Druze magazine that was established in 1982 by **Samih Natur** and is occasionally published in Haifa, **Israel.** The subtitle of this publication is "a cultural, social, literary, historical magazine." The magazine deals with local affairs but has also included feature articles on regional issues. *See also* LITERATURE.

'AMATTUR. An old town that likely takes its name from *'ayn ma' tur*, meaning "source of mountain water"; a Druze village in the southern **Shuf**. It is the home of several large Druze **families**, including those of **Abu Shaqra** and **'Abd al-Samad.**

AMBASSADOR. *See* QURASHI, ABU 'ABDALLAH MUHAMMAD, AL-.

'AMER. A large ancient Arabian tribe with some branches that joined the Druze **movement** in the 11th century. Different **families** of the 'Amers live today in **Lebanon**, **Syria**, and **Israel**. The Syrian 'Amers migrated there from Mount Hermon in 1805. Not all 'Amers are necessarily related.

'AMER, 'ABD AL-KARIM MAHMUD (1886–1951). *See* RIF 'ABD AL-KARIM AL-.

'AMER, SHAYKH SALIH (?–1905 or 1906). Often known as Salih Abu Milh. A devout **shaykh** from **Galilee, Israel**, who lived in **al-Buqay'a, Kisra**, and **Bayt-Jann** and for a brief period in **Khalawat al-Bayyada, Lebanon**. He is known for his high rank in spirituality and **asceticism** and for exhibiting signs of **thaumaturgies** (*karamat*), or working miracles. He was often referred to as the second devout shaykh of his time after Shaykh **Salih Jaramani**. He has a **visitation site** in al-Buqay'a.

'AMER, TURKI HASAN (1954–). An educator and poet from the village of **Hurfaysh, Israel**. He has written several **poetry** collections as well as various articles on social and literary critiques. Among his collections is *Arabian Nightmares* (1998).

AMERICAN DRUZE FOUNDATION (ADF). An **organization** established by some members of the **American Druze Society (ADS)** in 1989. The ADF's mission is to fund projects associated with the ADS or other Druze communities elsewhere. Since its inception, the ADF has sponsored presentations during the ADS annual conventions and has given grants to conferences and workshops on Druze subjects as well as fellowships to Druze students. The organization is presently chaired by **Ghassan Sa'b**. *See also* DIASPORA; ORGANIZATIONS; UNITED STATES.

AMERICAN DRUZE SOCIETY (ADS). The first organized association of American Druzes was founded in Seattle, Washington, in 1908 and was initially known as **al-Bakourat al-Durziyya**. Later, the title American Druze Society (ADS) was suggested and adopted. The ADS has organized annual conventions since 1946; purchased a large building as a community cultural center in Eagle Rock, California, in the late 1980s; and moved its national office from New York to Eagle Rock in the late 1990s. The ADS Center presently houses regular social activities during the Druze **holidays** and other monthly events as well as **educational** and cultural programs for both adults and young people.

The ADS Center has also founded the Arabic School, which is open to Druze and non-Druze children in the Los Angeles area. Moreover, the Center has become the permanent address of the Druze community in the **United States** and the location where Druze leaders and other dignitaries are received. Recent visitors to the Center included the Lebanese Druze leaders **Walid Junblat** and **Talal Arslan**.

During the past two decades, the ADS has established a number of committees to oversee the operation of the **organization** and to improve its outreach activities. These committees include the Committee on Charitable Affairs (COCA), which solicits and allocates funds; the Committee on Religious Affairs (CORA), which sponsors religious seminars and lectures; and the Committee on Research and Education (CORE), which develops educational programs. *See also* AMERICAN DRUZE FOUNDATION (ADF); AMERICAN DRUZE YOUTH (ADY); DIASPORA; ORGANIZATIONS.

AMERICAN DRUZE YOUTH (ADY). An **organization** and committee for young people, ages 17 to 38. The primary goal of the ADY is to organize diverse activities in which members can relate and give support to one another culturally and socially. Since it is an **American Druze Society (ADS)** organization, the ADY has organized activities in several ADS chapters, and its management is influenced by the ADS president and board of directors. *See also* DIASPORA; ORGANIZATIONS; UNITED STATES.

AMERICAN UNIVERSITY OF BEIRUT (AUB). One of the most prestigious universities in **Lebanon** and in the Middle East in general. It was established by American missionaries in 1866 as a Protestant college and was named the Syrian Protestant College. Since its inception, the AUB has influenced generations of students coming not only from Lebanon but from the entire world as well.

The university has also left its imprint on members of Druze communities in the region, as many have chosen it because of its close proximity to Druze concentrations. Some of the numerous Druzes who were educated at the AUB include **Muhammad Abu Izziddin**, **Najib 'Alam al-Din, As'ad Sleem, Dawud Sleem, Sa'id Taqi al-Din**, and **Diana Taqiyyidin**. Among faculty who have taught or are still teaching at the AUB are **Sami Nasib Makarem**, **Husayn Sariyy al-Din**, 'Abbas Abu Salih, Intisar 'Azzam, and Na'ila Taqiyiddin.

AMIN AL-DIN, AHMAD (?–1809). A prominent pious **shaykh** from **'Abey** in the district of **'Alay, Lebanon.** He was so popular and respected by all the Lebanese factions that both **Bashir Shihabi II** and **Bashir Junblat**, two prominent political opponents, attended his funeral and helped carry his casket. A **visitation site** (*mazar*) was later built for him in his town and financed by Bashir Shihabi.

AMIR. Prince, **emir.** *See also* EMIRATE.

AMIR AL-SAYYID, AL-. *See* TANUKHI, AL-EMIR AL-SAYYID JAMAL AL-DIN 'ABDALLAH.

'AMMAR (da'i). *See* MAGHRIBI, 'AMMAR AL-.

'AMMIYYA, 'AMMIYYAT. Peasant uprisings and revolts against landlords that took place in different parts of **Mount Lebanon** and **Syria** in the 19th century. The socioeconomic nature of these uprisings, however, was soon fueled with sectarian sentiments beginning in the 1820s and culminating in the **Maronite**-Druze (and, at times, Christian-**Muslim**) bloody confrontations of the 1840s–1860s. *See also* CIVIL WAR OF 1860; QA'IMAQAM; QA'IMAQAMIYYA.

'ANJAR, BATTLE OF. A battle waged against the Ottoman governor of **Damascus**, Mustafa Pasha, by the Druze **emir Fakhr al-Din al-Ma'ni II** in 1623. Mustafa Pasha had refused to comply with the Ottoman sultan's grant of the districts of Nablis and 'Ajlun to Fakhr al-Din in 1618. The pasha's forces were defeated, and the sultan acknowledged the dominion of the **Ma'ni** prince from **Aleppo** in the north to the Sinai in the south.

ANTAKI, SA'ID AL-. An 11th-century Christian historian who lived during the emergence of the Druze **movement** and later became known for his historical account documenting the period. Though Antaki's work has its own shortcomings, any serious study of the

Druze movement and that period in general must take into consideration Antaki's account.

ANTAKIA. *See* MIHNAT ANTAKIA.

APOSTATE, APOSTATES (*mulhid*, pl. *malahida*). A person accused of heresy (*ilhad*); a heretic. In the Druze **manuscripts**, the term is often used to refer to individuals who joined the Druze **movement**, became committed members (at times rising in the **da'wa** ranks), and then turned against the movement. One chief apostate was **Muhammad al-Darazi**, who has ever since the 11th century become the symbol of evil in the Druze tradition. *See also* PEOPLE OF APOSTASY.

'AQIL, 'AQILA (pl., *'uqqal* and *'aqilat*). The masculine and feminine forms, respectively, of the initiated members in the Druze society. These titles are derived from the term *'aql*, meaning "intellect." *See also* MASHAYIKH AL-DIN; SHAYKH AL-'AQL; 'UQQAL.

'AQL. Intellect; also often referred to as *reason* or *intelligence*. A concept discussed in Greek and **Islamic** philosophy in regard to the ideas of revelation and reason. The Greek Arksagoras of the fifth century B.C.E., for example, treated the *'Aql* as the actual ruler of the world. **Druzism** refers to this notion of *'Aql* as the **Universal Intellect** (*al-'Aql al-Kulli*) and the leader and source of power for all other luminaries (*hudud*). Druzism often refers to itself as the School of Reason or Intellect (*Madhhab al-'Aql*) because all things emanate from the *'aql*. *See also* MASHAYIKH AL-DIN; SHAYKH AL-'AQL; 'UQQAL.

'AQL AL-KULLI, AL-. *See* UNIVERSAL INTELLECT.

'AQL, SHAYKH AL-. *See* SHAYKH AL-'AQL.

ARAB, ARABS. A title used to designate an ethnicity or people who speak one of the **Arabic** dialects and identify with a common history, culture, and **politics**. Some observers have restricted the connotation to those living or originating in the Arabian Peninsula, while others have attributed it only to those who speak the Arabic language. Still others have included those who are culturally Arab regardless of their geographical origin or linguistic orientation. Throughout the history of the Druzes, some writers and rulers have attempted to reject the Arabness of Druzes based primarily on **politics** and at times on the distinctiveness of the Druze culture. *See also* ARAB AMERICANS; ARAB NATIONALISM; ARAB WORLD; EGYPT; JORDAN; LEBANON; QAF; SYRIA.

ARAB AMERICAN FUND. *See* NAJJAR, 'ABDALLAH.

ARAB AMERICANS. Arabs began migrating to the **United States** in the last three decades of the 19th century. Initially, the majority of these Arab migrants were Syrian-Lebanese. A small percentage of them were Druzes. Although these Druzes perceived themselves as part of Arab Americans, they have always emphasized their Druzeness as evident in the names of their primary **organizations, al-Bakourat al-Durziyya** (1908) and, later, beginning in 1946, the **American Druze Society (ADS)**. Relations between Druzes and other Syrian-Lebanese migrants have often been friendly but occasionally have reflected the political conditions in the homeland. However, homeland **politics** have not always impacted relations between, for example, Druze and Christian Americans of Lebanese descent. On the contrary, incidents of intermarriage took place even during the raging Lebanese **Civil War of 1975–1990**.

ARAB-ISRAELI WARS. Several wars were fought between **Israel** and its neighboring **Arab** states since the 1940s. These wars had a profound impact on Druzes and their sociopolitical identity. The independence of **Lebanon** (1943), **Syria** (1944), **Jordan** (1946), and Israel (1948) established Druzes as citizens in these four countries. Throughout the past six decades, Druzes have found themselves in the midst of tragic circumstances that have no satisfactory solution in sight. Many Israeli Druze **families** have relatives in one or more of these Arab countries. As a result of these political boundaries and ideologies, Druzes have developed strategies for improving their individual communities while maintaining strict loyalty to the nations in which they live. *See* also ISRAELI INVASION OF LEBANON;

OCTOBER 1973 WAR; SIX-DAY WAR; WAR OF INDEPEN-
DENCE.

ARAB NATIONALISM. An ideology that adheres to the notion that **Arabs** are a united political community separate from the rest of the world. It surfaced in **Syria** in the beginning of the 20th century, and from there it spread to other Arab lands in the Middle East. It also became a powerful ideology among many Arab migrants in the **diaspora**. During World War I, it was more popular as a result of the prospects of Arab independence, especially with the potential support of **Great Britain**. In the 1950s, the failure of **Egyptian** initiatives under **Jamal 'Abd al-Naser** for Arab union weakened the movement considerably.

Although many Arabs acknowledge the failure of Arab nationalism in its authentic project, some are still believers in its utility as an ideology that has the potential to unite them. The few hundreds of Arab nationalist Druzes scattered around the Middle East and in the diaspora are perhaps among the most loyal and at times zealous in their ideological attitudes. They are visible and very vocal in their communities. Druze Arab nationalists are likely to continue advocating Arab nationalism regardless of the increase in fragmentation in the Arab lands and communities, just as they continued supporting the Syrian-Egyptian Union long after its termination. *See also* ARAB AMERICANS; ARSLAN, 'ADIL IBN HAMUD; ARSLAN, SHAKIB IBN HAMUD IBN HASAN; EGYPT; SYRIA.

ARAB REVOLT OF 1936. A revolt of the **Arabs** in **Palestine** and in the neighboring regions against the increasing Jewish presence and settlement in the Land of **Palestine/Israel**. Some Arab nationalist Druzes joined the Arab forces and defended the Arab causes. Among Druzes from **Lebanon** and **Syria** who joined the Arab armies were **Mahmud Abu Yahya** (d. 1941) and **Hamad Sa'b** (d. 1941). The local Druzes in Palestine in the 1930s (and 1940s) were split between those who supported the Arabs and those who remained neutral because of ongoing feuds with some **Muslim** communities there. *See also* ARAB-ISRAELI WARS; ARAB NATIONALISM.

ARAB SOCIALIST BA'TH PARTY (Hizb al-Ba'th al-'Arabi al-Ishtiraki). *See* BA'TH PARTY.

ARAB WORLD. This term refers to the countries and lands in the Middle East that are inhabited by a majority of **Arabic**-speaking peoples. Approximately 90 percent of Druzes live in the Arab world, and the majority of those who live in the **diaspora** see themselves as part of the Arab world and are in close contact with their homelands. *See also* ARAB AMERICANS; ARAB NATIONALISM; ARABS; EGYPT; GOLAN HEIGHTS; JORDAN; LEBANON; SYRIA.

ARABIC. The mother tongue of almost all Druzes except those born in the **diaspora** where the Arabic language was not taught at home. The Druze Arabic dialect is often found to be different from the other regional Arabic dialects, especially in Druze rural areas. An example is their emphatic pronunciation of the 23rd letter of the alphabet, the *qaf*. *See also* ARABS.

A'RAF. This term is derived from the words *'arafa* (to know), *m'arifa* (knowledge), and *'irfan* (**esoteric** knowledge). It is often used to refer to those who know God, knowers. The title *A'raf* is used in the **Qur'an**, most notably as the title of *sura* 7, where it has been translated as "the Heights" or "the Wall between Heaven and Hell." In the Druze **manuscripts**, it is often used to refer to true Unitarians (*Muwwahhidun*).

'ARAYDI, NA'IM (1948–   ). An educator and poet from the town of Mghar, **Israel**. In addition to publishing several **poetry** collections in both **Arabic** and Hebrew, he has written several articles dealing with comparative **literature**.

ARGENTINA. A Druze community has existed in Argentina since the end of the 19th century. Among early Druze migrants to Argentina is the journalist **Salim Abu Isma'il**, who founded the **Arabic** newspaper *al-Arjantin* in 1915. Druzes in Argentina have established **organizations** such as the *Association de Beneficencia Drusa* in Buenos Aires. It helped bring members of the Druze community together for social and communal activities while maintaining close relations with the rest of the Lebanese and the larger **Arab** communities. Another early Druze immigrant to Argentina was the writer **Amin Arslan** (d. 1943), who also served as an Ottoman consul to Argentina. *See also* DIASPORA.

'ARIDI, AL-. A **family** mainly from **Lebanon** but with some branches living in **Israel** and **Syria**. In Lebanon, many 'Aridis live in **Baysur** along with the Mla'eb family. Presently, Ghazi 'Aridi is the minister of culture in the Lebanese government.

ARSLAN, ARSLANI. A leading princely **family** from **Mount Lebanon** that traces its genealogical roots to Malik Ibn Barakat Ibn al-Mundhir Ibn Mas'ud of the ancient Arabian tribe of Lakhm. Al-Mundhir Ibn Mas'ud was also known as **Tanukh**.

In the year 758, the two sons of Malik, al-Mundhir and Arslan, with some of their followers, joined the forces of the **'Abbasi caliph Abu Ja'far al-Mansur** (r. 754–775) in **Damascus** and were instructed to settle near the Lebanese-Syrian coasts and defend the **Islamic** frontiers from recurring **Byzantine** threats. They then spread throughout the region. Another caliph, al-Mahdi (r. 775–785), reaffirmed the 'Abbasi recognition of the Arslani-Tanukhi principality and its role in protecting the northern borders of the Islamic Empire. In 799, the prince Mas'ud Ibn Arslan moved and resettled with his family in what became known as **Shwayfat**.

When the **Yazbaki-Junblati** competition emerged in Mount Lebanon in the 18th century, the Arslanis maintained neutrality. But later they divided into two factions, one supporting the Yazbaki and the other the **Junblati**. Over time and because the Arslani faction that supported the Yazbakis was larger and stronger, observers perceived the Arslanis as a whole to be Yazbaki, and the conflict soon transformed into **Junblati-Arslani**.

In the first decades of the 20th century, many prominent Arslani leaders and writers were active and contributed to **Arab nationalism** and Islamic unity, including the two prominent brothers **'Adil** and **Shakib Arslan**. The city of Shwayfat has remained the seat of Arslani power, and today Prince **Talal Arslan**, who is minister of state in the Lebanese government, is the head of the Arslani faction. *See also* DUALISM; QAYSI-YAMANI.

ARSLAN, 'ADIL IBN HAMUD (1887–1954). A **Lebanese** Druze leader who was educated in **France** and Istanbul. He was a skillful writer, speaker, and poet and dedicated most of his life to **Arab** independence, becoming one of the early supporters of pan-Arabism and **Arab nationalism.**

'Adil served in numerous political and diplomatic posts, including representative of **Mount Lebanon** to Istanbul (1916–1918), adviser of Emir Abdallah of **Jordan** (1921–1923), military commander in the **Great Revolt of 1925–1927,** and ambassador to Turkey (1937–1938). Moreover, he participated in the radical wing of the **Syrian-Palestine Congress** after nearly being expelled from **Syria** in 1923 as a result of British pressure.

Because of his various political activities, 'Adil Arslan received the sentence of execution three times: in 1920, when the French entered **Damascus;** a year later, in 1921, as a result of his activism from outside Lebanon; and then in 1925, during the Revolt. One of the titles that were given to him is "the prince of the sword and pen" (*Amir al-Sayf wal-Qalam*). In addition to having published articles and poems in various newspapers, he left a three-volume memoir that was published in 1983.

ARSLAN, AMIN (1868–1943). A diplomat, playwright, and literary figure who was born in **Shwayfat** and educated in Paris. He served as an Ottoman consul to **Argentina** but resigned nearly four years later in order to dedicate his life to writing and public service. He lived 33 years in Argentina, wrote in **Arabic** and Spanish for numerous journals and newspapers, and established a number of publications, including *al-Istiqlal* (*The Independence*). In addition to several books in Arabic on various topics, Prince Amin also wrote 12 books in Spanish, including five plays. Some of his books were printed several times in Arabic, Spanish, and Portuguese. He died in Argentina.

ARSLAN, HBOUS (1768–1823/1824). Princess or Lady Hbous was well known for her eloquent and convincing speeches, and individuals often sought her advice. She took control of the Gharb region of **Lebanon** after the death of her husband, 'Abbas Arslan (d. 1809). Some argue that she was killed by Emir **Bashir Shihabi,** but others believe she died of natural causes. *See also* LEADERSHIP; WOMEN.

ARSLAN, 'IMAD AL-DIN MUSA (1004–1036). An early member of the Druze **movement**. He received the Lebanese principality of the Gharb region of **Lebanon** from his father in 1019. Voluntarily, 'Imad al-Din passed the **leadership** to Prince **Mi'dad al-Fawarisi**, who is well known in the Druze written and oral traditions.

ARSLAN, MAJID IBN TAWFIQ (1908–1983). The former head of the **Arslani** faction and a Lebanese minister 28 times (1937–1976), 19 of which as minister of defense. With his death, **Talal Arslan** emerged as the successor in the **leadership** of the Arslanis.

ARSLAN, NAHID AL-DIN BUHTUR (?–1157). Known also as Nahid al-Dawlah Abu al-'Asha'ir Buhtur al-**Tanukhi**, the patriarch of the **Buhturis**. He took control of the Gharb region and **Beirut** after the death of Prince Majd al-Dawlah Muhammad of the **Banu 'Abdallah** clan (another Tanukhi branch) in the battle of al-Burj in 1137. His **leadership** was supported by the governor of **Damascus**.

ARSLAN, NASIB IBN HAMUD IBN HASAN (1867–1927). Brother of **Shakib** and **'Adil Arslan** from the city of **Shwayfat** who resided in **Beirut** for some years. He was a poet and literary figure who promoted **Arab nationalism** and wrote at times under the pen name "A Free Ottoman" (*'Uthmani Hurr*). Nasib wrote more than 300 articles and poems that appeared in *al-Mufid, Fata al-'Arab, al-Zuhur*, and *Sada al'Arab* in addition to a volume of **poetry**. *See also* LITERATURE.

ARSLAN, SHAKIB IBN HAMUD IBN HASAN (1869–1946). A Lebanese Druze leader and activist who emerged as a prominent figure in the **Arab** and **Islamic** nationalist movements at the turn of the 20th century. He advocated the idea of a strong **Ottoman Empire** as a means of preventing the European powers from taking control of Arab lands. The Ottoman caliphate was, in his eyes, the legitimate rulership for the Arab and Islamic world. During World

War I, he moved to Turkey and continued to mediate between the Turks and the Arabs, who desired independence from Ottoman rule.

Shakib Arslan was also a prolific writer who was given the title "prince of eloquence" (*Amir al-Bayan*) for his hundreds of articles, books, and poems. He was elected to the Arab delegation to the **United Nations** in 1925, joined the **Syrian-Palestine Congress** during the French Mandate era, and became a representative in the League of Nations. Prince Shakib studied under Muhammad 'Abduh in **Beirut** and met and befriended major figures of his time, including **Sa'd Zaghlul** in **Egypt**, Jamal al-Din al-Afghani in Istanbul, and Rashid Rida in Switzerland and Egypt.

ARSLAN, TALAL (1963–). Son of Khawla and **Majid Arslan** and the contemporary leader of the **Arslani** faction after the death of his father. He is presently minister of state in the Lebanese government. Prince Talal has improved relations with the **Junblati** faction and its leader **Walid Junblat**, with the **Syrian** regime and its present leader **Bashshar al-Asad**, and with the **Maronites** through the leading figure **Sulayman Franjiyyah**. Talal Arslan holds a degree in political science from George Washington University, Washington, D.C.

ARSLANI-JUNBLATI. *See* QAYSI-YAMANI.

ARTICLES OF FAITH. *See* FAITH.

ARZ. *See* CEDARS OF LEBANON.

AS'AD, AS'AD. A former **Knesset** member in the Likkud Party from the town of **Bayt-Jann, Israel**. He has also served on several Israeli government delegations, including one to the **United Nations** and another to the Oslo Peace Conference. He is still active in community affairs and has recently established an **organization** for intercommunal cooperation in Israel.

ASAD, BASHSHAR AL- (1965–). President of **Syria** after the death of his father, **Hafiz al-Asad**, in 2000. He received his degree in ophthalmology in **Great Britain**. He has continued his father's policies and maintained close relations with the Druze **leadership** in both Syria and **Lebanon**. *See also* ARAB NATIONALISM; BA'TH PARTY.

ASAD, HAFIZ AL- (1930–2000). Former President of **Syria** who took office in 1970. Previously, he served as minister of defense after the 23 February 1966 coup. Asad has befriended Druzes in order to maintain the sectarian balance of power in Syria while deemphasizing sectarianism altogether. Syrian Druzes and many Lebanese Druzes have admired him and remained loyal to his regime, which continues today during the rule of his son, **Bashshar al-Asad**. *See also* ARAB NATIONALISM; BA'TH PARTY.

ASAS (Foundation). An important concept in **Isma'ili** and Druze **cosmology**. It refers to the helper of a prophet. It is believed that each prophet, that is, spokesman, has a close associate who assists in interpreting the revealed message to the masses. *See also* 'ALI IBN ABI TALIB; HUDUD; NATIQ.

ASCETIC, ASCETICISM. A religious form of self-discipline in which individuals commit themselves to a simple lifestyle with minimal involvement in the world and maximal devotion and worship. Asceticism is indeed one of the core teachings of the Druze **faith**, though only the advanced in **spirituality** adopt it. Some men and **women** have chosen the ascetic life and also practiced celibacy and rejected the married life in spite of pressures from **family** members. Examples include **Sitt Fakhara El-B'ayni**; **Abu Husayn Mahmoud Faraj**; **'Ali Faris**; and **al-Shaykh al-Fadil**. *See also* DRUZISM; SUFISM.

ASHRAFANI, MUHAMMAD IBN MALIK AL-. A 17th-century devout **shaykh** from Ashrafiyya in **Syria**. Because of an internal communal dispute, he left Ashrafiyya and lived in solitude in a remote cave for seven years until he was discovered by several community members and was persuaded to return.

Ashrafani is also known for his important three-volume **manuscript**, which is a primary Druze source linking **Druzism** to biblical **prophets**, Greek philosophers, and early **Islamic** history. In the third volume, he reconstructs the story of the Druze **movement**, its struggles with the larger neighboring communities, and its successes in developing strategies for survival.

ASMAHAN (1917–1944). Amal al-Atrash by birth; a popular singer and actress in the 1930s and early 1940s and sister of the singer, actor, and composer **Farid al-Atrash**. With their mother, both Asmahan and Farid escaped the events leading to the **Great Revolt of 1925–1927** and later decided to make **Egypt** their home. Asmahan became the leading prominent **Arab** singer after the legendary Um Kulthum. She incorporated Western performance techniques into her singing, enriching the **Arabic** song without abandoning its original characteristics. Among the songs that exhibited such qualities are *Dakhalt Marra fi Jenina* (I Once Entered a Garden) and *Ya Tuyur* (O' Birds). Asmahan died in a mysterious car accident. *See also* MUSIC.

ASSOCIATION DE BENEFICENCIA DRUSA. *See* ARGENTINA.

ASSOCIATION OF DRUZE REFORM. *See* 'ISRAWI, NAJIB SA'D AL-DIN.

'ATIR, BANU. *See* TANUKH.

ATRASH, AL-. A prominent Druze **family** of **Jabal al-Duruz**, **Syria**, beginning in the 18th century. The family is traced to a **shaykh** by the name of 'Abd al-Ghaffar, who lived in **Jabal al-A'la** near **Aleppo** and moved to **Mount Lebanon** while his grandson, 'Alam al-Din, settled in Iqlim al-Billan. The first of the Atrashs to migrate to **Hawran** was Isma'il, the son of 'Alam al-Din. The name al-Atrash was coined in reference to Isma'il, who was deaf (*atrash*). When Muhammad, the son of Isma'il, became the leader of the town of al-Qrayya, he was referred to as Muhammad al-Atrash.

Al-Atrash rose to prominence under the **leadership** of the son of Muhammad al-Atrash, Isma'il II. Isma'il II withstood the attacks of the **Bedouins** of the region, invited Druzes and Christians to settle in the area, and responded to Sa'id Junblat's request to send support to Druzes in Mount Lebanon in their 1860 conflict with the **Maronites**. The Atrash family took a center stage during the **Great Revolt of 1925–1927**, when the leading figure was **Sultan al-Atrash**.

ATRASH, AMAL AL-. *See* ASMAHAN.

ATRASH, DHUQAN (?–1910). Leader of the **Atrash family** and father of **Sultan al-Atrash**. He fought the Ottomans and was executed by their governor, Sami Pasha al-Faruqi, in **Jabal al-Duruz** when he led a team to negotiate with the governor. Sultan was at the time a soldier in the Ottoman army in Greece.

ATRASH, FARID AL- (?–1974). A popular singer, actor, producer, and composer. He was born in **Suwayda**, **Syria**, and in his youth was sent (along with his sister, **Asmahan**, and mother, 'Alya) to **Egypt** in 1923 during the events leading to the **Great Revolt of 1925–1927**.

Farid became one of the leading figures in Arabic **music**, composing hundreds of pieces, introducing new genres, and directing a number of award-winning films. He initially produced his self-composed songs that made him famous, including *Ya Zahratan Fi Khayali* (Oh Flower That Is in My Imagination) and *Ya Raitni Tayr* (I Wish I Was a Bird). Among his many movies are *Intisar al-Shabab* (The Victory of Youth), *Lahn al-Kholoud* (The Eternal Musical Note), and *Gharam wa-Intiqam* (Love and Revenge).

Toward the end of his life, he lived in **Lebanon** and Syria. Farid al-Atrash has mentored many **Arab** singers, dancers, and actors, including his sister Asmahan and the Syrian **Fahd Ballan**. *See also* MUSIC.

ATRASH, SHIBLI AL- (1850–1904). A political activist from **Jabal al-Duruz**, **Syria**, who became the leader of the **Atrash family** after the death of Ibrahim Ibn Isma'il al-Atrash in 1892. Later, in the 1890s, he was exiled with several other leaders, including Husayn al-Hajari, who was the *shaykh al-'aql* at the time. But in 1897, some of the leaders escaped, returned home, and declared a revolt against the Ottomans. This led to Sultan 'Abd al-Hamid's decree, which forced all the leaders to flee, including Shibli, in 1900.

Shibli al-Atrash is also known for his poems describing the Druze struggles against the **Ottoman Empire**. Some consider him to be the last representative of the early school of Druze **poetry** and, at the same time, the one who marks the beginning of its modern era. In addition to his political and nationalist poetry, he also wrote religious and romantic poems.

ATRASH, SULTAN AL- (1891–1982). A prominent Druze leader who led the **Great Revolt of 1925–1927** and stimulated the successive **Syrian** independence movements. Sultan's father, **Dhuqan al-Atrash**, was executed by the **Ottoman Empire** while Sultan was in the Turkish army, where he served for nearly two years (1910–1912). Sultan's activism began in 1912 against the Ottoman support for confiscation of lands. He succeeded in persuading the authorities to return the lands to their legitimate owners.

A few years later, Sultan became active in the **Arab** resistance forces, and in 1918 he joined the army of King Faysal in taking **Damascus**. In the battle of al-Dayr and Tilal al-Mani', Sultan captured the Turkish commander Rida Pasha. He later used the arrest of **Adham Khanjar**, a Shi'i who was taken into custody while visiting Sultan to solicit support for his armed struggle against the French forces. The Great Revolt of 1925–1927 was triggered by Sultan's insistence in protecting Adham Khanjar, who had fled from the French after killing one of their officials.

ATRASH, ZAYD AL-. Deputy commander of the **Great Revolt of 1925–1927** and brother of **Sultan al-Atrash**. He led a number of battles against the French forces and is remembered as one of the primary Druze heroes of that conflict. Zayd was among those individuals pursued by the French authorities.

'ATSHI, ZAYDAN (1940–   ). A Druze activist, politician, and diplomat from **'Isfiya, Israel**. In the 1970s, he was the first Israeli Druze to serve as a consul for Israel in New York and as a member of the Israeli delegation to the **United Nations**. In 1977, he was elected to the **Knesset** as a member of the Shinui Party, representing the young educated elite in the Israeli Druze community.

AUSTRALIA. Druzes have lived in Australia for more than a century and have established three cultural centers, including one in Adelaide (the first ever outside the Middle East), known as the **Levant**. The other two cultural centers are the Australian Druze Association of

New South Wales in Sydney and the Australian Druze Association of Victoria in Melbourne.

'AYHA. A town in **Lebanon**; the site of an early bloody feud that took place in 1041 leading to a massacre of residents by the **family** of Jandal. Those who suffered most were the **Sibat** (Al Shbat) family, who migrated as a result of the massacre to different parts of the region.

'AYN DARA. The site of an important battle that took place in 1711 between the **Qaysis** and the **Yamanis**, the northern and southern Druze factions, respectively. The Yamanis lost the battle, and many of their **families** migrated to the **Hawran** region of **Syria**. This battle provoked an unprecedented large-scale **migration** of Druzes as well as the decline of the Yamani presence in **Mount Lebanon**. The exodus reduced the size of the Druze community in Mount Lebanon and created a vacuum, leading to the demand for farmworkers and the increase of **Maronite** migration into Druze areas.

'AYN JALUT. The site of a battle in September 1260 in which the **Mamluks** defeated the **Mongols**. The Mamluks' victory marked the retreat of the Mongol threat and the rise of the Mamluk power hold in **Syria**. Since the Druzes aided the Mamluks, they were able to maintain their control of their areas. But later, Mamluk-Druze relations deteriorated. *See also* MARJ DABIQ, BATTLE OF.

'AYN QINYA. *See* GOLAN HEIGHTS.

'AYN AL-TINAH. A battle that took place in 1151 between the **Tanukhi-Buhturi** prince **Nahid al-Din Arslan** and the crusaders. Nahid al-Din won the battle and reasserted his control over the region, raising his principality's importance in the eyes of the **Islamic 'Abbasi** central government in Baghdad. *See also* CRUSADES.

AYYUB, NABI (Prophet Job). *See* JOB.

AYYUBI, AYYUBIS (r. 1171–1250). A ruling dynasty that was founded by the prominent military commander, Salah al-Din (1138–

1193), who is known in the west as **Saladin**. The Ayyubis under Saladin defeated the crusaders in the famous battle of **Hittin** in 1187 and regained control over Jerusalem in 1188. Beginning with Saladin, the Ayyubis recognized and supported the efforts of the Druze princes of **Mount Lebanon** in fighting the crusaders. *See also* 'ABBASI; BUHTURI; FATIMI.

'AZAYIM, BANU. *See* TANUKH.

AZHAR, AL-. An institution of learning founded by the fourth **Fatimi caliph, al-Mu'iz** (r. 952–975), who had conquered **Egypt** and began building **Cairo** in 969. Al-Azhar initially served as a seminary for religious sciences, training preachers and missionaries for propagating the **Isma'ili**-Fatimi doctrine. Later, al-Azhar developed into what remains today a leading **Islamic** university. It is also regarded as one of the principal architectural monuments of the Fatimi period. Because of its historical roots in the Isma'ili-Fatimi traditions, Druzes have viewed al-Azhar with a sense of spiritual nostalgia, and, therefore, some Druzes have pursued their education in this prestigious institution.

'AZIZ BILLAH, AL- (r. 975–996). The fifth **Fatimi caliph** after **al-Mu'iz** and before **al-Hakim bi-Amr Allah**. In addition to being the **imam** of his time, Al-'Aziz is considered one of the stations (*maqamat*) in Druze **cosmology**.

AZRAQ, AL-. *See* JORDAN.

'AZZAM. A large ancient **Arab family** with some Druze branches in **Lebanon, Syria**, and **Israel**. It originates in the Banu 'Azzam tribe, some of which joined the **emir Ma'n** and moved to **Wadi al-Taym** around the same time, in the early 12th century.

'AZZAM, FAYIZ (1942–   ). An educator and writer from **'Isfiya, Israel**. He is a major participant in the Druze Education Curriculum in Israel with **Salman Falah** and others. He is currently the head of the **Druze Research Institute (DRI)** at Haifa University. 'Azzam has written, coedited, and compiled many articles and books on the Druzes, including the memoirs of **Sultan al-Atrash**.

– B –

B'ABDA. A Christian town to the southeast of **Beirut**. The town was the administrative capital of **Mount Lebanon** during the *Mutassar-rifiyya*, from 1861 to 1914. Beginning in 1969, it also housed the presidential palace and served as the seat of power for the Lebanese president.

BADDOUR, SLEIMAN (1888–1941). A journalist and founder of one of the first **Arabic** newspapers, *al-Bayan*, in the **United States** in 1910. He was known for his anticolonialist activism; *al-Bayan* was discontinued with Baddour's death.

BAHA' AL-DIN. *See* SAMUQI, BAHA' AL-DIN AL-.

BAKOURAT AL-DURZIYYA, AL-. The first Druze association in the **United States**. It was formed by 76 Druzes who met in 1908 in Seattle, Washington. Some of them were from the northwestern region of the United States, and others came from a handful of different states. Later, the association changed its name to **American Druze Society (ADS)** and, beginning in 1946, convened an annual gathering that continues today. *See also* AMERICAN DRUZE FOUNDATION (ADF); AMERICAN DRUZE YOUTH (ADY); DIASPORA.

BALLAN, FAHD (1933–1997). A Syrian Druze singer and actor. At some point, he traveled to **Egypt** and was mentored by the famous composer and singer **Farid al-Atrash**. Fahd Ballan became popular beginning in the 1960s as a result of his traditional **Hawrani** dialect of southern **Syria** and northern **Jordan**. But one of his tracks, *Ma-aqdarshi 'ala Kidah* (I Cannot Handle It), is done in an Egyptian dialect, while another is done in standard **Arabic,** *Jassa al-Tabibu Liya Nabadi* (The Physician Checked My Heartbeat). His lyrics are down to earth, applying his deep and masculine voice, which often overshadows the **music** soundtrack.

BANU 'ABDALLAH. One of the tribes that migrated with the **Emir Tanukh** from Iraq to northern **Syria** in the seventh century and later to **Mount Lebanon** in the early ninth century. They are mentioned in the Druze **manuscripts**, though the reference "Banu 'Abdallah" may include **families** from other tribes in Mount Lebanon. Some of the Banu 'Abdallah **shaykhs** were praised for their piety in the early days of the establishment era (996–1043) of the Druze **movement**.

BANU MA'RUF. This title means "sons of beneficence" or "sons of mercy" and is often used to refer to Druzes. The term *ma'ruf* is also derived from the words *'arafa* (to know), *ma'rifa* (knowledge), *'irfan* (**esoteric** knowledge), and *A'raf* (the knowing, knowers). *See also* DRUZISM; MUWWAHHIDUN.

BANU TANUKH. *See* TANUKH.

B'AQLIN. A town in the central **Shuf, Lebanon**, that has been a center of the Druze **faith** since the emergence of the Druze **movement** in the 11th century. Thus, it is a historic town with many important sites, including the first home of **Fakhr al-Din al-Ma'ni II**, a well named after him, Mustafa Arslan's palace, and an old church.

BARAKI, AL- (?–1375). A title given to Shaykh Muhammad Abu 'Alwan. He was an early Druze **shaykh** of the 'Alwans, a large **family** that participated in the early **Islamic** conquests. Al-Baraki is known for his *Majrawiyyat al-Qiyamah*, a long poem on the events of the **Judgment Day**.

BASHIR II. *See* SHIHABI, BASHIR, II.

BA'TH PARTY. A political party known as the Arab Socialist Ba'th Party (*Hizb al-Ba'th al-'Arabi al-Ishtiraki*). It was founded originally in 1940 in **Syria** and later established in Iraq. The party advocates a secular government, and its ideology revolves around the idea of **Arab nationalism**. In Iraq, the **leadership** was seized by Saddam Hussein and collapsed when the regime was defeated in 2003. In Syria, it has been in power since 1963; the most prominent figure and leader of the Ba'th Party since 1970 was **Hafiz al-Asad**, who was succeeded by his son **Bashshar al-Asad** in 2000. The Ba'th Party membership has been drawn disproportionately from different minority groups, including the Druzes. Some Druzes are very ideological in their support of the Ba'th Party despite the losses that the Druze community incurred as a result of the party's policies.

BATIN. *See* ESOTERIC.

BATTLE OF THE MOSQUE. *See* WAQ'AT AL-JAMI'.

BAYAN, AL-. One of the pioneer **Arabic** newspapers established in the **United States** in 1910 by **Sleiman Baddour**. Because of its anticolonialist, anti-European, and anti-Ottoman outlook, it was banned from distribution in **Mount Lebanon**. Among prominent authors who contributed articles to *al-Bayan* were **Shakib Arslan**, **'Adil Arslan**, **'Arif al-Nakadi**, and **'Abbas Abu Shaqra**. *Al-Bayan* was discontinued after the death of its founder in 1941.

B'AYNI, HUSAIN MAHMOOD (1911–1944). A military officer who served in the **Lebanese army** for 40 years and later became the mayor of his town, Mazra'at al-Shuf. He participated in the activities leading up to **Lebanon**'s independence and received a number of awards and recognitions for his services, including the **Cedars of Lebanon** Award.

BAYSUR. A small Druze town in **Lebanon** overlooking the coastline and, according to archaeological evidence, the site of an old city that dates back to the Stone Age. Baysur is home of the **'Aridi** and Mla'eb **families**.

BAYT AL-DIN (or Beiteddine). A popular historical city in the **Shuf** region, **Lebanon**, and the seat of power of Emir **Bashir Shihabi** (r. 1788–1840). The **emir**'s palace there was built in the years 1812–1815 and was recently restored, along with its museum and exhibition of Porphyrion's mosaic, under the supervision and personal financing of the present Druze leader, **Walid Junblat**. Porphyrion was a successful trade city under the **Byzantines** in the sixth century. Junblat's substantial funding of several million dollars enabled the preservation of the city's ruins and relocated valuable artifacts to Bayt al-Din. The restoration of this historical site has earned Junblat praise from many groups around the world, such as archaeologists and environmentalists.

BAYT-JANN. A large all-Druze town in upper **Galilee, Israel**, with nearly 9,000 residents. Several **Knesset** members were elected from Bayt-Jann, including Shafiq As'ad, **As'ad As'ad**, and more recently **Mjaleh Wahbeh**. In Bayt-Jann, there is a **visitation site** that was built in the early 1990s in honor and memory of the fifth Druze luminary, **Baha' al-Din al-Samuqi**.

BAYT AL-YATIM. *See* ORPHANAGE.

BEDOUINS. Nomads who often subsist on pasturing their sheep and camel herds. As a result of state policies throughout the Middle East, many Bedouins chose (or were forced) to become sedentary. Historically, competition between Bedouins and Druzes over land and water rights in the **Hawran** and the **Galilee** regions has led to armed struggles that were eventually resolved by mediations and signed treaties. In 2000, clashes erupted again in **Suwayda**, and the **Syrian leadership** under **Bashshar al-Asad** sent the military to intervene and keep the peace.

BEIRUT. The capital and largest city in **Lebanon** with a population estimated at half a million. The city has served as a financial and sociopolitical center not only for Lebanon but for the entire region as well. It has often served as the summer homes for the affluent in the region. The city and its surrounding communities have also attracted large numbers of tourists. During the recent **Civil War of 1975–1990**, many sections of the city were destroyed, and reconstruction work continues in different neighborhoods. Many Druze **families** have roots in Beirut going back to the 11th century, including Halabi, Deak, and Sariyy al-Din. Beirut is today the home of the Druze Administrative Communal Center.

BEITEDDINE. *See* BAYT AL-DIN.

BEKÁA. A valley in central **Lebanon** between **Mount Lebanon** and the Anti-Lebanon region. Its population is largely **Shi'i** but with pockets of **Sunnis** and Christian minorities. Several wars were fought in the Bekáa Valley, including one led by the army of **Fakhr al-Din al-Ma'ni II** against the Ottomans in the 1620s and more recently between **Syrian**-backed militias and **Israeli Defense Forces (IDF)**.

BIBLE. Both the Hebrew Bible (*Tanakh*) and the New Testament are central to the Druze teachings. The Druze **manuscripts** are replete with biblical references. Druzes also seek the **esoteric** dimension of these scriptures and believe that the esoteric complements the **exoteric.** Moreover, the esoteric dimension of scriptures does not undermine the importance of the exoteric. Actually, some Druze sages have argued that Druzes are not true Unitarians (*Muwwahhidun*) if they do not master the exoteric knowledge found in the Bible. Among the biblical figures who are significant in Druze **cosmology** are **Adam**, **Noah**, **Abraham**, Moses, and **Jesus**; they are considered the five spokesmen. Additional important personages are **Job**, David, **John**, and others. *See also* 'IRFAN; QUR'AN; SHU'AYB.

BIQ'ATHA. *See* GOLAN HEIGHTS.

BIRRI, NABIH (1938–). A Lebanese **Shi'i** lawyer and politician who rose to prominence in the 1970s and became president of the Amal movement in 1980. He was an occasional ally of the Druze leader **Walid Junblat** during the **Civil War of 1975–1990**.

BOHRAS (or Bohoras). An **Isma'ili** sect of Hindu descent from Gujarat. In recent decades, some of their members initiated pilgrimages to their **Fatimi** heritage in **Cairo**. With the approval of the **Egyptian** government, they have recently begun to restore and maintain the **mosque** of **al-Hakim**. Some scholars have speculated that the Bohras are the closest of the Isma'li branches to **Druzism** in their doctrines and practices. Attempts by scholars to arrange meetings between leading religious figures on both sides have taken place during the past decade. *See also* HAKIMICALL, THE; ISMA'ILIS; SHI'IS.

BQA'SAMANI, SA'ID IBN 'ALI. A 15th-century Druze sage from the village of Bqa'sam and a student of **al-Emir al-Sayyid al-Tanukhi**. He was given an expensive cloak as a gift by al-Emir al-

Sayyid in recognition of his devotion and services. But he then sold it, bought different material, and made 10 white and black cloaks to give to his master al-Sayyid and to all the other students. The significance of this type of newly made cloak is that it later became the traditional clothing of **initiated** Druzes who reach high spiritual rank. Shaykh Bqa'samani became one of the prominent Druze sages and has a **visitation site** today. *See also* AJAWID; ASCETIC; 'UQQAL.

BRAZIL. Druze presence in Brazil began at the end of the 19th century. Later, Druzes there organized gatherings and established a community center and an association. The center is known as *Dar Druzo Brasilloro*, and the association, as *La Druze Brazileiro* (the Druze Association of Brazil, São Paulo). Among early Druze immigrants to Brazil was **Najib 'Israwi** (d. 1987). *See also* DIASPORA.

BRITISH DRUZE SOCIETY (BDS). The BDS is relatively new and small compared to other Druze **diaspora** communities, although some Druze exiles already lived in **Great Britain** in the late 19th century. The society has a board of directors that meets regularly and organizes social and **educational** events for the community. They have also been active in maintaining strong ties with other Druze communities elsewhere and in contributing to Druze social **organizations** both in the diaspora and in **Lebanon**. Some say that there are over 500 Druzes residing in the London area with a smaller number in other parts of Great Britain.

BROTHERLINESS (Hifz al-Ikhwan). This is one of the primary **commandments** of **Druzism**, second to **truthfulness**. It instructs "guarding one's brothers and sisters" (*Hifz al-Ikhwan*). Brotherliness is described in the **manuscripts** as the quality in individuals that reflects pure senses (*jawarih nazihah*). One's heart must be open to doing every superior deed (**fadilah**), and his or her thoughts must always be enlightened by the presence and power of God. One must also be dedicated (*mukibban*) in pursuing spiritual knowledge (*ma'rifa*) and meditative recitation (*mudhakarah*), for only by doing so is one able to "do good unto others" as other traditions have it.

BUHTUR, NAHID AL-DAWLAH ABU AL-'ASHA'IR. *See* AR-SLAN, NAHID AL-DIN BUHTUR.

BUHTURI, BUHTURIS. A branch of the **Tanukhis** and cousins of the **Arslanis**. The Buhturis can be traced to the prominent prince **Mi'dad al-Fawarisi** (d. 1040), who was active in the Druze **movement**. They supported and were acknowledged by the **Mamluks**, **Seljuks**, and **Ayyubis** in their fight against the crusaders and at times the **Mongols**. For example, the Mamluks granted 'Add al-Dawlah Buhtur (d. 1137) a principality, the Seljuks expanded it during the reign of his son Zahr al-Dawlah, and the **Ayyubis** gave prince **Jamal al-Din Haji** (d. 1222) a land grant.

At the turn of the 13th century, the Mongols reinvaded the area, and the Druzes, as well as **Shi'is**, **Maronites**, and **'Alawis**, cooperated with the invaders as a result of the Mamluks' poor treatment of the inhabitants of **Mount Lebanon**. This angered the Mamluk sultan Nasr al-Din, who sent an army to defeat and suppress the population. This confrontation was approved by the renowned medieval jurist **Ahmad Ibn Taymiyya** (d. 1328). Ibn Taymiyya issued a religious ruling (**fatwa**) that proclaimed this invasion a holy war (**jihad**) against the residents of the Lebanese Mountains, among them the Druzes. Subsequently, **Muslim** opponents of the Druzes have often relied on Ibn Taymiyya's religious ruling to justify their attitudes and actions against Druzes.

Despite the Mamluk invasion, the Buhturis remained in charge of protecting the northern coastal areas and reporting to the Mamluks any infiltration by crusaders. By renewing their recognition of Mamluk dominance, the Buhturi **emirs** managed to maintain their control over the area until the takeover of the **Arab** lands in 1516 by the Ottoman sultan Selim (r. 1512–1520). Based on some accounts, Sultan Selim is said to have been encouraged to invade the area by a Druze prince, **Fakhr al-Din al-Ma'ni I** (r. 1516–1544).

BUQAY'A, AL- (Piki'in). A predominantly Druze village in upper **Galilee**, **Israel**, with Christian and Sunni minorities. There is also a small Jewish presence with a synagogue that goes back to medieval times. The rabbi Shim'un Bar Yuhai used one of the caves in the village to escape from the Romans. The total population is approximately 5,000 with roughly 70 percent Druzes. In the village there is also the tomb and **visitation site** of **Shaykh Salih 'Amer.**

BURHAN, AL. *See* ABU SHAQRA, 'ABBAS IBN MAHMUD.

BUSTAN, SHUYUKH AL-. *See* DAMASCUS.

BYZANTINE EMPIRE. Also known as the Eastern Roman Empire. The Byzantines were in conflict with **Muslim** armies throughout the **Umayya** (r. 661–750) and **'Abbasi** (r. 750–1258) caliphates. Muslim armies made several attempts at conquering the Byzantine capital, Constantinople, but were unsuccessful until the Ottoman forces captured it in 1453. Byzantine power declined steadily through the 12th and 13th centuries as a result of, among other things, the rise and expansion of Ottoman power. The Druze forefathers, the **Tanukhis**, received 'Abbasi support and defended the Lebanese coastal fronts against the Byzantines.

– C –

CAIRO. Capital of **Egypt** and one of the most important **Islamic** cities in the world, housing more than 700 historical monuments. It was founded by the **Fatimi caliph al-Mu'iz** (r. 952–975) after he conquered Egypt in 969. It is considered the point of departure for **Druzism** before the teachings were spread into the **Levant**. *See also* AZHAR, AL-; HAKIM BI-AMRALLAH, AL-; RIDAN MOSQUE; WAQ'AT AL-JAMI'.

CALIPH (Khalifa). A term used to refer to the successors of the Prophet **Muhammad**, first with the Rightly Guided caliphs (r. 632–661) and then with the **Umayya** (r. 661–750) and **'Abbasi** (r. 750–1258) dynasties. In Druze religious circles, it is at times used to refer to the *shaykh al-'aql*'s successors.

CALL. See DA'WA.

CALLIGRAPHY. Several Druze calligraphers have excelled in their creative and precise artworks, including Shaykh **Nasib Makarem** (d. 1971) and **'Adil Salman Maher** (d. 1997). Both have received many awards for their works from various governments and institutions.

There were, however, earlier Druze calligraphers, such as Shaykh **'Izziddin 'Alam al-Din** (d. 1356).

CANADA. Druzes arrived in Canada at the end of the 19th and early 20th century. In recent decades, they have formed a number of centers, including the ones in Calgary, Toronto, and Edmonton. Druzes of the province Alberta, for example, were officially recognized by the Canadian government in 1987; they subsequently purchased land from the government and built the Druze Home in 1993. Among early prominent Canadian Druzes was the surgeon **Dawud Sleem** (d. 1913). *See also* DIASPORA.

CARMEL. A mountainous region in the northern part of **Israel** where the coastal city of Haifa is located. There are two large Druze towns on the eastern slopes of **Mount Carmel**; one is **Daliyat al-Carmel**, and the other is **'Isfiya**. In the early centuries of the sect, it is said that additional Druze villages had existed on Mount Carmel.

CEDARS OF LEBANON. The official emblem of the state of **Lebanon** found on the Lebanese flag and other national symbols. It is borrowed originally from what is mythically referred to as *Arz al-Rab* (Cedars of God), instilling a religious connotation to the Cedars of Lebanon. The state has instituted a national award tradition in which distinguished contributors to society are granted the Cedars of Lebanon Medal as recognition. Many Druzes were granted the medal, including **Mahmoud Abu Khuzam** and **Husain Mahmood B'ayni** as military officers, **'Afifah Sa'b** and **Najla Sa'b** as writers and social activists, **Husayn Sariyy Al-Din** as a medical doctor, and **Amin Shams** as a judge, to mention only a few.

CELIBACY. *See* ASCETIC, ASCETICISM.

CHAMOUN, CAMILLE (1900–1987). Second president of **Lebanon** (1952–1958) and Lebanon's first ambassador to **Great Britain**. His politics often undermined leftist and Arabist movements and platforms, giving impetus to the **Civil War of 1958**. He was perceived as anticommunist, anti-Naserist, and a political opponent of the Druze leader **Kamal Junblat** and his leftist **Progressive Socialist**

Party (PSP) as well as the broader-based **Lebanese National Movement (LNM)**.

CIVIL WAR OF 1860. A rebellion in **Mount Lebanon** initially instigated by peasants against their feudal lords. This war has been viewed as a culmination of a period of turmoil beginning in 1858 but with roots in the 1840s or perhaps as early as the 1820s. The rebellion soon manifested itself as a sectarian war between Druzes and **Maronites** and occasionally led to sectarian sentiments in the region between **Muslims** and Christians. This civil conflict led to the subsequent European intervention and then to the establishment of the *Mutassarrifiyya* governate for Mount Lebanon in 1861; the *Mutassarrifiyya* was supervised by the European powers. *See also* 'AMMIYYA; IQTA'; QA'IMAQAM; QA'IMAQAMIYYA.

CIVIL WAR OF 1958. A Lebanese crisis that led to the mobilization of the **Lebanese National Movement (LNM)** and the **Progressive Socialist Party (PSP)** forces against the rightist government of **Camille Chamoun**, president of **Lebanon** at the time. Chamoun requested help from the **United States**, and the latter ordered U.S. Marines to land in **Beirut** and assist the government to remain in control. As a result, the tension was suppressed, and a relative calm followed until the eruption of the **Civil War of 1975–1990**. *See also* JUNBLAT, KAMAL.

CIVIL WAR OF 1975–1990. This bloody crisis exploded in April 1975 when a militia of the right-wing **Lebanese Phalanges Party (LPP)** committed a massacre in 'Ayn al-Rummanah against a bus carrying a group of **Palestinians**. The LPP, along with other rightist groups, resented the presence of the Palestine Liberation Organization (PLO) in **Lebanon** and gradually promoted a policy of Christian Lebanon. Subsequent events involved the Phalanges joining forces with national liberal parties on one side against the left-wing **Lebanese National Movement (LNM)** backed by the PLO on the other. The LNM, which consisted of a loose coalition of Druzes, **Muslims**, and some Christians, was led by the prominent thinker and leader **Kamal Junblat** until his assassination in 1977. The death of Junblat was a major blow not only to Druzes everywhere but also to the left in Lebanon, for he attracted individuals from a wide religious and political spectrum.

In 1980, Kamal's son, **Walid Junblat**, was elected to lead the LNM, and he immediately faced several challenges in regard to the community and to the LNM. The Druzes found themselves losing some territories to the LPP. The LPP was backed by the Israelis, who invaded Lebanon in 1982, reached **Beirut**, defeated the PLO, and intended to support the LPP in their fight against the Druzes and the LNM as a whole. But Walid emerged victorious in the **War of the Mountain** (*Harb al-Jabal*) in 1985 and reasserted his control over previously lost Druze territories. He established a temporary Druze administration of these areas, appearing to many as though he created a nation within a nation. But he publicly emphasized that his administration is indeed temporary until the Lebanese government regains its control over the country.

The **Ta'if Agreement** of 1989 was, in the eyes of many Lebanese, a good move in the right direction, but it has not yet delivered what it had promised. Nevertheless, many Lebanese, regardless of religious and political affiliation, remain optimistic and continue to work toward a harmonious and peaceful state of affairs.

COMMANDMENTS. *See* WORSHIP.

COMMITTEE ON CHARITABLE AFFAIRS (COCA). *See* AMERICAN DRUZE SOCIETY (ADS).

COMMITTEE ON RELIGIOUS AFFAIRS (CORA). *See* AMERICAN DRUZE SOCIETY (ADS).

COMMITTEE ON RESEARCH AND EDUCATION (CORE). *See* AMERICAN DRUZE SOCIETY (ADS).

CONTRACT. *See* MITHAQ.

COSMOLOGY. Druze cosmology is rooted in the **Judeo-Christian–Islamic traditions** and emerges from the **Isma'ili-Fatimi** doctrine. Two ideas may be considered central: **cycles** and **intermediaries.** **Druzism** teaches that there are two cycles of human history: **Cycle**

of Concealment (*Dawr Sitr*) and **Cycle of Disclosure** (*Dawr Kashf*). The first cycle refers to a period in which religious truth was concealed, that is, not fully revealed to humanity. The latter cycle was initiated 1,000 years ago with the emergence of the Druze **movement** and the reign of the sixth Fatimi **caliph, al-Hakim**. This Cycle of Disclosure will come to an end with the events of the **Judgment Day**.

The second central idea of Druze cosmology involves three types of intermediaries (between God and mankind). These were, first, the **prophets** or spokesmen and included **Adam, Noah, Abraham**, Moses, **Jesus, Muhammad**, and **Muhammad Ibn Isma'il**. Second, for each spokesman (*natiq*), there was a helper or foundation (*asas*) to assist in the prophetic mission. In addition to spokesmen and helpers, there were the luminaries (*hudud*) who are neither prophets nor helpers and represent spiritual entities. Moreover, in each phase, it is believed that God has manifested His power, glory, and illumination in pure personages, several of whom are known as stations (*maqamat*). A *maqam* makes use of God's illumination as he wills and does not become God, just like an image in the mirror does not become the person looking into the mirror. There are eight *maqamat* in Druze cosmology: Abu Zakariya, al-'Aliyy, al-Mu'ill, al-Qa'im, al-Mansur, **al-Mu'iz, al-'Aziz**, and **al-Hakim**. *See also* TAWHID.

COURT SYSTEM. The leaders of the Druze **movement** in the early 11th century adopted the **Islamic Sunni** Hanafi code of law with some modifications. The community has always enforced these reforms on its members informally, as Druzes were under the **Muslim** court system.

The Druze legal code differs from that of the Hanafi on several issues. These include marriage (where Druze males are restricted to one wife and prohibited from remarrying one's divorcée), **inheritance** (where female heirs are granted a higher share than was customary), and **women**'s rights (where women are able to initiate divorce and participate equally in the decisions of the household).

It was not until the 1890s that the Ottoman sultan in Istanbul officially acknowledged the status of the Druze community as a *millet* (*milla*). Thereafter, the sultan or his governors usually assigned the duties of judge (*qadi*) to a learned member in the various Druze communities.

A Druze court system with an elaborate legal code was officially established first in **Lebanon** in 1948. The **Syrian** and **Israeli** Druze communities have subsequently adopted this code for their own court systems. There are five Druze courts in Lebanon, in **Beirut**, **'Alay**, **B'aqlin**, Rashaya, and **Hasbaya**. In Syria, the primary court is in **Suwayda**, while in Israel the main court is in Haifa.

COVENANT. *See* MITHAQ.

CRUSADES. Religious expeditions of western Europeans to recover the Holy Land from **Muslims** but with political motivations to control the entire area and stop the Muslim threat to Europe. Because they wore the cross (*crux* in Latin), they became known as crusaders. The first series of Crusades took place between 1095 and 1204; Jerusalem was captured in 1099, and Baldwin was crowned as king of Jerusalem in 1100. Later the **Ayyubi** Muslims under **Saladin** regained Jerusalem in 1188, leading to additional Crusades that failed to recapture Jerusalem. The **Islamic** power was on the rise, and the papacy decided to redirect its focus to internal affairs in Europe.

Druzes fought crusaders in many battles, such as **'Ayn al-Tinah** (1151). Almost all Muslim governments during these Crusades supported the Druze princes in guarding the Lebanese coastal areas and in preventing any infiltrations. *See also* 'ABBASI; BUHTURI; MAMLUK.

CYCLE (*dawr*, pl. *adwar*). A term meaning a phase of history. Two prominent cycles are usually emphasized in **Druzism**: **Cycle of Concealment** (*Dawr Sitr*) and **Cycle of Disclosure** (*Dawr Kashf*). The two often correspond with the years 996–1017 and 1017–1043, respectively. *See also* COSMOLOGY; TAWHID.

CYCLE OF CONCEALMENT (Dawr Sitr). The period between 996 and 1017. The Cycle of Concealment may also imply the entire history of humankind up to the **Cycle of Disclosure**. In this era, spiritual knowledge and teachings were limited or unavailable, for humans were not ready to absorb them fully. *See also* COSMOLOGY; DRUZISM; TAWHID.

CYCLE OF DISCLOSURE (Dawr Kashf). The cycle or phase of uncovering *Tawhid*. *Dawr Kashf* is the final cycle in *Tawhid*, which was announced at the beginning of the 11th century by the founders of **Druzism**. It implies an advanced understanding of the unity of God and the nearness of the **Judgment Day**. *See also* COSMOLOGY; CYCLE OF CONCEALMENT.

– D –

DA'I (pl. *da'is, du'at*). Literally, summoner or caller. One who engages in *da'wa* (call) and summons others to **faith**; a religious missionary or propagator of religion. The leaders of the Druze **movement** trained many *da'is*, some of whom became sages or **saints** (like **Mi'dad Fawarisi**) in the Druze tradition and others who deviated from the doctrine and became **apostates** (like **Muhammad al-Darazi**). *See also* ASAS; HUDUD; MAQAM; NATIQ.

DALIYAT AL-CARMEL. One of the two large Druze towns on the eastern slopes of **Mount Carmel, Israel**. It is the largest predominantly Druze town in Israel with a total population of over 12,000; Druzes make up more than 95 percent. Some residents of the town moved there from **Aleppo** three centuries ago. There is a **visitation site** in Daliyat al-Carmel dedicated to the legendary **Abu Ibrahim**. *See also* 'ISFIYA.

DAMASCUS. This very ancient city (established in 3000 B.C.E., if not earlier) is the capital and largest city in **Syria**. It was conquered by **Muslims** in 635 and was made the capital of the **Umayyas** (r. 661–750) under their founder, Mu'awiya Ibn Abi Sufyan (r. 661–680). The city is the seat of power for the **Ba'th Party** regime and its present leader, **Bashshar al-Asad**.

The size of the Druze community in Damascus has varied over the centuries, but a small Druze presence in the city persists. During the emergence of the Druze **movement**, a number of important **shaykhs** lived in Damascus and were referred to as Shuyukh al-Bustan, including the prominent shaykhs Abi Ya'la and Nasr Ibn Futuh.

DAMASCUS MASSACRE (July 1860). A Sunni-Druze uprising against Christian townsmen that lasted several days. Anti-Christian sentiment had been building as a result of the 1831–1840 **Egyptian** occupation of the region and the Egyptian commander **Ibrahim Pasha**'s favorable treatment of Christians. The uprising led to the destruction of homes, churches, and shops as well as the murder of several thousand Christians.

DAR AL-HIKMAH. *See* HOUSE OF WISDOM.

DAR AL-'ILM. *See* HOUSE OF WISDOM.

DARAZI, MUHAMMAD (OR NASHTAKIN) AL-. One of the early Druze missionaries turned **apostate** (*mulhid*). He is referred to by Druzes as the **adversary** (*didd*), which is equivalent to the devil. The Druze **manuscripts** refer to him as "a deviant," "the first [Druze] apostate," and the movement's "greatest heretic." Ironically, Darazi's name gave the title *Duruz* to followers of the **movement**.

Of Persian or Turkish origin, he came to **Cairo** in the year 1015 and worked under **al-Hakim** in the **Fatimi** state's treasury. He then participated in the new religious movement under the direction of **Hamza Ibn 'Ali**. But soon thereafter, he deviated from the instruction of Hamza and decided to claim the position of the **imam** for himself. He went further and decided to give himself the title of "**Master of Guides**" (*Sayyid al-Hadin*), intending to promote himself above Hamza, whose title was "**Guide of Believers**" or guide of respondents (*Hadi al-Mustajibin*) to the new movement.

Darazi also decided to attribute a divine status to al-Hakim, hoping that al-Hakim would favor him in return. Instead, Darazi was subsequently executed in 1019. Many observers overexaggerated his role and significance in the movement, especially after his death. Many scholars and other writers wrongly continue to treat Darazi as the founder of **Druzism**. *See also* DA'I; DA'WA; HUDUD; PEOPLE OF APOSTASY; SATAN.

DAW. *See* ZAR'UN.

DA'WA (Call). Often a "religious" call; a term used in **Islamic** discourse. In **Druzism**, it commonly refers to the period between 1017 and 1043, when the Druze doctrine was being propagated. But the term is also applicable to the initial stage of the **movement**, during the covert activity of the *nudhur* between 996 and 1017. *See also* DA'I; HUDUD.

DAWR (pl. *adwar*). *See* CYCLE.

DAWR KASHF. *See* CYCLE OF DISCLOSURE.

DAWR SITR. *See* CYCLE OF CONCEALMENT.

DAWUD PASHA. The first Ottoman governor (**mutasarrif**) of **Mount Lebanon** in the 1860s. He initiated several projects that benefited all religious factions, and as a result he gained reputation of a strong and wise governor. Dawud Pasha approved and supported the building of the famous Dawudiyya School in 1862, which was named after him (al-Madrasah al-Dawudiyya). The Dawudiyya School was administered and supported by the Druze endowments (*waqf*) authorities, the spiritual leaders (*shaykh al-'aqls*), and the acting governor (*qa'i-maqam*).

DAWUDIYYA SCHOOL. *See* DAWUD PASHA.

DAY OF JUDGMENT. *See* JUDGMENT DAY.

DAYF, 'ALI IBN AL-. *See* SAMUQI, BAHA' AL-DIN AL-.

DAYR AL-QAMAR. A historical town in the central **Shuf** and seat of power for **Fakhr al-Din al-Ma'ni I**, who moved there from **B'aqlin**. Fakhr al-Din built an impressive **mosque** that is still there along with many other historical sites. After the **Civil War of 1860**, the first *mutassarrif*, **Dawud Pasha**, forced the Druze **families** that were still living in Dayr al-Qamar, including Ghannam, al-Qadi, Najjar, and Abu Durgham, to relocate to neighboring villages and towns as a part of the compromises made to **Maronites**. The town became the seat of power for the *mutassarrif* as well as later Lebanese Maronite leaders, such as **Camille Chamoun**.

DAZBARI, ANUSHTAKIN AL-. An 11th-century Turkish military commander who served in the **Fatimi** army in **Syria** during the emergence of the Druze **movement**. Some authors have confused Dazbari with **Darazi** and, in doing so, have contributed to the misconceptions about **Druzism**. The relationship (if any) between Dazbari and members of the Druze movement is not discernible from the available Druze **manuscripts** and other early sources.

DEVIL. *See* SATAN.

DIALOGUE. *See* JABER, BOBBY.

DIASPORA. Although Druzes within the Middle East have always lived in several permanent mountainous regions in **Lebanon**, **Syria**, and **Israel**, some **families** or individuals have often moved from one part to another within the region. For example, a massive Druze exodus took place after the battle of **'Ayn Dara** (1711), in which many **Yamanis** were forced to relocate and settle in **Hawran**, Syria, when they lost that battle against the **Qaysis**. Between 1840 and 1860, during the turmoil in **Mount Lebanon**, additional Druzes also migrated voluntarily to Hawran and other parts of the Middle East. Moreover, during the **Great Revolt of 1925–1927**, some Druze families relocated and settled in **Jordan**, **Egypt**, and **Palestine**.

Migration of Druzes to other places in the world out of the Middle East began taking place at the end of the 19th century. Many Druzes found homes in the Americas, **Australia**, New Zealand, the **Philippines**, and elsewhere. Although some Druzes found a host country in **Europe** early in the 20th century, most European Druzes are new immigrants who left the Middle East in the past three decades. Overall, the Druze diaspora communities outside the Middle East are predominantly Lebanese; some authors have estimated that 10 percent of Lebanese Druzes have resettled outside the Middle East. *See also* AMERICAN DRUZE SOCIETY (ADS); ARGENTINA; BRAZIL;

CANADA; GREAT BRITAIN; MEXICO; UNITED STATES; URU-
GUAY; VENEZUELA.

DIDD (Adversary). *See* SATAN.

DIR'A. Administrative capital of the **Hawran** district in southern **Syria**
and a Sunni **Muslim** stronghold. It is in close proximity to the three
main Druze concentrations in **Jabal al-Duruz**, the **Golan Heights**,
and **Wadi al-Taym**.

DISSIMULATION. *See* TAQIYYA.

DIWAN. *See* MADAFA.

DRUZE (Durzi). The singular form of *Duruz* (Druzes). A title given
to the community by outsiders. It is derived from the name of an
early member of the community, **al-Darazi**, who later deviated from
the **movement**'s teachings and was declared an **apostate** (*mulhid*).
Even though the title is not used in the early 11th-century authentic
Druze **manuscripts**, it has become the dominant name for the community. *See also* BANU MA'RUF; MUWWAHHIDUN; TAWHID.

DRUZE ASSOCIATION OF TORONTO. *See* CANADA.

**DRUZE CHARITABLE ASSOCIATION (al-Jam'iyyah al-Khairi-
yya al-Durziyya).** A charity established in **Lebanon** in 1929. A
women's section was added in 1960, and in 1988 a university housing project was inaugurated to help Druze female students from faraway villages pursue their higher education.

DRUZE CULTURAL CENTER. *See* AMERICAN DRUZE SOCI-
ETY (ADS).

DRUZE FOUNDATION FOR SOCIAL WELFARE (DFSW). A
nonprofit social **organization** based in **Beirut, Lebanon**. Its mission
is to provide moral support and financial assistance to members of
the Druze community in the forms of relief, health, rehabilitation,
and various **educational** programs.

DRUZE IMAN ASSOCIATION, AL-. *See* 'ALAY.

DRUZE INITIATIVE COMMITTEE (Lajnat al-Mubadarah al-Durziyya, LMD). This **organization** is rooted in the 1956 **Israeli** legal decision regarding the three-year compulsory service of Druze males in the **Israeli Defense Forces (IDF).** LMD members objected to the service and have since worked unsuccessfully to abolish it. The **politics** of most members of the LMD is directed toward **Arab** and **Palestinian** nationalism, and many are members of the Israeli Communist Party (ICP). The LMD publishes occasional papers that compile excerpts from previously published articles, statements, and poems.

DRUZE RESEARCH INSTITUTE (DRI). This institute is located at Haifa University, **Israel**, where a two-year program for educators and other interested parties has been launched through the External Studies Division of the university. The program is run in conjunction with the Education Ministry's supervisor of Druze **education**. The institute has also created a library collection of books, articles, and documents. *See also* 'AZZAM, FAYIZ; FIRRO, KAIS.

DRUZISM. This term was used for the first time in the 1920s to refer to the religious teachings of the Druzes. Druzism defines itself as a reform **movement** (*harakat islah*) rather than a separate religion and advocates the use of the intellect (*'aql*) side by side with revelation. The Druze teachings may be analyzed as consisting of two components: Articles of **Faith** and Acts of **Worship**. The Articles of Faith reflect primary beliefs and include Unitarianism (*Tawhid*), veneration (*taqdis*), and metempsychosis (*taqamus*). The Acts of Worship are personal practices and include speaking the truth (**truthfulness**), assisting others (**brotherliness**), and abandoning one's sinful nature (**sinlessness**).

Druzism also delves into the spiritual and **esoteric** meanings of the biblical and **Quranic** verses and instructs that the **exoteric** dimension of religion, though useful and required for believers, is not sufficient to advance in spirituality and reach the Truth. In other words, Druzism advocates that the esoteric must complement the exoteric as two mutually inclusive elements of religion and spirituality. *See also* COSMOLOGY; DUALISM.

DUALISM. The Druze community may be characterized by two types of dualism: societal and familial. Societal dualism divides Druzes into the religious initiated (*'uqqal*) and the nonreligious uninitiated (*juhhal*). Familial dualism is rooted in the old Arabian tribal competition or conflict known as the **Qaysi-Yamani**, which evolved among Druzes later as the Yazbaki-Junblati and most recently as the **Arslani-Junblati** competition. This familial dualism is also often found in many towns and villages in which small **families** align themselves with the two largest families in the community. It is often observed that while the societal religious dualism is almost always fixed, the familial or sociopolitical alliances are not static but often change. *See also* AJAWID; 'AYN DARA; SHAYKH AL-'AQL.

DUBAYSI, YUSEF SELIM (1926–). A Syrian Druze and educator who was born in al-Kafr, south of **Suwayda**, **Syria**. He was appointed to work in the Ministry of Education and then Ministry of Foreign Affairs during the Syrian-Egyptian Union (1959–1961). For this position, he was stationed in **Cairo**, where he attended Cairo University until the union was discontinued, and he returned to Suwayda. He is also known for his five-volume account on the Druzes, which has sparked praise as well as criticism by members of the community.

DUHA, AL-. The official publication of the Druze *Mashyakhat al-'Aql* in **Lebanon**. The subtitle of *al-Duha* is *A Journal of Unitarian, Islamic, Nationalist Thought* (*Majallat al-Fikr al-Qawmi, al-Islami, al-Tawhidi*). The publication includes short reports on relevant developments in the region and in the world, articles on the Druze and *Tawhidi* heritage and principal virtues and values, and stories about important figures, such as **shaykhs**, politicians, scientists, and artists.

– E –

EDUCATION. General education among Druzes began improving in the second half of the 19th century, but more emphasis has been placed on it since the 1950s. Historically, Druze religious education has been pursued, if at all, through local and informal settings resembling what is colloquially known as homeschooling. At times, in each small village there were one or more learned individuals who taught the youth selected precepts about the Druze **faith** and tradition. But overall, the specific knowledge about the Druze doctrine has always been reserved only to those who commit themselves to the religious life and become initiated (*'uqqal*). Thus, religious education has always been limited.

In **Lebanon** in the 1860s, an institution was built by the devout female **Nayfeh Junblat**, daughter of **Bashir Junblat**, for those who are initiated and wish to further their knowledge and contemplation of the religious and spiritual dimensions of **Druzism**. This institution and retreat place is in **Hasbaya**, is known as **Khalawat al-Bayyada**, and is the central religious institution for Druzes everywhere; many **shaykhs** visit it from other parts of the Druze-inhabited areas outside Lebanon as well. Visitors may stay for short or extended periods of time.

In 1971, the **'Irfan Tawhid Foundation (ITF)** was established in Lebanon, and in 1973 it developed a system of Tawhidi-Druze education. Later, the ITF expanded and opened several branches serving a few thousand students.

In **Israel** beginning in the 1960s, the state separated Druzes from other **Arabs** in the minorities section of the Ministry of Education. Druze history, culture, tradition, and overall heritage were incorporated in the new school curriculum. Instructors, inspectors, and committees were appointed specifically for teaching and reemphasizing Druze education. Later, a two-year program for educators was launched through the External Studies Division of Haifa University. The program is run in conjunction with the Education Ministry's supervisor of Druze education. *See also* 'AZZAM, FAYIZ; DAWUD PASHA; DRUZE RESEARCH INSTITUTE (DRI); FALAH, SALMAN.

EGYPT. Egypt is where the Druze **movement** emerged during the reign of the sixth **Fatimi caliph**, **al-Hakim**, in the first part of the 11th century. However, Druzes were persecuted in Egypt and the surrounding regions under al-Hakim's successor, al-Zahir. In the modern era, friendships developed between Druze leaders and Egyptian statesmen and literary figures, including the friendship of **Shakib Arslan** with Muhammad Rashid Rida as well as that of **Shawkat Shuqair** and **Kamal Junblat** with Egypt's former president **Jamal 'Abd al-Naser**.

Many Druzes have lived and worked in Egypt in recent times, beginning in the 1920s and 1930s. These include such prominent Druze figures as writers **Sulayman Abu Izziddin** and **'Abbas Abu Shaqra** and musicians **Farid al-Atrash** and **Asmahan**. *See also* CAIRO; DRUZISM; MAMLUK.

EID AL-ADHA (Feast of Sacrifice). In **Islam**, this feast is celebrated to mark the end of the annual **pilgrimage** (*hajj*) to Mecca. Those not performing the pilgrimage usually attend a communal prayer and sacrifice an animal. The feast also serves to commemorate **Abraham**'s obedience and sacrifice of the ram instead of his son.

Most Druzes today do not undertake the pilgrimage, and therefore the act of "sacrifice" for them is spiritual and refers to giving up one's own worldly desires and redirecting one's energies toward the **Judgment Day**. On the day of *Eid al-Adha*, many Druzes join in a communal prayer and sacrifice an animal for the celebration. This feast is also the main holiday and is referred to as "the Great Feast" (*al-Eid al-Kabir*). *See also* EID AL-FITR.

EID AL-FITR. In **Islam**, this feast marks the breaking of the fast at the end of the holy month of Ramadan. Although many Druzes have abandoned this holiday, it is still being celebrated in certain Druze villages and among some **families.** It is also referred to as "the lesser feast" (*al-Eid al-Saghir*).

EID AL-KHIDR. *See* KHIDR, AL-.

EID AL-NABI AYYUB. *See* JOB.

EID AL-NABI SABALAN. *See* SABALAN.

EL B'AYNI, SITT FAKHARA (1764–1849). A devout female **ascetic** from Mazra'at al-**Shuf**. She was dedicated to her spiritual pursuits and led a life of **celibacy**, solitude, and devotion to God. Sitt Fakhara is said to have rejected a marriage proposal from the prominent Druze leader **Bashir Junblat**. She became a symbol of piety for Druze **women** and men in subsequent generations. *See also* ASCET-ICISM.

EL-RIF, 'ABD AL-KARIM. *See* RIF, 'ABD AL-KARIM AL-.

EMIR (Prince). *See* EMIRATE.

EMIR AL-LIWA. *See* HNEIDI, FADLALLAH.

EMIR AL-SAYYID. *See* TANUKHI, AL-EMIR AL-SAYYID JAMAL AL-DIN 'ABDALLAH.

EMIRATE. Principality; an area ruled by a prince or emir (*amir*). There are a number of emirates throughout the history of the Druze community, including the **'Alam al-Dins**, **Arslanis**, **Buhturis**, **Ma'nis**, and **Tanukhis**. The Ma'ni Emirate during the reign of **Fakhr al-Din al-Ma'ni II** included vast territories and a large number of non-Druze inhabitants.

ENDOWMENTS. *See* WAQF.

EPISTLES OF WISDOM. A collection of epistles sent by the leaders of the Druze **movement** in the early 11th century to **families**, missionaries, rulers, enemies, **apostates**, or whole communities. These **manuscripts** were not collected in one volume until later; some authors attribute the compilation to the famous Druze sage Emir **al-Sayyid al-Tanukhi**, who is also known for having written several commentaries on some of these epistles. Since then, epistles have been organized into one, two, three, five, or six volumes, most of which seem to consist of 111 epistles, varying in length, style, content, and spirituality.

Beginning in the 16th century, these epistles or some sections of them found their way to some European libraries. The first systematic study of the *Epistles of Wisdom* was completed by the French Arabist

Silvestre de Sacy in the 1790s and published in two volumes in 1838.

Scholars and laypersons, Druzes and non-Druzes, have almost always referred to these 111 epistles as the Druze holy books, neglecting the complex and elaborate processes and requirements of canonization. Moreover, unlike other sectarian developments in other world religions, these texts themselves do not consider the Druze movement an independent religion. They refer to it as a reform movement (*harakat islah*). The epistles are certainly incomplete, as some have been lost, judging by references in the manuscripts themselves. *See also* DRUZISM; DUALISM; FAITH; TAWHID.

ESOTERIC, ESOTERICISM. A tradition within many religions that emphasizes the importance of the spiritual and transcendental dimensions of religiosity. It points to the inner or allegorical meanings of scriptural sources, commentaries, or other secondary texts. Esotericism has a predominant role in the Druze doctrine, as Druzes seek the inner interpretation of texts like the **Bible** or the **Qur'an** in addition to the initial **exoteric** perspective. Esotericism is also central in almost all mystically oriented traditions. *See also* DRUZISM; EXOTERIC; 'IRFAN; ISMA'ILIS; SUFISM.

EXOTERIC, EXOTERICISM. The outer or literal meaning of scriptural sources, commentaries, or other secondary texts. **Druzism** advocates that scriptural and other spiritual sources are often interpreted exoterically and that a higher and complementary level of meaning resides in the **esoteric** dimension of such sources. **Islam** is often described in the Druze **manuscripts** as the exoteric phase of Unitarianism (*Tawhid*). *See also* ISMA'ILIS; SUFISM.

– F –

FADIL, AL-SHAYKH AL-. *See* SHAYKH AL-FADIL, AL-.

FADILAH (pl. *fada'il*). A good deed done unto others without any intention or regard for self-interest or benefit. It is often sought after by initiated (*'uqqal*) Druzes. According to the teachings of **Druzism**, men and **women** are put on earth to live a life full of good deeds (*fada'il*) and null and void of bad ones (*radha'il*). *See also* BROTH-ERLINESS; FAITH; TAWHID; TRUTHFULNESS; WORSHIP.

FAHD. *See* ABU LATIF.

FAITH. The Druze **manuscripts** describe the Druze faith as a reform **movement** (*harakat islah*) or sect (**madhhab**) that emerged in the early 11th century out of the **Isma'ili, Shi'i, Islamic,** monotheistic tradition. The word *religion* (*din, diyana*) is used in reference to Islam, Christianity, and Judaism. Whether **Druzism** is a movement, sect, or religion, non-Druzes cannot become members of the community; proselytizing and conversion have been prohibited since 1043.

The Druze faith is a mystical tradition with **esoteric** teachings and a system of initiation. Members of the community are required to go through a process of initiation in order to become religious and advance in spirituality. Once the individual seeker joins the ranks of the religious, he must transform his lifestyle and be focused on the teachings of the faith. If one behaves in an unacceptable manner, he is reprimanded and dismissed from the ranks of the religious or banned from attending services for a specified period of time. **Women** are also held with the same standards as men, except that they are at times perceived as more inclined to spirituality; the process of their initiation is less rigorous. Several articles of faith may be derived from the manuscripts, including Unitarianism (**Tawhid**), veneration (***taqdis***), and metempsychosis (***taqamus***). *See also* DA'WA; DRUZISM; JUDEO-CHRISTIAN–ISLAMIC TRADITIONS; JUHHAL; 'UQQAL; WORSHIP.

FAKHR AL-DIN I. *See* MA'NI, FAKHR AL-DIN AL-, I.

FAKHR AL-DIN II. *See* MA'NI, FAKHR AL-DIN AL-, II.

FALAH, SALMAN (1935–). An educator from Kafr Smay', **Israel**. After a career in journalism and as founder and head of the Druze Boy Scouts, he was appointed in the 1960s as director of Druze **education** in Israel to develop the Druze curriculum for elementary schools with regard to Druze history and culture. *See also* EDUCA-TION; 'AZZAM, FAYIZ.

FAMILY, FAMILIES. Druze society in general, and in rural areas in particular, has remained largely unchanged in its perception of the importance of the family unit and in its prioritization of the needs of the community over those of the individual. Extended families live in close proximity to one another; brothers build their homes on adjacent land when possible, and decisions are often made in consultation with other members of the family whether in regard to political elections or large purchases such as a car, house, or land. The more important the decision, naturally, the greater the number of family members involved in the decision-making process. Consultation with members of the family is also mandatory in cases of marriage and divorce. The initiated (*'uqqal*) often play a larger role in influencing decision. Thus, almost all major decisions are made collectively.

Moreover, in towns and villages, families frequently align themselves into two competing camps, usually behind the two dominant families. This is especially evident in the larger tribal alignments of the **Junblat** and the **Arslan** in **Lebanon**. In almost all Druze communities, large families have always occupied the positions of political **leadership.** Consensus building among large families (or groups of families) has been necessary for peaceful governance of the community on the one hand and high economic and political achievements on the other. *See also* BROTHERLINESS; DUALISM; LEADER-SHIP.

FAMILY LAW. *See* COURT SYSTEM.

FARAJ, ABU HUSAYN MAHMOUD (1862–1953). An **ascetic shaykh** from **'Abey, Lebanon,** who built a place of retreat in the mountains and worked the land for sustenance while dedicating most of his time to worshipping God. He shied away from big events and from situations where attention was directed at him. Shaykh Faraj has a **visitation site** in his hometown of 'Abey. *See also* AJAWID.

FARHUD, MUHAMMAD. *See* TARIF, MUHANNA.

FARIS, 'ALI (?–1753). An important **shaykh** who is known for his **ascetic** practices and mystical **poetry.** He was born in Yarka in present-day **Israel**, lived a life of poverty, and sought solitude in a cave near that town. He befriended the **family** of **Tarif** in the nearby town of Julis, spent some time in **Khalawat al-Bayyadah** in **Hasbaya, Lebanon**; and later returned to his hometown. He has a **visitation site** in Julis. *See also* AJAWID.

FARISI, MUHAMMAD AL-. *See* TARIF, MUHANNA.

FARISI, SALMAN AL- (?–655 or 656). A prominent companion of the Prophet **Muhammad** (d. 632) and a central figure in **Shi'ism, Isma'ilism**, and **Druzism**. Historically, he is remembered for having suggested digging a trench around the city of Medina in 627 in order to protect the city from the invading Meccan forces. This trench may have saved the city and **Islam**. The confrontation between **Muslims** and the Meccan army of several thousand became known as the Battle (or Incident) of the Trench (*al-Khandaq*). Although he came to Arabia from Persia (Farisi means Persian) to join the emerging religion of Islam, he was declared by Muhammad to be a member of the Prophet's immediate **family** (*Ahl al-Bayt*).

He has also become one of the most prominent figures and symbols in Druzism. Druze folk songs and poems praise him for his high spiritual status in Unitarianism (***Tawhid***). His name is often invoked and juxtaposed with that of **Hamza Ibn 'Ali**, the 11th-century **imam** and leader of the Druze **movement**. Although historians seem to agree about the approximate time of his death, they disagree about his age when he died; figures range from 90 to 350 years.

FASKH. *See* TAQAMUS.

FATH. A spiritual power or entity that acts as a mediator between the spiritual and physical worlds. In **Druzism**, the term refers to one of the luminaries, the seventh in the hierarchy. *See also* DA'I; DA'WA; HUDUD.

FATIMA (?–633). Daughter of the Prophet **Muhammad** (d. 632) and wife of **'Ali Ibn Abi Talib** (d. 661). Her two sons, Hasan and Husayn, are considered by **Shi'is** to be the legitimate successors of 'Ali and therefore the second and third **imams**, respectively. **Fatimis** consider themselves descendants of Fatima and 'Ali.

FATIMI, FATIMIS (r. 909–1171). A Shi'i Isma'ili empire that began its rule in Mahdiyya, Tunisia, and 60 years later expanded its territories east to **Egypt** and later to **Syria**. During the time of **Caliph al-Mu'iz** (r. 952–975), **Cairo** was built and the Fatimi capital was reestablished there.

The Fatimi power in Syria declined slowly after the reign of the sixth caliph, **al-Hakim bi-Amr Allah** (r. 996–1021), especially with the assaults of the **Seljuks**. The Druze **movement** emerged under al-Hakim's rule. According to almost all historians, the Druze doctrine was either founded, approved, supervised, or at least tolerated by al-Hakim. In 1171, the Fatimis were overthrown by **Saladin** (Salah al-Din), who was the founder of the **Ayyubi** dynasty.

FATWA. A religious ruling issued by a *mufti*, a learned religious figure in **Islam**. There are several *fatwas* that were issued by Sunni **Muslim** jurists against the Druzes and the Druze sect. The first and most important one is that of **Ahmad Ibn Taimiyya** (d. 1328). Subsequent *fatwas* have relied heavily on Ibn Taimiyya's ruling. The relationship between **Sunnis** and Druzes remain tainted by these *fatwas*. *See also* JIHAD.

FAWARISI, MI'DAD IBN YUSEF (?–1040). One of the early important princes of the Gharb region of **Lebanon** and son of **'Imad al-Din Arslan**. Prince Mi'dad was appointed by the leader of the Druze **movement**, **Baha' al-Din al-Samuqi**, to fulfill the mission of delivering a message to the Druze **apostate Sukayn** and his followers. The mission aimed to bring an end to Sukayn's corruption. Although Sukayn escaped and only later was murdered, his followers were killed in the confrontation.

Druze sources tell the story of Mi'dad receiving information from a devout female member by the name of **Salha**, daughter of one of Sukayn's followers. Mi'dad is often considered to be the first *shaykh al-'aql* of the Druze community, known at the time as the shaykh of shaykhs (*shaykh al-mashayikh*). *See also* BUHTURI; PEOPLE OF APOSTASY; TANUKH.

FEUDALISM, FEUDALISTS. *See* IQTA', IQTA'IS.

FIQH. Law, or jurisprudence. The Druze **legal system** is based on the Sunni Hanafi school of law with some modifications, primarily with regard to laws on **women** and **inheritance**. *See also* COURT SYSTEM.

FIRAS, BANU. *See* TANUKH.

FIRGHANI, AL-HASAN IBN HAIDARA. Also known as al-Akhram and al-Ajda'. Based on **al-Kirmani**'s account in his Counseling Epistle (*al-Risala al-wa'iza*), he was an 11th-century religious activist who was responsible for the claim of divinity attributed to the **Fatimi caliph al-Hakim**. At times, some authors have erroneously thought Firghani to be a member of the Druze **movement**, but he is never mentioned in the Druze **manuscripts**, and his beliefs are inconsistent with **Druzism**. Firghani was assassinated by a person named al-Karkhi, who is also not related to Druzes.

FIRRO, KAIS. A contemporary historian at the University of Haifa, **Israel**. He has also served as the chair of the Department of Middle Eastern History in the same university. Firro received his academic training in **France** and has written extensively on Israel, **Syria**, and **Lebanon** in general and on the Druzes in particular. *See also* 'AZZAM, FAYIZ; DRUZE RESEARCH INSTITUTE (DRI).

FLAG. The Druze flag is made up of five colors: green, red, yellow, blue, and white. The flag is rooted in theology rather than **politics.** The five main luminaries (***hudud***) are represented by five colors that form the Druze flag (or the five-pointed Druze star). In recent decades, as many other peoples have been emphasizing their ethnic and religious identities, the five-colored Druze flag and star have been politicized as well and have therefore become more visible and at times ubiquitous in Druze communities, namely, on houses, cars, and even clothing.

FLEHAN, HENRY (?–1999). Often known as "Uncle Henry." He arrived in the **United States** in 1937 and served in the U.S. Army during World War II, where he earned a Bronze Star for his service. Henry then became an entrepreneur in the motel and restaurant business and later was involved in the **American Druze Society (ADS)**.

FOUNDATION. *See* ASAS.

FRANCE. France received a provisional mandate over **Lebanon** and **Syria** in 1920 and became responsible for the governing institutions, internal security, and foreign relations of that region. In 1925, the **Aleppo** and **Damascus** districts were combined to form a Syrian state, leaving the Druze and '**Alawi** regions under separate administrations. The first major uprising against the French rule was the **Great Revolt of 1925–1927**, and it was not until 1936 that Syria elected its first nationalist government and reincorporated the Druze and 'Alawi areas. The French withdrew entirely from Syria in April 1946.

Because of the French rule over much of the Druze regions and the active Druze role in the **Arab** independence movement, Druzes in Lebanon and Syria have often pursued or accepted close relations with France's opponent, **Great Britain**. France's competition with Great Britain over control of the Middle East as the **Ottoman Empire** was on the decline resulted in French influence over Lebanon and Syria. Throughout the competition with the British, the French favored the **Maronites**, while the British supported the Druzes. However, French policies have not remained the same, and some recent French presidents have chosen not to engage in Lebanese affairs.

FRANJIYYAH, SULAYMAN (1910–1992). A former president of **Lebanon**. He entered **politics** in the 1950s, becoming first Parliament member and then minister in the 1960s and president in 1970. His presidency witnessed a rise in the influence of the Palestinian Liberation Organization (PLO) in Lebanon and gradual decline toward the **Civil War of 1975–1990**. At times, Franjiyyah joined forces with the **Junblatis**.

FRANJIYYAH, SULAYMAN, JR. (1964–). Grandson of **Sulayman Franjiyyah** and son of Toni Franjiyyah. He was appointed minister in 1990 and won a seat in Parliament in subsequent elections. He is presently minister of public health. Franjiyyah is considered one of the most powerful contemporary **Maronite** leaders in **Lebanon**. He is a friend of some Druze leaders, such as **Talal Arslan**.

FREE OTTOMAN ('Uthmani Hurr). *See* ARSLAN, NASIB.

– G –

GALILEE. The northern mountainous region of **Israel** where a handful of Druze villages are located. Some of the large towns are **Bayt-Jann**, **Buqay'a**, and **Hurfaysh**. Some **families** in Galilee responded to and joined the Druze **movement** in the early 11th century. The Druze **manuscripts** of that period mention a few of these families, including Abu al-Saraya, Abu 'Arus, **Abu 'Abdallah**, and others, who were described as "the Pure" (*al-Tahara*). *See also* TURAB; PALESTINE.

GHAYBA. *See* OCCULTATION.

GHAYTH, BAHJAT. The present *shaykh al-'aql* in **Lebanon**, appointed in 1991. Like his predecessor, Shaykh **Muhammad Abu Shaqra**, he was initially a businessman who worked in various parts of the Middle East and then returned to Lebanon and pursued a religious lifestyle and **leadership**. Shaykh Ghayth is also a philanthropist who has made large contributions to community projects. He has survived the challenges of his critics; befriended diplomats, politicians, and intellectuals; and expressed some of his spiritual insights in a recently published book as well as in numerous public forums, communal and intercommunal. Although he has been in office for over a decade, some still regard him as an interim or acting *shaykh al-'aql*.

GHAZALA, NAWAF. A 20th-century **Syrian** Druze who is known for having pursued the former Syrian leader **Adib al-Shishakli** for 10 years and finally finding and killing him in **Brazil** on 28 July 1964. Nawaf's motive was to avenge Shishakli's attack on Druzes in 1954, which killed many Druzes, including some members of Ghazala's own **family**.

GHULAT. Literally, exaggerators; extremists in **Islam** who are perceived to have departed from the Islamic doctrine. Some Sunni and Western authors tend to lump the Druzes and some other non-Sunni sects with the Ghulat.

GHUTA, AL-. Oasis and farming district to the southeast of **Damascus**. It was an early center of **Druzism** during the emergence of the Druze **movement** in the 11th century. Druzes fought battles in this area both in the 11th century and during the **Great Revolt of 1925–1927**.

GNOSTIC, GNOSTICISM. This term comes from the Greek *gnosis*, which means "knowledge." Gnosticism is an intellectual school that dates back to early Christianity but has roots in earlier religious and philosophical traditions, including Judaism and Greek philosophy. **Druzism** adopted some gnostic ideas that relate to the soul, initiation, illumination, and metempsychosis (*taqamus*). *See also* DUALISM; ESOTERICISM; HUDUD; MAQAM; SUFISM.

GOD. *See* TAWHID.

GOLAN HEIGHTS. An area east of the Sea of **Galilee** and northeast of the state of **Israel**. It was previously a part of **Syria** but has been under the control of Israel since the **Six-Day War** (June 1967). It was originally located on the caravan route from **Damascus** and Baghdad to the Mediterranean sea. The Romans ruled the area from Qunaytra, the largest city. In the seventh century, it was conquered by the **Islamic** forces and renamed the Golan (*al-Julan*).

There are approximately 15,000 Druzes living in four villages on the Golan Heights: **Majdal Shams**, Mas'ada, 'Ayn Qinya, and Biq'atha. On 14 December 1981, the Israeli government annexed the Golan Heights, but three days later the **United Nations** pronounced the annexation null and void. The Golani Druzes have continued to assert their Syrian identity, and the chief Syrian objective in the Syrian-Israeli peace talks since 1992 has been to regain the entire Golan

Heights. Many Israelis have also believed that the area will eventually be handed back to Syria when a "land for peace" agreement is signed. On the other hand, some writers have treated Golani Druzes as a part of the Israeli Druzes.

GREAT BRITAIN. Great Britain played a major role in the lives and lands of Druzes throughout their involvement in the Middle East. Overall, the British have maintained good relations with the leading Druze **families**. This is due to the superpower competition between Great Britain and **France** as well as to the role that the **Ottoman Empire** was playing in the Druze areas. At times, both the Ottomans and the French have supported Druze opponents.

There is presently a small Druze **diaspora** community in Great Britain. They have established an **organization** known as the **British Druze Society (BDS)**, which works at maintaining close ties between its members and their homeland. *See also* 'ALAM AL-DIN, NAJIB; KHAYR AL-DIN, SALIM.

GREAT REVOLT OF 1925–1927. A revolt against the **French** forces in **Syria**, which began in **Jabal al-Duruz** and spread throughout the rest of the region. By July 1927, the French had successfully suppressed the revolt and either exiled many of its leaders or forced them to flee. The revolt, however, was the first major political **movement** in modern Syria and subsequently accelerated the independence movement of Syria and other **Arab** states.

The leader of the revolt was the Druze **Sultan al-Atrash**, who objected to French rule in 1922 and later, in 1925, used the rebel **Adham Khanjar**'s execution in **Beirut** by the French as a reason to mobilize against French interference with the population's customs and traditions of hospitality. Adham Khanjar had apparently sought the hospitality and protection of Sultan, who was not home at the time. The French rejected Sultan's appeal to release Adham since Adham had been charged with killing a French soldier. The revolt led to the strengthening of the Syrian (and Arab) nationalist movement and the end of European control over the Middle East. *See also* ARAB NATIONALISM.

GREEN PROPHET. *See* KHIDR, AL-.

GUIDE OF BELIEVERS (Hadi al-Mustajibin). Guide of those who responded to and accepted the Druze *Tawhid* Call (*Da'wa*) in the early 11th century. It is one of the titles used in the Druze **manuscripts** to refer to **Hamza Ibn 'Ali**. *See also* DRUZISM; MASTER OF GUIDES; MITHAQ; MOVEMENT, DRUZE.

– H –

HADI AL-MUSTAJIBIN. *See* GUIDE OF BELIEVERS.

HADITHAT ADHAM (The Incident of Adham). *See* KHANJAR, ADHAM.

HAFIZ, AMIN AL- (1920–   ). **Syrian** Sunni army officer who came to power with the **Ba'th** coup of 1963. He was overthrown in 1966. Druze officers joined forces with **'Alawi** officers to overthrow al-Hafiz.

HAJALI. *See* SA'B.

HAJARI. A prominent **family** in the **Jabal al-Duruz**, **Syria**, with several *shaykh al-'aqls*, the earliest being **Ibrahim al-Hajari** (d. 1840). It is said that this family is originally a descendant of the **Abu Hamzeh** family from the **Shuf** in **Mount Lebanon**. The father of Ibrahim moved to Ashrafiyya and then to **Suwayda**. Some derive the name Hajari from the **Arabic** root, which means "to migrate."

HAJARI, IBRAHIM IBN MAHMOUD AL- (?–1840). The founder and first *shaykh al-'aql* in **Jabal al-Duruz** in the beginning of the 19th century. Because of his spiritual insights, mediation skills, and wide-ranging knowledge in the religious sciences, he gained the respect and spiritual **leadership** of the various **families** in the region.

HAJI, JAMAL AL-DIN (?–1222). An early prince in **Mount Lebanon** and the son of Najm al-Din Muhammad. He excelled in administering the political affairs of the area and was acknowledged by **Saladin**. Toward the end of his life, he became a religious figure and an **ascetic**. He is the father of **Shuja' al-Din 'Abd al-Rahman**. *See also* BUHTURI.

HAJJ. *See* PILGRIMAGE.

HAKIM BI-AMR ALLAH, AL- (r. 996–1021). The sixth **Fatimi caliph** who took office at the age of 11 when **al-'Aziz**, the fifth caliph, died. He was initially known as Abu 'Ali Al-Mansur. Scholars have often viewed him as one of the most controversial and mysterious of the caliphs and **imams** throughout **Islamic** history. On the one hand, he was a devout and pious religious figure with **ascetic** qualities. On the other, he was often perceived as erratic and harsh in some of his edicts against Jews, Christians, and **Sunnis** at times, though he reversed some of these resolutions.

The controversies surrounding his personality and unusual or unprecedented actions have perhaps distracted some scholars from giving more attention to him as a religious reformer. Most notably, he separated church and state by appointing **Hamza Ibn 'Ali** as the imam and **al-Zahir** as the caliph.

Some historians link the Druze **faith** to al-Hakim. Several Druze **manuscripts** confirm that **Druzism** was approved by him, for such sources indicate that certain epistles were brought to his inspection by the **ambassador** before such writings were returned to Hamza Ibn 'Ali and then distributed among missionaries and members of the **movement**.

In 1021, al-Hakim went on one of his routine trips to Jabal **al-Muqattam** outside the city of **Cairo** and never returned. The fact that his body was never discovered has added to the mystery of his death. *See also* JAMI' AL-HAKIM; HAKIMI CALL, THE.

HAKIMI CALL, THE (Al-Da'wa al-Hakimiyya). Also the Hakimi sect (*al-Madhhab al-Hakimi*). A title coined after the name of the **Fatimi caliph al-Hakim**. It is often used by some early scholars and other writers to refer to **Druzism** or the Druze **movement** though at times more broadly to include all supporters of al-Hakim. *See also* DA'WA; HAMZA IBN 'ALI; ISMA'ILIS.

HALABI, ABU IZZEDIN AL-. A 16th-century devout **shaykh** and writer who wrote commentaries and spiritual guidance. His work was highly praised by **al-Shaykh al-Fadil** (d. 1640). He is also known for his long poem in which he describes in detail the events leading to the **Judgment Day**.

HALABI, JABIR IBN MUHAMMAD AL- (?–1640). A devout **shaykh** from **Ma'arrat al-Ikhwan** in the district of **Aleppo**. His depth of knowledge in the Quranic sciences was well known in the regions of Aleppo and **Damascus**. On one occasion, he delighted the Ottoman governor with his ideas and was subsequently invited to take a part in a contest with several prominent Sunni theologians. As a result of winning this contest, the governor appointed Shaykh Jabir to the position of *shaykh al-Islam* in the district of Aleppo.

After his death, the Ottoman sultan ordered the construction of a **sacred site** on his tomb in remembrance of his good deeds and contributions to the community of Aleppo. The shaykh was also known for his **thaumaturgies** (*karamat*) both while living and after his death; for example, attempts to harm his burial site or act with disrespect in the vicinity of the site were often reported as unsuccessful. His **visitation site** is today a place of sacredness and blessing for Druzes and non-Druzes.

HALABI, SALAH AL-DIN AL-. A 15th-century **shaykh** from **Jabal al-A'la**. He was a contemporary of Emir **al-Sayyid al-Tanukhi** in the 15th century and is said to have visited him and sought his advice. Shaykh Salah al-Din led an **ascetic** lifestyle and wrote important spiritual poems, but little is known about his life and genealogy.

HALABIYYA, MASHAYIKH AL-. A term used to refer to several devout **shaykhs** in **Aleppo** who visited **al-Shaykh al-Fadil** and subsequently maintained close contact with him through correspondence. They became prominent spiritual guides for the Druze community in the district of Aleppo. Among these shaykhs are 'Abdallah Ibn Yasin and Ahmad Ibn Abi 'Izziddin Sharaf al-Din.

HALAL. Something that is permitted, the opposite of *haram* (that which is prohibited). Both terms, *halal* and *haram*, are also often used in legal settings. *See also* COURT SYSTEM.

HAMADEH, FARID. *See* YAZBAKI LIBERATION FRONT.

HAMADI, MARWAN (1939–). Editor of *al-Nahar*, **Beirut**'s daily newspaper, during the 1970s. He emerged as **Walid Junblat**'s primary public relations representative and adviser and is known for his moderate policies. He won a seat in Parliament in 1992 and was re-elected in 1996 and 2000. He became minister of economy and trade in the Lebanese government in 2003 but resigned in 2004. He survived an assassination attempt on 1 October 2004.

HAMADY, HUSAYN (1862–1946). A *shaykh al-'aql* in **Lebanon** between 1915 and1946. He graduated from the **Dawudiyya School** and was later educated in the religious sciences by his father, who was also a *shaykh al-'aql*.

HAMADY, JACK (?–2001). An early 20th-century Druze immigrant to the **United States** who served as the chairman of the board of Hamady Brothers, established in 1911 in Flint, Michigan. He is a philanthropist and humanitarian with many honors, including an honorary degree, doctor of human letters, from Baker College in 1992. He also established a writing contest (Uncle Jack's Appreciate America Contest), which he cosponsored with the Flint Board of Education.

Uncle Jack was active in numerous business and community **organizations**, including the Big Brothers of Flint, the Flint Chamber of Commerce, Flint Area Conference Inc., March of Dimes Mothers Fundraising, the Salvation Army, the **American Druze Foundation (ADF)**, and the **American Druze Society (ADS)**.

HAMDAN. One of the prominent Druze **families** of **Lebanon** and **Syria**. In Syria, they were one of the two important families at the beginning of the 19th century, the other being **Abu Fakhr**.

HAMDAN, SALIM IBN 'ABBAS (1892–1968). A journalist who migrated to the **United States** in 1907 and worked in marketing and journalism but returned to **Lebanon** a decade later. After a career in teaching at the **Dawudiyya School** in **'Alay** and in editing the newspaper *al-Safa'*, he moved to **Egypt** and worked on the editorial staff of *al-Ahram* and then *al-Muqattam*. He then moved to Jerusalem to work for *al-Wafa'* newspaper and later with **'Ajaj Nuwayhid** for Jerusalem Radio. In 1942, he returned to Lebanon for several years and then moved to **Suwayda**, where he worked on the staff of *al-Jabal* newspaper. Salim published several **poetry** collections in addition to a few studies on various topics, including one on **women**'s issues.

HAMDAN, TALI' (1944–   ). A popular Lebanese folk poet (*zajal*) who joined Zaqhlul al-Damur's prestigious entertainment group in the late 1960s. He also published some collections of his **poetry** in the 1970s and has participated in many communal and ceremonial events in **Lebanon** and abroad. *See also* LITERATURE.

HAMMANA. Large Christian village in the eastern **al-Matn** region with a significant Druze minority. It was a site of a large defection by Druze soldiers from the **Lebanese army** in the **War of the Mountain** (*Harb al-Jabal*) in 1983–1985. The town is also a tourist attraction.

HAMUD, SALMAN. *See* TARIF, MUHANNA.

HAMZA IBN 'ALI. The first Druze luminary and the author of some of the 11th-century Druze **manuscripts**. Hamza was born in the city of Zawzan in Khurasan, obtained a degree in philosophy from the University of Jandisabur, and came to **Cairo** in order to join the faculty of the **House of Wisdom** (*Dar al-Hikmah*). He was appointed as **imam** by **al-Hakim** in 1017. He seems to have consistently kept a low profile, and, therefore, many sources do not mention him at all. Nevertheless, those authors who mention him indicate that he arrived in Cairo in December 1016 and met the main luminaries (*hudud*) of the Druze **movement** later that month in the **Ridan Mosque**. He had direct access to al-Hakim, but it seems that at times his epistles were brought to al-Hakim by another luminary who was referred to as the **Ambassador** of Power (*Safir al-Qudrah*).

In 1021, Hamza withdrew from public preaching to an undisclosed place of retreat outside Cairo. During the period of his retreat, the fifth luminary, **Baha' al-Din al-Samuqi**, tells us that his own writings and decisions had been approved by Hamza Ibn 'Ali. Based on the Druze traditions, Hamza Ibn 'Ali is referred to as the **Universal Intellect** (*al-'Aql al-Kulli*), but he is also known by many additional titles, including the Ruler of the **Judgment Day** (*Waliyy al-Zaman*), the Owner of the Judgment Day (*Qa'im al-Zaman*), and the **Guide of Believers** (*Hadi al-Mustajibin*). *See also* DARAZI, MUHAMMAD AL-; DRUZISM.

HAMZY, WILLIAM (1966–). Son of Nabih and Raja' Abu Hamzeh, who were originally from the town of **al-Khraibeh** in the **Shuf, Lebanon**. He is an American Druze attorney who was elected as the state representative of the 78th district of Connecticut in 1992. He has served on many committees in that state and was recently selected to serve as assistant minority leader for the 2003–2004 legislative sessions.

HAQIQA (pl. *haqa'iq*). Truth, ultimate reality, or knowledge of God. In some mystical circles, it is the third dimension after *Shari'a* (law) and *Tariqa* (path). Like other mystics, devout Druze **shaykhs** pursue *Shari'a* and *Tariqa* while aiming to reach *Haqiqa*.

HARAM. That which is forbidden based on the **Islamic legal system** as stipulated in the **Qur'an** and elaborated on in the *Hadith*. The Druze writings and commentaries adopt many of the **Judeo-Christian**–Islamic legal restrictions and prohibitions. *See also* COURT SYSTEM; HALAL.

HARB, NASIF HAMADEH (1880–1926). One of the fallen heroes of the **Great Revolt of 1925–1927** from the village of Doma. He is remembered for his initiative, courage, and fearlessness.

HARB AL-JABAL. *See* WAR OF THE MOUNTAIN.

HASBAYA. An ancient city in southeastern **Lebanon**. It is today a largely Druze town. Hasbaya is the administrative capital of the two northern and southern regions of **Wadi al-Taym**, where a Druze presence flourished during the emergence of the Druze **movement** in the beginning of the 11th century. The town is adjacent to the Hasbani River, which is central to the agricultural wealth of the town. It is also in close proximity to the main Druze **shrines** and center of spiritual learning known as **Khalawat al-Bayyada**. Historically, the **Shihabi emirs** of Lebanon (r. 1697–1842) had a stronghold in Hasbaya.

HASBAYA WOMEN'S ASSOCIATION. A social **organization** that aims at **education** and professional training for **women** in the area of **Hasbaya**. It later became a model for various women's organizations in other Druze regions.

HASSUN. *See* ABU AL-HUSN.

HATUM, SALIM (?–1967). A Druze army officer of the **Syrian Ba'th Party** who led an unsuccessful coup against the **'Alawis** in September 1966. He fled to **Jordan** but was executed in 1967 on his return to Syria.

HAWRAN. This term is often applied to the entire southern region of **Syria**, including the Druze mountain **Jabal al-Duruz**. Some sources, on the other hand, refer to Hawran as only the area adjacent to Jabal al-Duruz. *See also* 'AYN DARA; HAWRANIS; QAYSI-YAMANI.

HAWRANIS. A reference to inhabitants, both Druze and non-Druze, of **Hawran** in **Syria**. At times, the term is used by Druzes to refer to their coreligionists in **Jabal al-Duruz** in general. Hawranis have a distinct dialect of **Arabic**. *See also* BALLAN, FAHD.

HBOUS, PRINCESS. *See* ARSLAN, HBOUS.

HEALTH ESTABLISHMENT OF THE DRUZE COMMITTEE. Founded in 1978 by the former Lebanese *shaykh al-'aql* **Muhammad Abu Shaqra** (d. 1991) and others as a nonprofit health care **organization**.

HERMES. In Greek mythology, Hermes is the messenger of the gods. The "thrice-greatest" (Trismegistus) Hermes is the key figure in the mystical literature known as Hermetica. Hermes is regarded as a symbol of wisdom, power, and rule and as one who can save the world. In the **Qur'an**, he is the Prophet Idris, a man of truth and sincerity. In **Druzism**, he is also referred to as Akhnokh and Imhotep (2667–2648 B.C.E.). Historically, Imhotep is an **Egyptian** healer and architect who is said to have acquired the status of a god and became the first documented example of deification in 525 B.C.E.

HIFZ AL-IKHWAN. *See* BROTHERLINESS.

HIJAB. See NIQAB.

HIKMAH (Wisdom). When Druzes use this term, they refer to one of their main scriptural sources known as the *Epistles of Wisdom* (*Rasa'il al-Hikmah*). However, when the term is used in certain Druze **manuscripts**, it means wisdom in a generic sense. Thus, the distinction between *hikma* as wisdom and *hikma* as the volume of 111 Druze epistles is important. *See also* HIKMAH AL-SHARIFA, AL-.

HIKMAH, AL-. *See* 'ABBOUD, MAROUN.

HIKMAH AL-SHARIFA, AL- (The Noble Wisdom). A term used generally to refer to the world's religious, spiritual, and philosophical traditions. Most Druzes use it to refer to their **manuscript** known as the *Epistles of Wisdom* (*Rasa'il al-Hikmah*). *See also* HIKMAH.

HIKMAH, RASA'IL AL-. *See* EPISTLES OF WISDOM.

HILAL, BANU. *See* TANUKH.

HINAWI, ABU 'ALI. An early 19th-century Druze poet from **Jabal al-Duruz** who is known for his writings on Druze bravery and other characteristics in battles. In his poems, he provides a detailed account on the Druze battles against **Ibrahim Pasha** of **Egypt** in the 1831–1840 occupation of **Syria**.

HISN AL-DIN, NAHID AL-DIN IBN 'ABDALLAH. A 15th-century devout **shaykh** who was one of the disciples of Emir **al-Sayyid al-Tanukhi**. His grandfather, Hisn al-Din, came from **Aleppo** to become a tutor for the sons of the **Tanukhi emirs**. Shaykh Nahid al-Din grew up in **al-Mukhtara**, specialized in the religious sciences, met and then corresponded with Emir al-Sayyid, and eventually became his disciple. He died before his master.

HITTI, PHILIP. An early 20th-century American Lebanese historian who has written extensively on the **Arabs**. He published an influential book on the Druzes in 1928 (reissued in 1964) that is still popular despite its brevity and shortcomings. The book has been criticized by several Druze authors, though it provided some valuable insights.

HITTIN. A historical town near Tiberias, **Israel**, where the burial and **visitation site** of the biblical prophet Jethro (**Shu'ayb**) is located. Druzes visit the site regularly and hold an annual festival there every April. It is also the site where the famous **battle of Hittin** took place in 1187 between **Saladin** and the crusaders.

HITTIN, BATTLE OF (1187). The main decisive victory of the **Ayyubi** sultan **Saladin** (Salah al-Din, r. 1171–1193) over the crusaders after his initial victory in Marj 'Uyun in 1179. Druzes pride themselves on having participated in these two battles with the Ayyubi forces.

HIZB AL-KATA'IB AL-LUBNANIYYA. *See* LEBANESE PHALANGES PARTY (LPP).

HIZB AL-SHA'B. *See* PEOPLE'S PARTY.

HIZB AL-TAQADDUMI AL-ISHTIRAKI, AL-. *See* PROGRESSIVE SOCIALIST PARTY (PSP).

HNEIDI, FADLALLAH (1876–1926). One of the fallen heroes of the **Great Revolt of 1925–1927**. He was from the town of al-Majdal and was the son of Hazimah Hneidi. As a member of the Nationalist Party (*al-Hizb al-Watani*), Fadlallah was also active in the earliest struggle against the Ottoman occupation. He was among those who went to welcome Emir Faysal Ibn Sharif Hussein in the southern part of present-day **Jordan** in the city of 'Aqaba in 1916. Emir Faysal awarded him the title of brigadier general (*Emir al-Liwa*) on 28 December 1919. He died in battle in **Suwayda**.

HOLIDAYS. Druzes celebrate several holidays, though the nature of the celebrations may vary from one community to another. Almost all Druzes celebrate *Eid al-Adha* (Feast of Sacrifice), and some Druzes celebrate *Eid al-Fitr* (Feast of Breaking the Fast). Both celebrations symbolize meanings slightly different from the **Islamic** tradition. Additional celebrations include the Holidays of Jethro (**Shu'ayb**), **Job** (Ayyub), Sabalan, and the Green Prophet (**Khidr**).

HOUSE OF WISDOM (Dar al-Hikmah). Also known as House of Learning (*Dar al-'Ilm*). The term "*dar*" may be translated as "abode," "seat," and "center" of wisdom or learning. It was built by the sixth **Fatimi caliph**, **al-Hakim bi-Amr Allah**, in the year 1005 as an extension of his palace. It included a large library collection with several halls for lectures and public discussions. Early historians report that *Dar al-Hikmah* was accessible to all seekers and that people came to read, hand-copy books, or attend discussions and lectures. Earlier, the **'Abbasi** caliph al-Ma'mun (d. 833) also built an institution of learning called *Bayt al-Hikmah* (House of Wisdom).

HUDUD. In legal **Islamic** discourse, this term refers to punishment for certain crimes, as stipulated in the **Qur'an** and *Shari'a*. In Druze theology, **cosmology**, and eschatology, the concept means cosmic principles, luminaries, or limitaries. It refers to a large hierarchy of **intermediaries** who have spiritual functions that will again resurface on the **Judgment Day**. *See also* DRUZISM; HUDUD SUFLIYYA; HUDUD 'ULWIYYA.

HUDUD SUFLIYYA. Lower or secondary luminaries. In **Druzism**, it refers to the three luminaries, following the primary five ones; they are the sixth, seventh, and eighth and are known as Jadd, **Fath**, and Khayal, respectively. *See also* COSMOLOGY; HUDUD; HUDUD 'ULWIYYA.

HUDUD 'ULWIYYA. Upper or primary luminaries. In **Druzism**, the term refers to the five main spiritual principles or their representatives in the **Cycle of Disclosure** (*Dawr Kashf*) in the early 11th century: **Universal Intellect**, Universal Soul, the Word, the Former, and the Latter. *See also* COSMOLOGY; HUDUD; HUDUD SUFLIYYA.

HUJJAH. A figure in the **Isma'ili** *da'wa* hierarchy who represents evidence of God's will. In **Druzism**, it is a title given to **al-Tamimi** for being the medium between **Hamza Ibn 'Ali** and other missionaries.

HULUL. Incarnation of the divine essence; a belief that God's reality or spirit enters the soul of a human being. Although the doctrine of *Hulul* is often attributed to Druzes, it is not a belief advocated in the Druze **manuscripts**. Groups and individuals who believe in *hulul* have been referred to as *Hululiyya* by classical and some later authors.

HURFAYSH. A Druze town in upper **Galilee, Israel**, with a population approaching nearly 5,000. The **visitation site** of Prophet **Sabalan** is near the village and draws many visitors from the entire region.

HUSHA AND KASAYER. *See* RAMAT YUHANAN, BATTLE OF.

– I –

IBLIS. *See* SATAN.

IBN AL-BARBARIYYA. An early 11th-century opponent of the Druze **movement**. In 1029, he claimed to be an **imam** in the area of west of Alexandria, **Egypt**. He advocated that all matters belong to the imam and therefore denied God's supremacy. He is known in the Druze tradition as the "night thief" (*haramiyy al-layl*) because he declared himself imam while **Hamza Ibn 'Ali** was absent. This title is in contrast to that given to **al-Darazi**, the "day thief" (*haramiyy al-nahar*), because Darazi tried to steal the imamate in 1019 while Hamza was present. Later, however, Ibn al-Barbariyya feared confrontation with the leaders of the movement and withdrew his claims. *See also* PEOPLE OF APOSTASY.

IBN FUTUH, SHAYKH NASR. *See* DAMASCUS.

IBN JANDAL, ABI AL-KHAYR SALAMAH IBN HASM. One of the early 11th-century loyal members of the Druze **movement**. He advised the missionary **'Ammar** to confront the Druze **apostate Sukayn** and his followers in **Wadi al-Taym** unarmed. Ibn Jandal believed that 'Ammar may succeed in disuading Sukayn from apostasy if he approached him and his followers unarmed. Ibn Jandal's advice cost 'Ammar his life.

IBN SIBAT, HAMZA (?–1520). Son of **Shihab al-Din Ahmad Ibn Sibat** from 'Alay. He is a historian who is known for having chronicled events of the years 1132–1520. He is also known for his **poetry** as well as for his biographical account of Druze sages, such as that of Emir **al-Sayyid al-Tanukhi**.

IBN SIBAT, SHIHAB AL-DIN AHMAD. A 15th-century educator and devout **shaykh** from 'Alay. He excelled in the Quranic sciences. Shihab al-Din is the father of the historian **Hamza Ibn Sibat.**

IBN SUMER. *See* RAJBAL (RAJ PAL) IBN SUMER.

IBN TAIMIYYA, TAQI AL-DIN AHMAD (1263–1328). A prominent Sunni religious jurist who was also a prolific author and whose influence on **Islamic** puritan and fundamentalist movements extends to the present day. His writings are widely circulated in the Islamic world, and his teachings are highly appraised. He wrote a religious ruling (*fatwa*) against Druzes and other residents of the **Levant.** The *fatwa* was politically motivated and issued to enable the **Mamluk** sultan Nasir al-Din's army to attack and control the region. Although Ibn Taimiyya does not include any points of contention or any citation from the Druze **manuscripts, Muslim** jurists have, since Ibn Taimiyya's time, used this *fatwa* as the evidence for pronouncing **Druzism** a heresy and the Druzes **apostates.** *See also* JIHAD.

IBN YAHYA, SALIH. A 15th-century **Tanukhi** prince and historian who is known for his work on **Beirut**, in which he chronicles 300 years of the history of that city by shedding light on the **Tanukhi-**

Buhturi principality. He also wrote a book on the prominent imam al-Awza'i (d. 774) from **Damascus**.

IBN YA'LA. *See* PEOPLE OF APOSTASY.

IBN YASIR, 'AMMAR (?–657). One of the early companions of Prophet **Muhammad** whose parents were the first to be tortured and killed by the pagan Meccans. 'Ammar survived the early persecutions inflicted on the **Muslim** community but later died in the battle of Siffin between **'Ali Ibn Abi Talib** and Mu'awiyyah Ibn Abi Sufyan. In the Druze tradition, 'Ammar became a central figure in spirituality and a model of dedication and piety. *See also* FARISI, SALMAN AL-.

IBRAHIM IBN ADHAM (?–875). A **Muslim** prince turned **saint** who became a symbol of **asceticism** and piety. He is one of the early Muslim sages who was adopted in the Druze tradition as a model for discarding this world and focusing on devotion to God. **Emirs** like **Sayf al-Din al-Tanukhi** (d. 1455) have been described as Adham in their times. *See also* RABI'A OF BASRA.

IBRAHIM PASHA (1789–1848). Son of Muhammad 'Ali and commander of the **Egyptian** forces that invaded and occupied **Syria** from 1831 to 1840. His army defeated the Ottoman commander Uthman Pasha's forces in Tripoli and attempted to impose on Syria a central authority similar to that of Egypt. Ibrahim Pasha's favorable treatment of Christians and his alliance with Emir **Bashir Shihabi** fostered antagonism with the Druzes, most of whom had wished for an Ottoman victory.

In 1835, Ibrahim Pasha reached **Bayt al-Din** and controlled this Shihabi seat of power over **Mount Lebanon**. In 1837–1838, the Druzes rebelled against Ibrahim, and his troops suffered several minor defeats as a result of the Druze tactic, "attack and escape." However, the Druzes were unable to win a permanent victory.

The Ottomans had attempted to regain control over the area, but it was not until a European alliance of powers intervened that Egypt withdrew from the region in 1840. This invasion further provoked hostilities between Druzes and **Maronites**, hostilities that had begun before Ibrahim's arrival in the Lebanese Mountains but that then spread and intensified in the following two decades from 1841 to 1860.

'ID, NASIR AL-DIN AL- (?–1698). A Lebanese Druze sage from the town of **B'aqlin.** He is known for his wide-ranging knowledge in the religious sciences and has written commentaries on the Druze **manuscripts,** including a lexicon of religious terms.

IDRIS. *See* HERMES.

IHSAN. *See* IMAN.

IJTIHAD. Individual reasoning; the exercise of independent judgment in theology and jurisprudence. While in Sunni **Islam** the gate of *Ijtihad* was closed in the ninth century after the establishment of the four schools of law (Hanafi, Maliki, Shafi'i, and Hanbali), **Shi'i** jurists saw their role as interpreters of the law and the will or **intentionality** of the Hidden **Imam. Druzism** as a reform **movement,** based on the intellect (*'aql*), advocates a combination of scriptural perspective and human reasoning.

IMAM. The leader of prayers or ceremonial rituals in the **Islamic** and Druze traditions. The institution or office of the imam is known as *imamah.* **Shi'ism** has differentiated between *Imam Mustaqarr* (permanent imam) and *Imam Mustawda'* (acting or temporary imam). In scriptural and traditional Druze settings, the first luminary, **Hamza Ibn 'Ali,** is the Imam of the Times (*Imam al-Zaman*). *See also* CALIPH; DA'WA; HUDUD.

IMAN. Faith or belief. *Iman* is often perceived as the second stage after **Islam** and before that of *Tawhid,* the third stage. One of **Muhammad**'s famous sayings regards the distinction between Islam, *iman,* and *ihsan.* While Islam has been interpreted by later Islamic sects as the **exoteric** and ritualistic practices of the religion, *iman* has been perceived as the allegorical or **esoteric** interpretation of the Quranic verses and commentaries. *Ihsan,* which means goodness, has been explained as worshipping God as if one sees Him, for God sees the believer. *Ihsan* often corresponds with *Tawhid*. This view of three stages of progress toward spirituality gave birth to reform movements, including the Druzes, and directed believers to begin concentrating more on intentionality (*niyya*) than on practice. *See also* TANZIL, T'AWIL.

IMHOTEP. *See* HERMES.

INCIDENT OF THE MOSQUE. *See* WAQ'AT AL-JAMI'.

'INDANRI, BADR AL-DIN. A 16th-century leading **shaykh** who lived during the time of Emir **Fakhr al-Din al-Ma'ni**. Shaykh 'Indari advocated the teachings of **Emir al-Sayyid al-Tanukhi** and insisted that Druze shaykhs should emulate the spiritual qualities of al-Sayyid. *See also* ASCETICISM; 'AYN DARA; MASHAYIKH AL-DIN; SUFISM.

INHERITANCE. The Druze laws on inheritance are based on the 1948 legal code established in **Lebanon** and then in **Syria** and **Israel**. It is rooted primarily in the Sunni Hanafi school of law but with some modifications, such as the granting of female members in the **family** a larger share than is granted by the Hanafi school. *See also* COURT SYSTEM; WOMEN.

INITIATED. *See* 'UQQAL.

INSTITUTE OF DRUZE STUDIES (IDS). An academic nonprofit research **organization** that was established in the **United States** and registered in the state of California in 1998. The mission of the IDS is to promote academic discourse about the Druzes and Druze-related issues and to encourage research and studies on historical and contemporary Druze communities. The IDS has organized international conferences beginning in 1999 as well as panels at scholarly gatherings and has published several issues of its newsletter (**IDS Update**). The IDS journal (***Journal of Druze Studies***) was inaugurated in 2000 and is published occasionally.

INTENTIONALITY. *See* NIYYA.

INTERMEDIARIES. *See* TAQDIS.

INTERPRETATION. *See* PEOPLE OF INTERPRETATION.

IQTA', IQTA'IS. Feudalism, feudalists. Druze society was character-ized by a unique form of feudalism that flourished in the area during the previous few centuries; several **families** usually owned vast lands, while members of small families worked for landowners. In the 19th century, for example, Druze and non-Druze peasants rose against landowners beginning in the 1820s and later in the 1840s. This conflict between peasants and landowners was soon politicized as a sectarian conflict. Although many changes in society in general have taken place in the past century, some Druze families or individ-uals are still known as large landowners relative to the rest of the community. *See also* 'AMMIYYA; CIVIL WAR OF 1860.

'IRFAN. Esoteric knowledge; gnosis. It is often argued that such knowledge must remain secret and not be revealed except to individ-uals who are morally, intellectually, and spiritually ready to accept it. This esoteric and secretive practice is adopted from other, earlier traditions. For example, in Greek philosophy, Pythagoras had to es-tablish a secretive association that included only initiated members who could understand the esoteric teachings. In the Jewish tradition, Moses transmitted the written Torah to his followers but the oral Torah (*ha-Torah she-be'al peh*) only to the few selected elders.

The Druze tradition is an *'irfani* one. Only individuals with the right character are admitted into the ranks of the initiated (**'uqqal**). Lack of readiness will eventually lead to misunderstanding (*'irfan*), and therefore a lengthy and arduous process of initiation is usually required of interested individuals. *See also* JUHHAL; TAWHID; TA'WIL.

'IRFAN TAWHID FOUNDATION (ITF). A foundation that was es-tablished in **Lebanon** in November 1971 and became a nonprofit charitable **organization** in 1973. It aims to help orphans and other needy individuals. The ITF has developed a system of **Islamic-**

Druze education and started its first school in 1973, which expanded into several branches serving a few thousand students. In addition to the schools, there is also the *'irfan* hospital in **Simqaniya** in the **Shuf** region.

IRON HAND SOCIETY. *See* SHAHBANDAR, 'ABD AL-RAHMAN.

'ISFIYA. One of the two Druze towns on the eastern slopes of **Mount Carmel, Israel**. It is the smaller of the two; the other is **Daliyat al-Carmel**. The majority of the population in 'Isfiya is Druze (over 6,000) with Christian and **Muslim** minorities (over 2,000), totaling nearly 9,000. 'Isfiya has the **visitation site** of the Druze sage Abu 'Abdallah.

ISHTI, HAMAD YUSEF (1900–1992). One of the heroes of the **Great Revolt of 1925–1927**. He is remembered for having succeeded in infiltrating the French forces to collect intelligence. As a result, he was seriously injured and recovered only after many months. *See also* FRANCE.

ISLAH, AL-. *See* 'ISRAWI, NAJIB.

ISLAM. The term *Islam* means "submission (to God)." The Islamic religion emerged in the early seventh century when Prophet **Muhammad** (d. 632) began receiving and propagating the message of the **Qur'an**. The Qur'an was revealed to Muhammad over 22 years (610–632). The Islamic community soon after broke into **Sunnis** and **Shi'is**. The Druzes emerged from Shi'i Islam, though their **legal system** is rooted in the Sunni Hanafi school of law. The Druze **manuscripts** describe **Druzism** as a branch or a reform **movement** within Islam.

Some **Muslim** rulers and jurists have advocated the persecution of members of the Druze **movement** beginning with the seventh **Fatimi caliph** al-Zahir in 1021. Recurring periods of persecution in subsequent centuries, combined with the **esoteric** and secretive nature of the Druze teachings as well as the Druze failure to elucidate their beliefs and practices, have contributed to the ambiguous relationship between **Muslims** and Druzes. *See also* HAMZA IBN 'ALI; IBN TAIMIYYA, TAQI AL-DIN AHMAD; IBRAHIM PASHA; TAWHID.

ISLAMIC UNITY. *See* SYRIAN-PALESTINE CONGRESS.

ISMA'IL AL-TAMIMI. *See* TAMIMI, ISMA'IL IBN MUHAMMAD AL-.

ISMA'IL IBN JA'FAR (?–760). The seventh **Shi'i Isma'ili imam**. He is the elder son of the sixth Shi'i imam, **Ja'far al-Sadiq. Druzism** acknowledges Isma'il as one in the chain of imams who led to the emergence of the Druze reform **movement**.

ISMA'ILI, ISMA'ILIS. Seveners; **Shi'i Muslims** who revere **Isma'il Ibn Ja'far** as the **imam** instead of his younger brother Musa. The Isma'ilis are the forefathers of the **Fatimis** and the Druzes. The Druze doctrine is an Isma'ili one in origin but has several added reforms. These reforms include the transfer of the imamate from the sixth Fatimi **caliph** and imam **al-Hakim** to **Hamza Ibn 'Ali**, a transfer that is not recognized or accepted in Isma'ilism.

ISRAEL. The Druzes in Israel make up less than 1 percent of the country's population; they do not exceed 80,000. Most of them live on two mountain ranges: the **Galilee** and the **Carmel** (see map 4). They participate in many political parties, and as a result their **politics** has often granted them more seats in the Israeli Parliament, the **Knesset**, than they are proportionally entitled to.

In the 1930s and 1940s, the relationship of the Druze community with the surrounding neighbors was not peaceful. However, some Jewish settlers were able to win the support of several Druze leaders. During the same period, some other Druzes participated in the **Arab** armies' fight against the Jewish forces. But after the battle of **Ramat Yuhanan**, the Druze community's role in the Arab-Jewish struggle was strategically reduced, and they sought to save their community from a potential exodus.

Since the establishment of the state of Israel in 1948, Druzes began military service in the **Israeli Defense Forces (IDF)**, and this became compulsory after 1956. Israeli government policies have treated Druzes differently from other minorities within its borders. The state provided Druzes with limited upward mobility through military and government channels. Still, while this has not led to equality with the Jewish citizens of the state, there have been gradual improvements over the past several decades. This evolving state of affairs has provided fertile grounds for proponents and opponents to praise or criticize the Israeli government's treatment of Druzes. *See also* PALESTINE.

ISRAELI DEFENSE FORCES (IDF). Some Druzes joined the IDF voluntarily in 1948, but since 1956, male Druzes are drafted compulsorily for the regular three years of service between the ages of 18 and 21. Although some Christians and **Muslims** serve in the IDF, Druzes (as well as Circasians) are the only non-Jews subjected to compulsory service. The Druze advancement in the military officer ranks has been gradual. Initially, Druzes and Circasians served in a special minority unit, but over the past two decades, they have been allowed to serve in other IDF units and to rise in rank. *See also* IS-RAEL; PALESTINE.

ISRAELI INVASION OF LEBANON (1982). Israel invaded **Lebanon** in June 1982 in an attempt to put an end to the presence of the Palestine Liberation Organization (PLO) in the country. Although some Lebanese initially welcomed Israeli troops, soon thereafter they began viewing Israel as an occupier and not a liberator, especially when its troops did not pull out after accomplishing the mission. Today, over 20 years later, Israeli troops still occupy a small strip of Lebanese land for security reasons, and an official treaty between the two nations is most likely dependent on a treaty between Israel and **Syria**. *See also* CIVIL WAR OF 1975–1990; WAR OF THE MOUNTAIN.

ISRAELI PARLIAMENT. *See* KNESSET.

'ISRAWI, NAJIB SA'D AL-DIN (1891–1987). An activist who lived in **Lebanon** and **Syria**. He assisted the British agent Lawrence of Arabia in his activities against the **Ottoman Empire** in the **Arab**

lands. 'Israwi then migrated to South America in 1920, established the newspaper *al-Islah* in **Brazil**, and published many articles on various topics related to the Druzes and Arab and **Islamic** issues. He also established the short-lived Association for Druze Reform, which advocated detailed studies of Druze **faith**, history, and **politics**.

'**ISRAWI, SALIM (1936–).** Son of Yousef and Fouzia 'Israwi of **Btater, Lebanon**. He moved to Kuwait, **Venezuela**, West Virginia, and San Francisco, and finally settled in Los Angeles. Salim prospered in retail and then in the television and film fashion industry. His distinguished leadership has been utilized in a variety of **organizations**, including the World Lebanese Cultural Union, the **American Druze Foundation (ADF)**, the **American Druze Society (ADS)**, and the Rotary Club of Hollywood. 'Israwi is a philanthropist and humanitarian.

'**IZZ AL-DAWLAH, RAFI' ABI AL-LAYL.** An 11th-century prince of Bani Kalb (Kilab) who became a regional leader in 1028 and assisted the **Fatimi** army commander, al-**Dazbari**, in **Syria**. Rafi' is known for having used his good relations with the Fatimi state to protect members of the Druze **movement**. He also improved the security and safety in Druze areas and later was recognized in the Druze tradition as an early saint (*waliyy*).

'**IZZIDDIN.** *See* ABU AL-HUSN.

– J –

JABAL AL-A'LA. Mountainous region in northwestern **Syria**, also known as Jabal al-Sumaq. It has been populated by small communities of Druzes since the beginning of the Druze **movement** in the 11th century. Like other mountainous, remote, and hard-to-reach areas in the region, it provided a safe haven to members of the Druze community. *See also* CARMEL; GALILEE; JABAL AL-DURUZ; SHUF.

JABAL AL-'ARAB. *See* JABAL AL-DURUZ.

JABAL AL-DURUZ. The Mountain of the Druzes. A province in southern **Syria** inhabited mainly by Druzes (90 percent Druzes and 10 percent Greek Orthodox Christians). The city of **Suwayda** is the largest Druze center in Jabal al-Duruz.

Druzes began settling in the mountain in the late 17th century, but larger numbers of Druzes migrated there after the 1711 battle of **'Ayn Dara** between the **Qaysis** and **Yamanis**, in which the latter were defeated and many of them were forced to migrate. An additional but smaller Druze migration took place during the **Civil War of 1840–1860** in **Mount Lebanon**.

During the **Great Revolt of 1925–1927** against **France**, the Druzes received worldwide attention because of their leading role in the revolt. Their leader, **Sultan al-Atrash**, became a Syrian and **Arab** nationalist symbol. Although the French were able to crush the revolt by 1927 and force its leaders to flee, the resistance in that revolt has facilitated the independence of Syria and other Arab states and the departure of the French (and British) from the Middle East.

In a 1937 gathering of Druzes in Amman, **Jordan**, the title "Jabal al-Duruz" was declared by some Arab nationalist Druzes as Jabal al-'Arab. But the mountain is still commonly known as Jabal al-Duruz.

JABAL AL-MUQATTAM. *See* MUQATTAM, AL-.

JABAL AL-SUMAQ. *See* JABAL AL-A'LA.

JABER, BOBBY. A contemporary American-born Druze educator, businessman, and artist who makes porcelain pots called Porcelainia. Jaber's approach to design in porcelain draws from the works of other artists and scientists, especially from R. Buckminster Fuller, the founder of synergetic geometry and inventor of the geodesic dome. He is also known in the **American Druze Society (ADS)** and has contributed funds to children's **education** and to other social causes in both **Lebanon** and the **United States**. Jaber has also founded, edited, and distributed the newsletter *Dialogue*, which deals with community affairs.

JABHAT AL-TAHRIR AL-YAZBAKIYYA. *See* YAZBAKI LIBER-
ATION FRONT.

JABIR, SHAKIB (1932–1965). A Lebanese Druze lawyer who was
born in **'Alay** and became an activist in the 1950s and early 1960s.
He served as the spokesman of the **Progressive Socialist Party
(PSP)**, representative of many **organizations**, and head of the Lebanese delegation to the Afro-Asian Conference. He died in a car accident while attending this conference.

JADD. A cosmic principle or entity that acts as a mediator between
the spiritual and physical world. Jadd is the sixth luminary in Druze
cosmology. *See also* HUDUD.

JA'FAR AL-SADIQ (?–765). The sixth **Shi'i imam** and a prominent
figure in **Islamic** circles. His son **Isma'il** is the forefather of the **Isma'ilis** and Druzes. His other son, Musa, became the accepted patriarch of the Ithna 'Ashari (Twelver) Shi'is.

JAMAL AL-DIN, SHAYKH. *See* TANUKHI, EMIR AL-SAYYID
JAMAL AL-DIN.

JAMI' AL-HAKIM. The **mosque** of **al-Hakim bi-Amr Allah** in
Cairo. It was initially constructed by **al-'Aziz**, the fifth **Fatimi caliph**, and then completed by al-Hakim. Its location was outside the
old gates of Cairo, but it was included in the city when the gates were
reconstructed.

Initially, it was known as the mosque of the Friday congregational
prayer (*Jami' al-Khutba*) but later was given the name of al-Hakim.
In the past two decades, the **Egyptian** government has permitted the
Bohras of India to take over the mosque and carry out the necessary
renovations and maintenance, for the mosque had deteriorated considerably over the years.

JAMI' AL-KHUTBA. *See* JAMI' AL-HAKIM.

JAMI', WAQ'AT AL-. *See* WAQ'AT AL-JAMI'.

JARAMANI, ABU MUHAMMAD SALIH (?–1904). Originally
from the al-Kahhal family. A pious **shaykh** from Jaramana, near **Da-**

mascus, who led an **ascetic** lifestyle and rose to prominence throughout the region, he was considered the number one shaykh of his time and is known for having performed **thaumaturgies** (*karamat*), or miracles.

JAZIRA (pl. *jaza'ir*). A term that means "island" or "region" and that refers to the early followers of the Druze **movement** in **Syria** and **Lebanon**. The title implies that Druzes in those regions were in an island amidst antagonist political regimes and religious traditions.

JAZZAR, AHMAD PASHA AL-. *See* JUNBLAT, BASHIR.

JESUS (?–33). Jesus is known in the Druze tradition as the "True Messiah" (*al-Masih al-Haq*), for he delivered what Druzes view as the true message. He is also referred to as the "Messiah of the Nations" (*Masih al-Umam*) because he was sent to the world and as the "Messiah of Sins" because he is the one who forgives.

JETHRO. *See* SHU'AYB.

JIHAD. *Jihad* was declared against Druzes by various Sunni **Muslim** rulers and jurists throughout the history of the Druze **movement**. In 1021, the **Fatimi caliph** in **Cairo** and his loyalists in **Syria** fought and persecuted members of the Druze community for several years during a period that later became known as **Mihnat Antakia**. But the most important and lasting impact on Druzes and Druze-Muslim relations is rooted in **Ibn Taimiyya's** *fatwa*, which was intended to justify *jihad* against the Druzes by the **Mamluk** sultan Nasir al-Din's army.

JOB (750–610 B.C.E.). Also Ayyub; a biblical prophet who was tried by God but prevailed as having unshakable **faith** in God's wisdom and providence. He is highly regarded by Druzes as one of the important pillars of Unitarianism (*Tawhid*). Job has several **visitation sites** in the Middle East, one being in **Nayha**, in the **Shuf** region of **Lebanon**. Lebanese Druzes have an annual festival that is celebrated at the site.

JOHN (?–30). *See* YAHYA.

JORDAN. Several thousand Druzes live in Jordan, mainly in the cities of al-Azraq and al-Zarqa' and in the nearby areas northeast of the capital, Amman. Most members of the Jordanian Druze community moved and settled there during the **Great Revolt of 1925–1927**, but some relocated to al-Azraq and Amman nearly 10 years earlier during World War I. **Sultan al-Atrash** and other **Syrian** Druzes were welcomed as exiles there on two occasions, in 1926 and 1954. Overall, the Jordanian Druzes have maintained good relations with the ruling Hashimite **family** as well as with the surrounding communities. Moreover, several Druzes have served in various Jordanian governments, including those of **Ibrahim 'Alam al-Din** and **Najib 'Alam al-Din**.

On 26 October 1994, Jordan and **Israel** signed a peace treaty, and diplomatic relations were established thereafter between the two countries. This opened the doors for communal visitations between Israeli and Jordanian Druzes, as many have relatives on the other side.

JOURNAL OF DRUZE STUDIES (JDS). An occasional academic journal established in 2000 by the **Institute of Druze Studies (IDS)**. The journal publishes articles and book reviews on topics related to Druze history, **politics, literature,** and **faith**.

JUDEO-CHRISTIAN–ISLAMIC TRADITIONS. Known also as the Abrahamic, Western, or monotheistic traditions. The Druze **manuscripts** describe **Druzism** as a reform **movement** of such traditions; the Druze doctrine is characterized by abundant references and insights from the Hebrew **Bible**, the New Testament, and the **Qur'an**. The personalities and teachings of major figures such as **Abraham, Jesus, Jethro, Job, John,** Moses, and **Muhammad** have become central in Druze spirituality and **cosmology**.

JUDGMENT DAY. Also Day of Religion (*Yawm al-Din*), Day of Resurrection (*Yawm al-Qiyamah*), Day of the Hour (*Yawm al-Sa'ah*), and other titles. On that day, goodness will prevail over evil, justice over injustice, and truth over falsehood. **Druzism** adopts the central teachings of the **Bible** and the **Qur'an** in regard to the Judgment Day and leaves out the detailed descriptions of the worldly benefits that believers will be awarded on that day. Instead, the primary focus of the Druze **manuscripts** is on the chronology of events as well as the true knowledge, final illumination, and mystical union that true believers gain on that day. Emancipation from ignorance (*jahl*) is the essence of the Day of Judgment in the Druze **faith**. Druzes believe that that day is very near and that what is required of them is to contemplate and meditate that nearness. *See also* JUHHAL; MITHAQ; 'UQQAL; WORSHIP.

JUHHAL (Uninitiated). Literally, the "ignorant ones." They are members of the Druze community who are not initiated into the Druze **faith** because of their own choice or because of the religious elite's perception of them as "not ready" for a demanding, strictly spiritual lifestyle. Thus, the Druze society is divided between the *'uqqal*, a minority in the community, and the *juhhal* (sing. *jahil*), who constitute the majority. Each "ignorant" Druze who wishes to be initiated must go through a lengthy period of learning the doctrine and conforming with the *'uqqal*'s way of life.

JULAN, AL-. *See* GOLAN HEIGHTS.

JUMBLAT. *See* JUNBLAT.

JUNBLAT, JUNBLATIS. Etymologically, this name comes from the **Kurdish** *janbulad* (meaning "soul of steel"), and therefore the "n" instead of "m" in the Arabized and Anglicized forms is preferred here. The Junblats are often considered to be **Kurds**, but some scholars argue that they were the rulers of a largely Kurdish population, although they themselves are not Kurds. Proponents of this view base their argument on the fact that one of the Junblats' forefathers was known as Arabshah 'Abbas, which may suggest that they were **Arabs**.

The Junblatis emigrated after 1607 from **Aleppo** to **Lebanon** and settled in the **Shuf** mountains. They eventually emerged as the leading family against the **Yazbakis**. Beginning in 1712, their leader became known as *shaykh al-mashayikh*, or the shaykh of shaykhs. The most prominent recent Junblati leader is the prolific writer and nationalist politician **Kamal Junblat**, who was assassinated in 1977. The current leader of the Junblati faction is Kamal's son, **Walid Junblat**. *See also* ARSLAN; QAYSI-YAMANI.

JUNBLAT, 'ALI (1690–1778). One of the leading **Junblat family** members who is known for his political and religious **leadership** of the community. His reputation was spread among other communities in the region, and he mediated and resolved many conflicts among **Ma'ni** princes, between **Shihabis** and **Arslanis**, as well as between **Muslims** and Christians. The **shaykh** is also known for having encouraged religious diversity and granting land to the Christian clergy for building more churches in **Mount Lebanon**. He was a devout figure who gained the spiritual status of the shaykh of shaykhs (*shaykh al-mashayikh*).

JUNBLAT, BASHIR (1771–1826). Son of Qasim Junblat, who was loyal to Ahmad Pasha al-Jazzar, governor of **Acre**. However, Bashir, who was 14 years old, rebelled against the armies of al-Jazzar and called on residents of **Mount Lebanon** to join him and refuse to pay the tax demanded by al-Jazzar.

Shaykh Bashir was also known for his compassion toward non-Druzes. In 1791, he received a letter from the pope thanking him for allowing the **Maronites** to build more churches in the area. In 1811, he absorbed 400 Druze refugee **families** who had fled from **Aleppo** and helped them resettle in the **Shuf**.

In 1794, Shaykh Bashir was taken with Emir **Bashir Shihabi** to Acre as prisoners for four years. Junblat remained loyal to Bashir Shihabi, but the latter was aware of the prestige and popularity of the shaykh. For example, Junblat was given the title of "leader of leaders" (*shaykh al-mashayikh*) and the "pole to the heavens" (*'Amud al-Sama'*). Consequently, Bashir Shihabi sought to weaken Bashir Junblat's power and popularity.

In 1825, Junblat fought Bashir Shihabi in the **battle of al-Mukhtara** but lost and escaped to **Hawran** and then **Damascus**. He was later arrested and exiled to Acre, where he was executed with his friend Amin al-'Imad. The bodies of the two men were thrown out of the gates of Acre. Shaykh **Marzuq Mu'adi** of the nearby town of

Yarka was allowed to transport the two bodies and bury them in Yarka. Bashir Junblat's death marks the weakening of the Druzes in **Lebanon** and the rise of the Maronites. *See also* VATICAN, THE.

JUNBLAT, KAMAL (1917–1977). A prominent Lebanese Druze leader, thinker, and diplomat. He was born in **al-Mukhtara** in the **Shuf** region into a feudal **family**. His father, Fu'ad Junbalat, was assassinated in 1921 when Kamal was four years old. His mother, **Nazira Junblat**, became the leader of the **Junblatis** until Kamal matured and assumed the Junblati **leadership** in 1943. Kamal studied law and philosophy in the Sorbonne but had to return to **Lebanon** when World War II erupted. He completed his study at Saint Joseph University in **Beirut**.

In 1949, he established the **Progressive Socialist Party (PSP)** (*al-Hizb al-Taqadumi al-Ishtiraki*) as a secularist movement that attracted members from different religious communities. In the **Civil War of 1958**, he played a major role against the **Chamoun** coalition, which led to the intervention of the **United States** in Lebanon. He was elected member of parliament continuously until the beginning of the **Civil War of 1975–1990**. Junblat also served as a minister and ambassador in a number of governments.

He became one of the central figures in the early years of the Civil War of 1975–1990, acting as president of the **Lebanese National Movement (LNM)**, which consisted of a dozen different parties. Junblat and the LNM demanded the establishment of a democratic and secular Lebanon and called for immediate reform of the state laws. The LNM alignment with the Palestinian Liberation Organization (PLO), however, caused the **Syrians** to realign themselves with the **Maronites**.

Kamal Junblat is also a prolific writer, philosopher, poet, and mystic who has authored numerous books and articles dealing with **politics**, religion, spirituality, leadership, and diet. He has also been the subject of a number of biographies by both **Arab** and Western authors. He maintained close contacts with major Arab leaders including **Jamal 'Abd al-Naser** of **Egypt** and **Hafiz al-Asad** of Syria. Junblat was assassinated in 1977, and his son, **Walid Junblat**, became the leader of the Junblatis.

JUNBLAT, SITT NAYFEH (1810–1880). Daughter of Shaykh **Bashir Junblat**. She married the prominent leader Amin Shams of **Hasbaya**

but was widowed at the age of 30. Sitt Nayfeh then dedicated the remainder of her life to piety and charity. She was known for her generous contributions and for her assistance to members of all sects in the Hasbaya district. She is often referred to as the uncrowned queen of Hasbaya. Sitt Nayfeh contributed to the founding of the prestigious Druze spiritual center of learning and meditation known as **Khalawat al-Bayyada**. She is buried in one of the *khalwas* there.

JUNBLAT, SITT NAZIRA (1890–1951). Leader of the Junblati faction after the death of her husband, Fu'ad Junblat, in 1921 and until her son, **Kamal Junbalat**, who was at the time only four years old, matured and assumed **leadership** in 1943. She was a capable political leader who initially gained attention during the **Great Revolt of 1925–1927** for her representation of the **Shuf** region.

JUNBLAT, WALID (1949–). The present leader of the **Junblati** faction in **Lebanon**. In 1977, he assumed **leadership** after his father, **Kamal Junblat**, was assassinated. In 1980, he was also elected president of the leftist party, the **Lebanese National Movement (LNM)**.

In 1982, **Israel** invaded Lebanon, and one of its objectives was to enable the **Lebanese Phalanges Party (LPP)** to take control of the Druze **Shuf** region. The Druzes lost several towns in the process, but in 1983 Junblat's forces drove the Phalengists from the **Shuf** and regained control over the Druze areas. For the remaining seven years of the **Civil War of 1975–1990**, he succeeded in establishing an autonomous Druze region encompassing almost all the villages of Lebanon that are inhabited by Druzes. Walid Junblat remains the key figure in Lebanese Druze **politics**.

JUNBLATI-ARSLANI. *See* QAYSI-YAMANI.

JUNBLATI-YAZBAKI. *See* QAYSI-YAMANI.

JUNE 1967 WAR. *See* SIX-DAY WAR.

– K –

KABBALAH. The Jewish mystical tradition established in medieval times but with roots in earlier Jewish history. Certain Kabbalist doctrines on **cosmology**, the soul, and life after death are similar to those in **Druzism**. For example, the two **Adams**: the "Biblical Adam" and the "Primordial Adam" (*Adam Kadmun*). The latter is what Druzes and some other **Sufi** traditions refer to as the "Pure Adam" (*Adam al-Safa*).

KABBUL, ABU JABIR NASIR AL-DIN (?–1655). One of the **shaykhs** of Iqlim al-Billan from the village of 'Urnah. His **asceticism** was often compared to that of the well-known Druze sage **al-Shaykh al-Fadil**.

KABBUL, SALHA. *See* SALHA, SITT.

KAFR. A small village in **Jabal al-Duruz** where Druze forces, under the command of **Sultan al-Atrash**, destroyed a unit of **French** infantry on 21 July 1925 and ignited the **Great Revolt of 1925–1927**.

KAFRQUQI, YUSEF IBN SA'ID AL- (?–1560s). A devout **shaykh** who memorized the **Qur'an** and dedicated his life to **asceticism** and **worship**. His knowledge and wit won him a respectable place among the **Muslim** theologians and judges in the district of **Aleppo** and **Damascus**. Shaykh Kafrquqi is also a mystical poet who wrote a collection on repentance and nearness to God that resembles the works of the famous literary figure **Abu al-'Ala' al-Ma'ari**. *See also* AJAWID; LITERATURE.

KAFR YASIF. A large **Arab** village in western **Galilee**, comprised mostly of Christians and Muslims. It houses an important Druze **visitation site** for the Green Prophet (**Khidr**).

KAHHAL, ABU MUHAMMAD SALIH. *See* JARAMANI, ABU MUHAMMAD SALIH.

KALBI, RAFI' ABU AL-LAYL. *See* 'IZZ AL-DAWLAH, RAFI'.

KALIMA, AL- (The Word). See HUDUD.

KANJ, KAMAL ABU SALIH. A Druze leader from **Majdal Shams** in the **Golan Heights** who was charged with spying for **Syria** in

1967. The **Israelis** intended to create Druze and **Maronite** nations north of Israel that would serve as a buffer zone between Israel and its northern neighbors, **Lebanon** and Syria. To accomplish this, the Israeli secret service, the *Mossad*, instructed Kanj to meet **Kamal Abu Latif**, a close associate of **Kamal Junblat**, in Europe. In order to gain time and avoid deportation or exile of Golani Druzes, Kanj pretended to cooperate with the Israelis. The two men met and eventually decided that Abu Latif would reveal the Israeli plan to Kamal Junblat, who, in turn, informed **Jamal 'Abd al-Naser** and **Hafiz al-Asad**, the presidents of **Egypt** and **Syria**, respectively. Thus, the story of the two states, Maronite and Druze, became the subject of a number of books, essays, and editorials. Kanj spent several years in Israeli jails and later, when released and expelled to Syria, was honored by the Syrian government for remaining loyal to Syria.

KARAMAT. *See* THAUMATURGIES.

KARAMI, SITT UM MUHAMMAD. A pious Druze **woman** who has a **visitation site** in **Zar'un**, **Lebanon**. Members of the Karami **family** are said to have been massacred by other residents of Zar'un.

KARRA, AYYUB. A Druze activist in the **Israeli** right-wing party, the Likkud. He lives in **'Isfiya**. In January 2003, he was reelected as member of the 16th Israeli Parliament, the **Knesset**.

KASEM, CASEY (1932–). An American radio and television celebrity, Hall of Fame Broadcaster, philanthropist, and humanitarian. He has also appeared as a guest on many shows and other entertainment forums. As recently as 2004, he provided the voice of Shaggy in the children's cartoon show "Scooby Doo."

Casey Kasem has served on the boards of numerous **organizations**, including Fairness and Accuracy in Reporting (FAIR), the **American Druze Foundation (ADF)**, and the American Task Force for **Lebanon**. He has received numerous awards, including the Martin Luther King Drum Major Award from the Southern Christian Leadership Conference, the Nosotros Golden Eagle Award from the Hispanic Entertainment Society, the Special Image Award from the National Association for the Advancement of Colored People, and the Ellis Island Medal of Honor. Casey was born in Detroit, Michigan, and is the son of Amin Kasem, who migrated to the **United States** from **al-Mukhtara** in the **Shuf** region, Lebanon. *See also* AMERICAN DRUZE SOCIETY (ADS).

KASEM, SAMIH. *See* QASIM, SAMIH AL-.

KASHF, DAWR AL-. *See* CYCLE OF DISCLOSURE.

KATA'IB, AL-. *See* LEBANESE PHALANGES PARTY (LPP).

KATTER, NAFE (1898–1994). An American Druze originally from Bathloun, **Lebanon**. He migrated to the **United States** in 1920 to join his two brothers in Michigan and eventually became known as Uncle Nafe. He was active in many **organizations**, including the Mason Lodge, Shrine Club, Chamber of Commerce, and **American Druze Society (ADS)**.

KHADR, BANU. *See* TANUKH.

KHALAWAT AL-BAYYADA. A religious center with a number of secluded places, *khalwas*, for worship, study, and meditation. It is the Druze site for spiritual retreat and reflection. The center is located south of **Hasbaya** and was built in the 19th century with the support of the devout Druze female **Sitt Nayfeh Junblat**. Khalawat al-Bayyada is still perceived as the most prominent Druze religious center for initiated seekers (*'uqqal*) to visit and stay for short or extended periods of time.

KHALWA (pl. *khalawat, khalwas*). Literally, "a secluded place," where the **initiated** meet for spiritual readings or recitations. In some Druze areas, the term *majlis* is used more often, while *khalwa* is reserved for secluded remote places of worship. At times, however, *majlis* and *khalwa* are used interchangeably.

In recent centuries and after Druze **mosques** were on the decline, the *khalwa* or *majlis* became the Druze place for congregational prayers or socioreligious meetings. Each small town usually has one, two, or more of these houses of worship. Some devout **shaykhs** in certain areas left their room or home to the community, and it was turned into a *khalwa* or *majlis*. Almost all places of worship or **visitation sites** in Druze communities are modestly furnished with carpets and cushions. Extravagant furnishing is not permitted.

KHANJAR, ADHAM. An early 20th-century **Arab Shi'i** rebel from Jabal 'Amil who was sought by the French forces but who later succeeded in reaching the house of **Sultan al-Atrash** and seeking hospitality and protection. Though Sultan was not home, Adham was seated to wait in the guest room **(madafa)**. Meanwhile, the French reached the house, arrested Adham, and took him to **Beirut**, where they imprisoned and eventually executed him for killing one of their officials.

This incident helped trigger the **Great Revolt of 1925–1927**, because the negotiation between Sultan and the French over the release of Adham failed. Sultan al-Atrash insisted that it was his moral responsibility to defend his guest according to Arab traditions and customs. The French forces' insensitivity to such traditions worked in favor of Sultan and his followers, who sought a reason to instigate the revolt against French colonialism and the eventual independence of the Arab lands.

KHAYAL. A cosmic principle; spiritual power or entity that acts as a mediator between the spiritual and physical worlds. Khayal is the eighth luminary in Druze **cosmology**. *See also* HUDUD.

KHAYR AL-DIN. *See* SA'B.

KHAYR AL-DIN, SALIM. A prominent **Lebanese** Druze businessman who lives in **Great Britain** and is active in the **British Druze Society (BDS)**. He has contributed funds for various projects and helped establish the Druze Heritage Foundation, which sponsors and promotes publications on Druze and Druze-related topics.

KHAZIN, AL-. A notable **Maronite** family in **Mount Lebanon**. Some sources indicate that the **family** hosted and protected **Fakhr al-Din al-Ma'ni II** during his childhood after his father was murdered by the Ottoman Turks.

KHIDR, AL-. Also *al-Khadir*; the Green Prophet. A mythical figure who at times is associated with the biblical Prophet Elijah. Though not mentioned directly in the **Qur'an**, he is alluded to in *sura* 18, verse 64. The early **Islamic** and later **Sufi** stories were carried on in the Druze tradition. Al-Khidr has many **visitation sites** in the Middle East and the Islamic world. One such site is in the predominantly non-Druze village of **Kafr Yasif, Israel**. The site is frequently visited by Druzes from the entire region. Some communities celebrate a holiday after his name and perform a pilgrimage to one of al-Khidr's **shrines** or visitation sites.

KHISHIN, FOUAD AL- (1921–). A poet from **Shwayfat** who lived in **Venezuela** for several years and then returned to **Lebanon**. His **poetry** appeared in *al-Adab* and *al-Adib* and in several collections of poetry. He also translated Bulgarian poetry into **Arabic**. Al-Khishin won a number of literary awards.

KHRAIBEH, AL-. A village in **Lebanon** with a *majlis* named after **Isma'il Ibn Sa'b Abu Hamzeh** (d. 1798), who served in his time as spiritual leader, a *shaykh al-'aql*.

KIRMANI, AHMAD HAMID AL-DIN AL-. An 11th-century **Isma'ili** theologian from the area known today as Iraq and Iran (*al-'Iraqayn*) who defended the **Fatimi caliph al-Hakim.** He came to **Cairo** in 1017 and assisted in refuting the claim of divinity attributed to al-Hakim. Thus, Kirmani wrote his famous Counseling Letter (*al-Risala al-Wa'iza*) addressed to **al-Hasan Ibn Haidara Firghani**, who (based on this letter) was the source of the divinity claim. Some sources say that it was al-Hakim who invited Kirmani to Cairo for this particular mission because of his widely known reputation.

Although al-Kirmani's ideas and statements about al-Hakim are consistent with the teachings of **Druzism**, the Druze **manuscripts** remain silent about al-Kirmani's position regarding the Druze **movement**. Thus, neither Kirmani nor the main author of the Druze manuscripts, **Hamza Ibn 'Ali**, refers in their writings to one another.

KISRAWAN. A region of **Lebanon** to the northeast of **Beirut**. It was populated by Druzes and **Shi'is** until the battle of **'Ayn Dara** in

1711, when many Druzes migrated primarily to the **Hawran** region. Earlier, in the 16th century, the Druze prince **Fakhr al-Din al-Ma'ni II** (r. 1590–1635) invited **Maronites** to settle in Kisrawan.

KNESSET. The parliament of **Israel**. There are 120 members who serve four-year terms. Because of their diverse political affiliations, Druzes have occupied between one and four seats in the Knesset. In the present 16th Knesset, beginning January 2003, two Druze members were elected on the Likud list, **Mjalleh Wahbeh** and **Ayyub Karra**. The Labor candidate, **Salih Tarif**, who was a member in the 15th Knesset, was not reelected, as the Labor Party lost several seats in this last election.

KUFIYA. A black (or red) and white head covering often worn in the Middle East, especially in rural areas. It is often worn by the traditional Druze uninitiated (*juhhal*) men. *See also* 'AMAMAH.

KULL AL-'ARAB (All the Arabs). *See* QASIM, SAMIH AL-.

KURDI, MAS'UD AL-. *See* SUKAYN.

KURDS. A Middle Eastern ethnic group that lives predominantly in northern Iraq but also in **Jordan**, **Syria**, and Turkey. There are **Muslim**, Christian, and Jewish Kurds. The **Junblatis** of **Lebanon** are often said to be Kurds. Their name is derived from the Kurdish *janbulad*.

– L –

LAFFA. *See* 'AMAMAH.

LAHIQ IBN AL-SHARAF AL-'ABBASI. An early 11th-century religious activist who joined the Druze **movement**, served as a missionary (*da'i*), and then turned against the movement. Initially, one of the movement's leaders, **Baha' al-Din al-Samuqi**, promoted Lahiq to the highest rank among the missionaries. He called him the "moving star" (*al-Kawkab al-Sayyar*). But Lahiq soon thereafter helped spread corrupted ideas. Baha' al-Din sent him a reprimanding message (*tawbikh*) and removed him from the ranks of the missionaries. *See also* APOSTATE; PEOPLE OF APOSTASY.

LAHUT. Divine nature as used in the monotheist and mystical traditions. It refers to the Creator. In **Druzism**, it means the Absolute Essence, which cannot be conceived by human minds. *See also* COSMOLOGY; NASUT; NATIQ.

LAJAH. An area located east of **Hawran** in southern **Syria**. The Lebanese Druzes of the **Yamani** faction fled to this land after they were defeated in the battle of **'Ayn Dara** in 1711. They later settled in the area that became known as **Jabal al-Duruz**. *See also* DUALISM; HAWRANIS; QAYSI-YAMANI.

LAJNAT AL-MUBADARAH AL-DURZIYA (LMD). *See* DRUZE INITIATIVE COMMITTEE.

LAKHM. *See* TANUKH.

LEADERSHIP. Leadership among the Druzes is often concentrated in the hands of the large **families**, whether in the local village or in the national or regional setting. Small families usually ally themselves with one of the large families. The political leaders of the community often seek advice from—or at least maintain good relations with—the spiritual leaders. *See also* CALIPH; DUALISM; EMIR; IMAM; MASHAYIKH AL-DIN; SHAYKH AL-'AQL; WALIYY AL-'AHD.

LEBANESE ARMY. The Lebanese army was initially formed during the French Mandate and was then strengthened with increased number of Lebanese soldiers and officers after independence in 1943. During the **Civil War of 1975–1990**, the army disintegrated along sectarian lines. After 1990, efforts were directed to reuniting the various militias under the army as a part of the plan of restructuring **Lebanon** and its military and **politics**. During the **War of the Mountain** (1983–1985) (*Harb al-Jabal*), a large defection by Druze soldiers in the Lebanese army took place as the army was being redirected against the Druzes. Throughout its history, the Lebanese army included Druze officers, such as the distinguished **Shakib Wahhab**, **Husain B'ayni**, **Mahmoud Abu Khuzam**, and **Shawkat Shuqair**.

LEBANESE CIVIL WAR (1975–1990). *See* CIVIL WAR OF 1975– 1990.

LEBANESE DRUZE COMMUNITY, INCORPORATED. *See* AUSTRALIA.

LEBANESE FORCES. The Lebanese forces were established during the first year of the **Civil War of 1975–1990**. Although the power base of the Lebanese forces is Christian **Maronite** right wing, it has attracted some non-Maronite members, including Druzes. The Lebanese forces were supported by **Israel**, and it fought against the Druzes in the **War of the Mountain** (1983–1985) (*Harb al-Jabal*). It was also able to attract some of the **Lebanese army** troops and later to establish a political party after all the militias in **Lebanon** were dismantled. *See also* HAMADEH, FARID.

LEBANESE NATIONAL MOVEMENT (LNM). A leftist, nationalist, and progressive movement consisting of a dozen different parties that was established in **Lebanon** in the 1960s. The movement was reorganized and then recognized as the LNM in the 1970s. One of the leaders and founders was **Kamal Junblat** (d. 1977). **Walid Junblat** was elected president in 1980. The LNM aimed at introducing social and political reforms in Lebanon but also aided the military operations of the Palestinian Liberation Organization (PLO) against **Israel** at some point during the **Civil War of 1975–1990**. In the early years of the civil war, the LNM perceived the PLO as a vital force in the politics of Lebanon and the region as a whole. *See also* PROGRESSIVE SOCIALIST PARTY (PSP).

LEBANESE PHALANGES PARTY (LPP) (Hizb al-Kata'ib al-Lubnaniyya). The right-wing Christian political party in **Lebanon** founded in the 1930s by Pierre Gemayel (d. 1984), father of Bashir and Amin Gemayel, former presidents of Lebanon. In recent years, they were supported by **Israel**, especially during the **Israeli invasion of Lebanon (1982)**. In the **War of the Mountain** (1983–1985)

(*Harb al-Jabal*), the Druzes resisted and regained control of the previously lost areas and towns in **Mount Lebanon**.

LEBANESE WAR OF 1982. *See* ISRAELI INVASION OF LEBANON.

LEBANON. Lebanon's mountain ranges have served as a place of refuge for many cultural minorities and religious sects in the region. One of these communities was the Druze tribal forefathers who began settling in the region in the middle of the eighth century. Modern Lebanon is often traced back to the 16th-century Druze **Ma'ni** dynasty and especially during the reign of **Fakhr al-Din al-Ma'ni II** (r. 1590–1635). Some historians glorify the role and period of Fakhr al-Din II for nationalist and other purposes.

Beginning in the 18th century, the area was dominated by Druzes and **Maronites**. Later, the events of the 1840s led to the recognition of two lieutenancies (**Qa'imaqamiyyas**), one Maronite in the north and the other Druze in the south. The years 1840–1860 marked uprisings that were slowly developing into a religious conflict. These two decades of turmoil ended with the intervention of the European powers and the establishment in 1861 of the *Mutassarrifiyya*, which lasted until World War I. The end of the war and the Sykes-Picot agreement put greater Lebanon under the French Mandate until 1943, when Lebanon was declared independent.

The problem of confessionalism in Lebanon was never resolved, and therefore it surfaced in the brief **Civil War of 1958** (which was suppressed with the help of the American intervention) and then in the bloody **Civil War of 1975–1990**. Governments and coalitions rose and fell, and in 1989, a session of the Lebanese Parliament convened in **Ta'if** in Saudi Arabia and adopted a plan for reforms. The application of such reforms are still the concern of not only Druzes but of all Lebanese. More recently, there has been relative calm and some signs for economic recovery.

Today the Lebanese Druzes comprise 7 percent of the population and live mostly in **Mount Lebanon** and **Wadi al-Taym** (see map 2). Some Lebanese Druzes reside in the city of **Beirut**, where the judiciary and administrative center of the community is located. Two of the predominant **family** groupings that play major social, economic, and political roles in the present Lebanese state are the **Junblatis** and **Arslanis**.

LEGAL SYSTEM. *See* COURT SYSTEM.

LEVANT, THE. The eastern Mediterranean area from Izmir in Turkey to Alexandria in **Egypt**. Later, the term was modified to refer only to the Fertile Crescent. It is also the name of one of the Australian Druze **organizations**. *See also* DIASPORA.

LISAN AL-MU'MININ (The Believers' Tongue). *See* SAMUQI, BAHA' AL-DIN AL-.

LITERATURE. Several prominent **Arab** literary figures have dealt with Druzes in their works, including **Maroun 'Abboud, Ahmad Shawqi**, and Ibrahim al-Yaziji. These non-Druze literary figures have either lived in close proximity with Druzes or developed lasting friendships with some members of the Druze community; thus, they relied on their firsthand experiences when they addressed Druzes in their accounts.

Druze literature may be classified as, first, the mystical poetry of prominent sages and **shaykhs**, such as **al-Shaykh al-Fadil, 'Ali Faris, Yusef Kafrquqi, Abu Hasan Hani Ridan**, and **Shuja'al-Din 'Abd al-Rahman**. These mystical poets have inspired generations of Druzes who have become intrigued by the religious life. A second category of literature includes poetry, short stories, and novels. Examples of well-known authors include **Shibli al-Atrash, Nasib Nakadi, Samih al-Qasim, Fandi al-Sha'ar**, and Nadia Tueni. The third category of literature includes the folk poets (*zajal*) who recite their poetry in public forums. Some have also published their works. Examples include **Fuad Abu Ghanim** and **Tali' Hamdan**. *See also* 'ABD AL-SAMAD, YUSEF; 'AMER, TURKI HASAN; 'ARAYDI, NA'IM; MASRI, KARIM AL-; MUHANNA, HUSAYN.

LUMINARIES. *See* HUDUD.

–M–

MA'ARAT AL-IKHWAN. A town near **Aleppo, Syria**. It has a **visitation site** for the famous **shaykh Jabir al-Halabi**, who was appointed by the Ottoman sultan to the position of *shaykh al-Islam* for the district of Aleppo.

MA'ARAT AL-NU'MAN. A place near **Aleppo**, **Syria**, and hometown of the famous **Arab** literary figure **Abu al-'Ala' al-Ma'arri**. Some of the **Tanukhi** tribes initially settled in Ma'arat al-Nu'man in the eighth century and then relocated to **Mount Lebanon**.

MA'ARI, ABU AL-'ALA' AL- (973–1057). An important figure in classical **Arabic poetry** and prose. Ma'ari is also well known for his **ascetic** lifestyle, which included vegetarianism and a vow of celibacy. He was often referred to as "the philosopher of the poets and the poet of the philosophers." His *Epistle of Forgiveness* (*Risalat al-Ghufran*) became popular in the West and is said to have influenced Dante's famous work *The Divine Comedy*.

Ma'ari corresponded with **Isma'ili** *da'is* such as al-Mu'ayyid fil-Din as well as with the forefathers of the Druze **movement**. Some Druzes believe that Ma'ari was one of the secret admirers and possibly a member of their **faith**.

MADAFA (pl. *madafat*). The hospitality room or reception hall in a traditional **Arab** home where guests are received and welcomed. In some Druze regions, the synonym *diwan* is also often used to refer to the same thing.

MADHABIH AL-SITTIN. Literally, "the Massacre of the Sixty." A term that was coined by some authors to refer to the **Civil War of 1860**.

MADHBAHAT AL-NAKADIYYA. *See* NAKADIYYA MASSACRE.

MADHHAB (pl. *madhahib*). An Islamic school, sect, or **movement**. Druzes often refer to their **faith** as a school within **Islam**, *al-Madhhab al-Durzi al-Islami*.

MADHHAB AL-'AQL. *See* 'AQL.

MAGHRIBI, 'AMMAR AL-. An 11th-century missionary (*da'i*) in the Druze **movement**. He was born in North Africa but moved to

Egypt to join the newly founded **Fatimi** house of learning, *Dar al-Hikma*. 'Ammar rose in the ranks of missionaries of the new movement and, as a result, was granted the mystical-spiritual title of *Abu al-Yaqzan* (Father of the Awakened).

The fifth Druze luminary and leader of the community, **Baha' al-Din al-Samuqi**, was very pleased with 'Ammar's devotion and dedication and, therefore, sent him on difficult missions and eventually promoted him to a high rank among the missionaries. On one of these assignments, he was sent to persuade the Druze apostate **Sukayn** to repent and rejoin **Druzism**. 'Ammar visited Shaykh **Abi al-Khayr Salamah Ibn Jandal**, and the latter advised him to visit Sukayn unarmed. This advice proved fatal, for Sukayn and his followers attacked 'Ammar as he was reading Baha' al-Din's letter to them. Although 'Ammar managed to escape, he later died of his injuries a few miles away and became one of the early martyrs of the Druze movement. He has a **visitation site** in Bikfaia, **Lebanon**, and is highly revered among Druzes everywhere. *See also* APOSTATE; PEOPLE OF APOSTASY.

MAHER, 'ADIL SALMAN (1914–1997). A calligrapher and inventor with 27 patents, including the 1936 Calendar Clock, which showed the leap year (February 29) automatically every four years. He received several awards and honors; for example, in 1947, he was awarded the Egyptian Medal of Honor by King Farouk of **Egypt** for inscribing a Quranic passage on a miniature silver plate. Maher was born in the **Shuf**, **Lebanon**, and migrated in 1988 to the **United States**. *See also* 'ALAM AL-DIN, 'IZZIDDIN JAWAD; CALLIGRAPHY; MAKAREM, NASIB SA'ID.

MAHMOUD. *See* ABU LATIF.

MAJDAL SHAMS. The largest of the four Druze towns in the **Golan Heights**. Its population exceeds 8,000. The area has been under **Israeli** rule since the **Six-Day War** (June 1967). *See also* KANJ, KAMAL ABU SALIH.

MAJLIS. A place of congregation; a community center or hall where the Druze-initiated (*'uqqal*) members meet to **worship** and recite the scriptural sources. In each village or town, there is usually at least one *majlis* but often two or more *majlises* based on the size and number of **families** in the community. *See also* DUALISM; FAITH; KHALWA.

MAKAREM, NASIB SA'ID (1889–1971). A prominent calligrapher from 'Itat, **Lebanon**. He received many awards from governments, leaders, and academies in both the Middle East and the West. At some point in his career, he decided to follow the example of **'Izziddin 'Alam Al-Din** (d. 1356), who had written a 50-word Quranic verse on a grain of rice. Shaykh Makarem advanced his skill, wrote 61 words on a grain of rice, and won the first prize of the art fair in Zahle, Lebanon, in 1909. Later, he also engraved the national anthems of **Syria** and Lebanon. In 1939, he drew a map of the **United States** on another grain of rice, which was exhibited at the New York World's Fair along with other works by him. He also became an expert on handwriting for the courts and subsequently established an office in **Beirut** for **calligraphy** and calligraphy training. *See also* MAHER, 'ADIL SALMAN.

MAKAREM, SAMI NASIB. Son of Shaykh **Nasib Makarem** and professor of **Islamic** and **Arabic** studies at the **American University of Beirut (AUB)**. He has written extensively on **esoteric** and **Sufi** movements in Islam as well as on the Druze **faith**. He received his **education** in the **United States** in the 1960s.

MAMLUK, MAMLUKS (r. 1250–1516). Rulers of **Egypt** until the Ottoman sultan Selim (r. 1512–1520) defeated them in the battle of **Marj Dabiq** (1516) and conquered the **Arab** lands. The Druze prince **Fakhr al-Din al-Ma'ni I** is said to have supported the Ottomans against the Mamluks. Over two centuries earlier, the Mamluks had won the famous battle of **'Ayn Jalut** against the **Mongols** in 1260.

At the turn of the 13th century, the Mongols reinvaded Mamluk areas, and the Druzes, as well as **Shi'is**, **Maronites**, and **'Alawis**, cooperated with the Mongol invaders. As a result, the Mamluk sultan

Nasr al-Din sent an army to defeat and suppress the population. This confrontation was witnessed by the renowned medieval jurist **Ibn Taimiyya** (d. 1328), who issued a religious ruling (*fatwa*) proclaiming this invasion a holy war (*jihad*) against the inhabitants of the area. *See also* AYYUBI; BUHTURI.

MA'N. Ancestor of the **Ma'nis**. He migrated with his supporters to the **Shuf** mountain region around the year 1120 and, with the help of the **Buhturis** (who had been there since the eighth century), established towns such as **B'aqlin** and **Dayr al-Qamar**.

MANDIL. *See* NIQAB.

MA'NI, MA'NIS (r. 1516–1697). This princely ruling **family** of **Mount Lebanon** is a descendant of the **Tanukhi** tribe. The Ma'nis remained a relatively insignificant power until the emergence of **Fakhr al-Din al-Ma'ni I** (r. 1516–1544). The Ottomans allowed the Ma'nis to become an independent political force within the region, as long as the regular taxes from these territories reached the central government in Istanbul. Though Istanbul continued to support the Ma'nis, the local Ottoman governors in **Damascus** were at times antagonistic toward the Druzes and their Ma'ni princes. Fakhr al-Din I continued to cooperate with the Ottoman central government, but his son Qurqumaz (r. 1544–1585), with the support of both Druzes and Christians in the area, rebelled against the **Ottoman Empire** and its governors in the region.

The two sons of Qurqumaz, **Fakhr al-Din al-Ma'ni II** (r. 1590–1635) and Yunis, fled with their mother to **Kisrawan**, where, based on some sources, they were protected by the **Maronite al-Khazin** family until events quieted down in the **Shuf** in 1590. The boys' uncles of the **Arslani** clan administered the estates of the Ma'ni princes during their absence and later assisted their return. With the support of the Ottomans, the elder of the two sons, Fakhr al-Din II, extended the Ma'ni principality north to the city of Palmyra and south to the Sinai Peninsula.

Fakhr al-Din II initially restored good relations with Istanbul, but later the Ottoman Empire began suspecting his increasingly expansionist ambitions. Consequently, the Ottomans defeated his army at **Hasbaya** in 1635 and executed him and two of his sons in Istanbul. The Ma'nis, however, were allowed to continue their rule until 1697, when the last prince, who was living in Istanbul, decided not to exercise his right to govern. The rule of Mount Lebanon was then passed to the **Shihabi** Emirate after consultation among clan leaders of the area, both Druze and non-Druze.

MA'NI, FAKHR AL-DIN AL-, I (r. 1516–1544). A Druze prince of the **Ma'ni family** and grandfather of **Fakhr al-Din al-Ma'ni II**. He is said to have supported the Ottoman sultan Selim's forces in the famous battle of **Marj Dabiq** (1516) against the **Mamluks**. The battle facilitated the Ottoman rule over the **Arab** lands. Fakhr al-Din's actions won the Ma'nis a place in the Ottoman plan for the region.

MA'NI, FAKHR AL-DIN AL-, II (r. 1590–1635). A prince of the **Ma'ni family** and grandson of **Fakhr al-Din al-Ma'ni I**. At some point in his career, he turned against the Ottomans and refused to comply with their heavy taxes. He is known for his expansion of the Ma'ni Emirate, for his trade and diplomatic relations with Europe, and for the quality of his **leadership**.

Fakhr al-Din II is treated in many sources as a Lebanese nationalist hero and as a symbol of religious and political tolerance as well as a symbol of resistance against foreign powers. Druzes use him as a source of inspiration and nostalgia regarding their role in modern Lebanese politics, although some Druzes are aware of the fact that his land grants to **Maronites** have reduced their power and perhaps that of the **Shi'is**. He was one of the most prominent Druze leaders who sought to advance the project of a greater **Lebanon** and to improve the relations between the religious sects in the region. For example, he invited Maronites to live in Druze and Shi'i areas and advocated communal and sectarian harmony among the Lebanese. However, these ideals have often been exaggerated by both Druze and other **Arab** historians. *See also* BUHTURI; SHIHABI.

MA'NI, NASAB. *See* NASAB, PRINCESS.

MANSUR BI-ALLAH, AL- (r. 946–952). The third **Fatimi caliph** and **imam**. He is essential to both **Isma'ilis** and Druzes. In Druze **cosmology**, he is the fifth station (*maqam*).

MANUSCRIPTS. The Druze religious and spiritual doctrine is still predominantly in manuscript format. These manuscripts can be divided into three distinct types: scriptural, biographical, and dialogical. The scriptural manuscripts refer to the more revered ones and include a well-known manuscript titled *Epistles of Wisdom* (*Rasa'il al-Hikmah*), which consists of 111 epistles compiled into one, three, five, or six books. Different versions of these epistles are available in various research libraries around the world. In addition to being commentaries on the **Bible** and the **Qur'an**, the epistles include letters sent by the early leaders of the sect to its supporters, challengers, and **apostates**. Many scholars, Druze and non-Druze, have mistakenly referred to the *Epistles of Wisdom* as the Druze "Holy Book" or "Canon," equating it with the Bible and Qur'an. Additional scriptural manuscripts include three that were discovered in the middle of the 20th century: *al-Shari'a al-Ruhaniyya* (*The Spiritual Path*), *al-Munfarid Bidhatihi* (*In Solitude with Oneself*), and *Rasa'il al-Hind* (*The Epistles to India*).

The biographical manuscripts seem to have been written between the 12th and the first half of the 18th century. These biographical accounts of prophets, mystics, and other well-known historical figures address general moral issues and provide rich references to the meanings of some doctrinal principles and their consequential values. They also cover the lives and teachings of some biblical personages, such as **Job, Jethro, Jesus, John,** Luke, and others. Examples of biographical manuscripts include *'Umdat al-'Arifin* (*The Chief Sages*) and *al-Safinah al-Mubarakah* (*The Blessed Ship*). Other biographical manuscripts are based on the writings and lives of Druze sages, such as **al-amir al-Sayyid al-Tanukhi** (d. 1479), **al-Shaykh al-Fadil** (d. 1640), and al-Shaykh **'Ali Faris** (d. 1753), to mention only a few.

The dialogical manuscripts are instructional texts, often in a question-and-answer format. Although they were written and copied in later periods, they elaborate, in part, on the establishment era between 996 and 1043 C.E. The sources in this category are meant to teach Druze youth their socioreligious history. They aim at educating young members of the sect about the *Tawhid* doctrine and assisting them in coping with the outside world. For example, one presents a dialogue between a father and his son where the latter raises questions about Druze history and belief system and the former answers them. The content of the dialogical manuscripts, unlike the other two categories, often indicates an awareness of negative appellations directed at the Druzes by the outside world and an attempt on the part of the author of the manuscript to offer a rebuttal and perhaps to correct misunderstandings from the inside. *See also* LITERATURE.

MAQAM (pl. *maqamat*). One meaning of this term is "spiritual and mystical," referring to a station in which God reveals Himself to humankind through illumination (*ishraq*). God does not become the station or the station God. Individuals who advance in spiritual purity and mystical clarity are the only ones who experience God's illumination through the station. In Druze **cosmology**, there are eight *maqamat*.

The second meaning is "spatial." When used, the term refers to **sacred sites** or holy shrines. It usually includes the tomb of the sage, but some of these may include only a symbolic tomb-like structure and a large hall for reception. *See also* KHIDR, AL-; SABALAN; SAMUQI, BAHA' AL-DIN AL-; SHU'AYB.

MARJ DABIQ, BATTLE OF (1516). A famous battle between the invading Ottoman army of Sultan Selim (r. 1512–1520) and the **Mamluks**, resulting in the Ottomans taking control of the majority of the **Arab** lands. Although the Druzes under the **leadership** of **Fakhr al-Din al-Ma'ni I** were asked to assist the Mamluks, they decided to welcome and join Sultan Selim and the Ottoman forces.

MARJ 'UYUN. *See* HITTIN, BATTLE OF.

MARONITE, MARONITES. A Christian community that traces itself to seventh-century Syria and often to St. Maro or Maroun (d. 407 or 410). Since 1182 (and especially since the 16th century), the Maronite Church has been in communion with the Roman Catholic Church. The Maronite patriarch is elected by a synod of bishops and confirmed by the pope in Rome. Initially, Maronites were encouraged to settle in **Kisrawan** by **Fakhr al-Din al-Ma'ni II** in the 16th century. After the intracommunal battle of **'Ayn Dara** between the two

Druze factions, the **Qaysis** and **Yamanis**, in 1711, more Maronites moved and settled in **Mount Lebanon**.

Maronites today live mostly in Mount Lebanon but with smaller communities in other parts of the Middle East and in the **diaspora**. Some Lebanese Maronite factions have fought Druzes beginning with the 1840–1860 turmoils and up to the recent **Civil War of 1975–1990**. Although there have been many periods of peace between Maronites and Druzes, their relationship has at times been tumultuous.

MAS'ADA. *See* GOLAN HEIGHTS.

MASHAYIKH AL-DIN. The initiated religious members (*'uqqal*) of the Druze community. At times, the phrase refers to those in leading positions among the initiated. *See also* LEADERSHIP; SHAYKH AL-'AQL.

MASHAYIKH AL-ZAMAN. *See* LEADERSHIP.

MASHYAKHAT AL-'AQL. The leading Druze religious and spiritual institution. It is usually determined by region or faction. *See also* SHAYKH; SHAYKH AL-'AQL.

MASIH AL-HAQ, AL- (The True Messiah). *See* JESUS.

MASKH. Degradation. A form of reincarnation in which a person is believed to be reborn as an animal. *Maskh* is not a part of the Druze teachings. *See also* TAQAMUS.

MASRI, KARIM AL-. A contemporary Lebanese Druze poet who lives in the **United States**. He has recited his poetry on numerous occasions and has recently published a collection of **poetry** titled *Aghani al-Qalb* (*The Songs of the Heart*) in which he includes some of his poems on love, life, land, and youth. *See also* AMERICAN DRUZE SOCIETY (ADS); LITERATURE.

MASSEY, FRED (1895–1986). Born Farid Ibn Ibrahim Abu Muslih. A Lebanese Druze who migrated to the **United States** in 1910, joined the U.S. Army, and fought in World War I. Later, he wrote for *al-Bayan* and *al-Mithaq* and translated several works from **Arabic** and French into English, including two popular books: **'Abdallah Najjar**'s *The Druze Sect* and Narcisse Bouron's *Druze History*. He was active in the U.S. Druze **organization al-Bakourat al-Durziyya** and later in the **American Druze Society (ADS)**.

MASTER OF GUIDES (Sayyid al-Hadin). A title claimed in the 11th century by the heretic **Darazi** to elevate himself above **Hamza Ibn 'Ali**, whose title was **Guide of Believers** (*Hadi al-Mustajibin*). Darazi was killed or executed shortly after he claimed this title. *See also* PEOPLE OF APOSTASY.

MATN, AL-. A predominantly Christian subdistrict in the **Mount Lebanon** province with a small Druze minority. Historically, it includes the **B'abda** subdistrict to the south, where a larger Druze population resides.

MAWLA. Master, **saint**; a spiritual honorary title used among **Sufis** and **Shi'is**, and at times among other **Muslims**. In **Druzism**, it refers primarily to the luminaries (*hudud*) and to the stations (*maqamat*).

MAZAR, MAZARAT. *See* VISITATION SITE.

MERHI, AMEEN JOSEPH (1882–1962). An American Druze originally from Btater, **Lebanon**, who migrated to the **United States** in 1902 and settled in Elsedale, West Virginia. He was elected as the first president of the **American Druze Society (ADS)**.

MERHI, SAMI. A contemporary American Druze who is the representative of the *Mashyakhat al-'Aql* in North America. He is active in the **American Druze Society (ADS)** and has served as president of the society.

METEMPSYCHOSIS. *See* TAQAMUS.

MEXICO. The Druze community in Mexico is relatively small and can be traced to Druze **migration** to the Americas in the late 19th and early 20th centuries. The Druze association there is known as La Lega Drusa.

MIDIAN, MIDIANITES. *See* SHU'AYB.

MIGRATION. *See* DIASPORA.

MIHNA (pl. *mihan*). A hardship, struggle, or trial of the early members of the Druze **movement** in the 11th century. It is described in the **manuscripts** as a testing phase for believers. The term has since then been used to refer to any hardship that Druze communities or individual members face. *See also* MIHNAT ANTAKIA; WAQ'AT AL-JAMI'.

MIHNAT ANTAKIA. The hardship or trial of Antakia. A period of persecution of Druzes beginning in 1021, instigated by **al-Zahir**, the seventh **Fatimi caliph**. His governor in **Aleppo**, **Salih Ibn Mirdas**, was instrumental in attacking Druzes in that region. The hardship continued until 1026, when the fifth luminary and leader of the community at the time, **Baha' al-Din al-Samuqi**, was instructed by the first luminary, **Hamza Ibn 'Ali**, to resume missionary activity, as the danger of persecution was reduced.

MILITARY COMMITTEE. A secret faction within the **Ba'th Party**, **Syria**, consisting of **'Alawi**, Druze, and Sunni officers. They took over the government in the 23 February 1966 coup, but in 1970 **Hafiz al-Asad** asserted his control, marking the end of this committee. Druzes remained loyal to Hafiz al-Asad and presently to his son **Bashshar al-Asad**.

MILLET. Turkish term for community (in **Arabic**, *millah*). In the Ottoman system of government, each religious community within the empire was ruled by its own ecclesiastical law and **leadership**. In the 1890s, for the first time the Druze *millet* was recognized as an independent community by the Ottoman sultan. Consequently, Druze judges were appointed to adjudicate cases of **family law** in the community. *See also* COURT SYSTEM.

MIMASANI, ABU HUSAYN HASAN. A devout **shaykh** and poet who was born in Maymes near **Hasbaya**. He is known for his spiritual poems praising God and the luminaries (*hudud*) and for having been imprisoned in Sidon by the Ottoman governor.

MIRDAS, SALIH IBN (r. 1023–1029). Governor of **Aleppo** under the seventh **Fatimi caliph, al-Zahir**. He is known for his persecution of Druzes during **Mihnat Antakia** (1021–1026). *See also* MIRDASI DYNASTY.

MIRDASI DYNASTY. The tribal rulers of **Aleppo** in the 11th century. They created a buffer zone between the **Byzantine** and **Fatimi** lands. Their rule ended in 1079, when they came under the control of the **Seljuk** sultans. During their reign, there was a large Druze community in the district of Aleppo. The Mirdasis were in competition or conflict with the Druzes.

MISSIONARY, MISSIONARIES. *See* DA'I, DA'IS.

MITHAQ. Pact or covenant; also contract, promise, or commitment. A document given to and signed by prospective members in the Druze **movement** between 1017 and 1043 in which the new members committed themselves to the *Tawhid* **faith**. The *mithaq* specifies that the commitment must be comprised of *Tawhid* in its totality, that is, its teachings and conditions, **commandments**, and prohibitions. The signature implied that the new member accepted the teachings of *Tawhid* and pledged to transform his or her life according to these teachings.

The *mithaq* is also a record of witness (*hujjah*) for (or against) the members of the community to be displayed on the **Judgment Day**. The signed *mithaqs* were then given to the missionaries, who in turn passed them on to their superior, **al-Tamimi**. He gave them to **Hamza Ibn 'Ali**, and the latter sent them to **al-Hakim** through the ambassador, **al-Qurashi**. Al-Hakim inspected the *mithaqs* and returned them to al-Qurashi and to Hamza Ibn 'Ali, who kept them in a place from where they could be retrieved on the Judgment Day.

MITHAQ, AL-. *See* NAKADI, 'ARIF AL-.

MLA'EB, SA'DA. A 19th-century leading Druze **woman**, especially during the years 1896–1897. She became famous for her inspirational speeches to the Druze fighters against the Ottoman forces near Salkhad and **Qanawat**.

MONGOL, MONGOLS. A Turkic-speaking people who created a vast empire, which at times extended its borders from Central Asia to the Sinai Peninsula. In the 13th century, they destroyed the **'Abbasi** caliphate in Baghdad and invaded and occupied **Syria**. After a number of confrontations, in 1303 the **Mamluks** finally defeated the Mongols in a decisive victory and drove them out of Syria. The Druzes, as well as **Shi'is**, **Maronites**, and **'Alawis**, at times cooperated with Mongols because of the Mamluk suppression of these populations. *See also* 'AYN JALUT; BUHTURI; MARJ DABIQ.

MONOTHEISM. The belief in and **worship** of one God. The Druze doctrine combines teachings from the three monotheistic traditions— Judaism, Christianity, and **Islam**—and has often been described as "strict monotheism." *See also* DRUZISM.

MOSES (15th–13th c. B.C.E.). A Hebrew **Bible** prophet and lawgiver who led the people of Israel out of **Egypt** through Sinai toward the Promised Land and was given the Ten Commandments by **God** (Yahweh) on Mt. Sinai. He is also the son-in-law of **Jethro** (*Shu 'ayb*). In Druzism, Moses is the fourth spokesman (*natiq*) after **Adam, Noah,** and **Abraham.** *See also* COSMOLOGY.

MOSQUE (Masjid). House of **worship** for **Muslims**. Traditionally, Druzes worshipped in mosques, and some of their mosques have survived until the 19th century. In the past 150 years, however, Druzes have used the terms *majlis* and *khalwa* for their place of worship.

MOSQUE'S BATTLE, THE. *See* WAQ'AT AL-JAMI'.

MOUNT CARMEL. A mountain range in **Israel** with two large Druze towns, **'Isfiya** and **Daliyat al-Carmel**, located on its eastern slopes.

In previous centuries, there were more Druze villages on Mount Carmel.

MOUNT LEBANON. A district in **Lebanon** inhabited by a large Druze community. In the past, it housed several Druze **emirates**, including **Buhturis** and **Ma'nis**. Presently, it is the home to many Druzes and **Maronites**, and it still serves as the Druze seat of power for the two Lebanese Druze factions, **Junblatis** and **Arslanis**.

MOUNTAIN WAR. *See* WAR OF THE MOUNTAIN.

MOVEMENT, DRUZE. When this term is used, it refers to the emergence of the Druze **faith** in the first half of the 11th century, 1017–1043. Some sources include the covert activity of 21 years that took place before 1017 and argue that the dates are therefore 996–1043 because of the significance of that preparatory period.

The term *movement* was preferred by early leaders of the community and is used in the Druze **manuscripts**. The manuscripts often characterize it as a "reform movement" (*harakat islah*) and as a sect or branch (**madhhab**). Nevertheless, specialists and laypersons continue to classify the movement as a religion. *See also* DRUZISM; HUDUD; JUDEO-CHRISTIAN–ISLAMIC TRADITIONS.

MU'ADI, JABR. A prominent Druze from **Israel** who rose to **leadership** in the 1950s. He was instrumental in Jewish-Druze relations. Shaykh Jabr served in the Israeli **Knesset** for several terms until his retirement.

MU'ADI, MARZUQ. A 19th-century **shaykh** of one of the leading Druze **families** from the village of Yarka. In 1825, he transported the bodies of **Bashir Junblat** and Amin al-'Imad after they were executed in **Acre**. Mu'adi recovered their disposed bodies and buried them in Yarka.

MU'ALLIM, AL-. Literally, "the teacher"; a title that is often used to refer to the prominent Lebanese Druze leader, thinker, and political figure **Kamal Junblat**.

MU'ASSASSAT AL-KHADIMAT LIL-MUGHTARIBIN AL-DURUZ. An institution that provides services to Druze members in the **diaspora**. It was established in **Lebanon** in 1988 by Na'im Sa'id Hasan, 'Arif Yusef al-A'war, 'Isam Fayiz Makarem, and Shaykh Mursal Kamil Nasr. Among the services provided is spiritual counseling by authorized personnel.

MUBDA' AL-AWWAL, AL. *See* UNIVERSAL INTELLECT.

MUHAMMAD (570–632). The prophet, servant, and messenger of God in **Islam** as described in the traditional Islamic sources. He received the revelations of the **Qur'an** from God through the angel Gabriel between 610 and 632. In the Druze **manuscripts**, Muhammad is the sixth spokesman (*natiq*) after **Adam**, **Noah**, **Abraham**, Moses, and **Jesus**. *See also* COSMOLOGY; DA'IS; HUDUD.

MUHAMMAD ABU HILAL. *See* SHAYKH AL-FADIL, AL-.

MUHAMMAD IBN ISMA'IL. The seventh **imam** in **Isma'ili Islam**. In the Druze **manuscripts**, he is considered the seventh spokesman (*natiq*) after **Adam**, **Noah**, **Abraham**, Moses, **Jesus**, and **Muhammad**. *See also* COSMOLOGY; DA'IS; HUDUD.

MUHANNA, HUSAYN (1945–   ). A poet and educator from the village of **al-Buqay'a**, **Israel**. His first volume appeared in 1978, and since then he has published several collections of **poetry** as well as short stories. *See also* LITERATURE.

MU'IZ LE-DIN ALLAH, AL- (r. 952–975). Fourth **Fatimi caliph** and **imam**. In 969, he defeated the Ikhshidis, representatives of the 'Abbasis in **Egypt**. Under him, Egypt became Fatimi, and **Cairo** was built and made the Fatimi capital. A year later, the **Al-Azhar mosque** was built, which subsequently became one of the major institutions of learning in the **Islamic** world. In Druze **cosmology**, al-Mu'iz is one of the stations (*maqamat*).

MUKHTARA, AL-. A town in the **Shuf** region; the home and seat of power of the **Junblat family**. There is a historic palace there that was built by **Bashir Junblat** (d. 1826).

MUKHTARA, BATTLE OF AL- (1825). A battle between **Bashir Junblat** and **Bashir Shihabi**. The **Junblatis** lost, and Bashir escaped to **Hawran** and then to **Damascus**. He was later arrested and exiled to **Acre**, where he was executed in 1826.

MULHID (pl. *malahida*). *See* APOSTATE.

MUNDHIR III, AL- (514–563). One of the **Lakhmi** kings, also known as Ibn Ma' al-Sama'. He is said to be the forefather of the **Arslanis** in **Lebanon**.

MUNTALAQ, AL- (The Starting Point). *See* RIDAN MOSQUE.

MUQATTAM, AL-. A place east of **Cairo** where the **Fatimi caliph al-Hakim** (r. 996–1021) is said to have gone on regular retreats and in 1021 disappeared and never returned. Since scholars have not resolved the mystery of al-Hakim's disappearance, they continue to link it to al-Muqattam.

MUQTANA, AL-. *See* SAMUQI, BAHA' AL-DIN AL-.

MURID. Disciple; a seeker on the spiritual or mystical path. The term is used in some Druze circles to refer to the new initiates or to the companions or disciples of some Druze sages, such as **al-Shaykh al-Fadil** and **al-Emir al-Sayyid al-Tanukhi**. *See also* FARIS, 'ALI.

MUS'AB. An early 11th-century religious activist who was a friend of **Baha' al-Din al-Samuqi** in learning the *Tawhid* **faith**. He later departed from the ranks of the **movement**. Moreover, he repeatedly attempted to incite the **Fatimi caliphs al-Zahir** (r. 1021–1036) and al-Mustansir (r. 1036–1094) against Baha' al-Din and other members of the new movement. Al-Mustansir, however, eventually executed Mus'ab. *See also* APOSTATE; PEOPLE OF APOSTASY.

MUSIC. Music education in schools was not central in Druze towns and villages until recent decades. Many Druze musicians have distinguished themselves and became prominent in their areas and in the region. Examples include the singers **Asmahan** and **Fahd Ballan** and the composer and singer **Farid al-Atrash**. *See also* TAQIYYI-DIN, DIANA.

MUSLIMS. *See* ISLAM.

MUSTAJIB. A respondent or initiate in the **Isma'ili** tradition. In the Druze **manuscripts**, the term refers to adherents (pl. *mustajibin*) of the **movement** in the early 11th century, specifically between the years 1017 and 1043. Subsequently, the term has been used to refer to members of the Druze community as *Mustajibin*.

MUTASSARRIFIYYA. The governate of **Mount Lebanon** between 1861 and 1914 imposed by the Ottomans and the Europeans in which a non-**Maronite** Christian governor (*mutassarrif*) was appointed under the supervision of the Ottomans. The *Mutassarrifiyya* ended the over 20-year period of turmoil in Mount Lebanon. *See also* CIVIL WAR OF 1860; QA'IMAQAM; QA'IMAQAMIYYA.

MUWWAHHIDUN (pl. of *muwwahhid*). Adherents of *Tawhid*; believers in the absolute Oneness and Unity of God. The Druze **manuscripts** and the Druzes themselves refer to members of the Druze community as *Muwwahhidun*. However, it is clear in the manuscripts that not all Druzes are *Muwwahhidun* and that not all *Muwwahhidun* are Druzes. *See also* BANU MA'RUF.

– N –

NABI AYYUB, AL- (Prophet Ayyub). *See* JOB.

NABI SHU'AYB, AL-. *See* SHU'AYB.

NABWANI, NAJIB (1935–   ). An educator from Julis, **Israel**. He contributed numerous articles and short stories to various publications, including *al-Yawm*, *al-Anba'*, *al-Hadaf*, and *al-Sharq*. He has served as the president of the Arab Teacher's College in Haifa.

NAFA', MUHAMMAD (1939–). A writer and educator from **Bayt-Jann, Israel**. He has written many short stories and has long been an active member of the Israeli Communist Party (ICP).

NAFISEH, SITT. A 15th-century Druze female from **Mount Lebanon**, the daughter of the judge Zayn al-Din 'Abd al-Wahhab, and the niece of **al-Emir al-Sayyid al-Tanukhi**. She became a subject of intrigue for many people in her time. For example, she composed metered **poetry** at the age of six and memorized the entire **Qur'an** and other scriptural and literary sources before she reached the age of seven. She passed away at the age of eight, as her uncle al-Emir al-Sayyid had predicted. *See also* WOMEN.

NAFS AL-KULLIYYA, AL-. *See* UNIVERSAL SOUL.

NAHID AL-DAWLAH, BUHTUR. *See* ARSLAN, NAHID AL-DIN BUHTUR.

NAJJAR, 'ABDALLAH. A contemporary American Druze who has served for three decades as an expert on international health management. Initially, he trained Third World physicians and health professionals and later served as senior adviser to the **United States** Agency for International Development. Najjar founded the Arab American Fund of Georgia and has served on a number of social and cultural **organizations**, including the American Arab Anti-Discrimination Committee (ADC), the National Association of Arab Americans (NAAA), the **American Druze Foundation (ADF)**, the **American Druze Society (ADS)**, and others.

NAJJAR, 'ABDALLAH IBN MANSUR (1898–1976). A prominent diplomat and social activist. In the early 1920s, Najjar worked in **Jabal al-Duruz** and often mediated between the Druzes and the French representatives until the latter grew suspicious of him. He fled to **Cairo**, to **Australia,** and then back to the Middle East, where he served in the Iraqi government in 1940 as the head of the Information and Publication Department. In 1944, he was appointed **Lebanon**'s ambassador to **Jordan** and then to various diplomatic positions in

Argentina, the Soviet Union, and **Canada**. Najjar and his wife were killed in 1976 in their home during the **Civil War of 1975–1990**.

In 1965, Najjar wrote the book *The Druze Sect and Tawhid*, which initially sparked controversy in the Druze community and was subsequently banned by the Lebanese government. Many Druzes thought that Najjar revealed too much, especially in regard to the luminaries (*hudud*). However, the book was reprinted in 1967 and later translated into English by **Fred I. Massey** in 1973. The book led to the publication of another book by **Sami Nasib Makarem** that has a lengthy introduction by **Kamal Junblat**. The heated debate also inspired a favorable response to Najjar's work by **Najib 'Israwi** of **Brazil** in 1966. Najjar's book has initiated the first Druze debate over their religious doctrine.

NAJJAR, SA'ID (1923–2001). A World War II veteran who served in the **United States** armed forces and was responsible for assisting in the delivery of American supplies to the Soviet Union through the Persian Gulf. He was honored with a military funeral accorded to the veterans of World War II and buried in the Beaufort, South Carolina, National Cemetery.

NAKAD. Also Nakadi and Abu Nakad. An important Druze **family** originating in the Taghlib tribe that joined the **Islamic** forces in the early expansionary wars. Some settled in **Egypt**, migrated to West Africa, and then joined the **Fatimi** forces of the **caliph al-Mu'iz** to conquer (and then settle in) Egypt. From Egypt, they moved to **Mount Lebanon** and lived in **B'aqlin** and **Dayr al-Qamar**. In 1845, many migrated to the **Shuf**.

NAKADI, AMIN AL-. An important judge in **Mount Lebanon** who lived in 'Alay but moved between **B'abda** and **Bayt al-Din**. Later he settled with his **family** in **Beirut**. He is the father of **'Arif al-Nakadi**.

NAKADI, 'ARIF AL- (1887–1975). Son of the judge **Amin al-Nakadi**. 'Arif worked first as a clerk in the **court system** and later as a judge in **B'abda** until 1918, when **France** took control of **Lebanon**. He was forced to migrate to **Syria**, where he served in a number of positions in the courts, in teaching, and also as the legal representative of **Jabal al-Duruz**. He was the founder of the Druze **Orphanage** (*Bayt al-Yatim*), both in Lebanon and in Syria, and the editor of the two Druze serials, *al-Duha* and *al-Mithaq*, in addition to authoring many books and articles.

NAKADI, NASIB IBN SA'ID (1875–1922). A literary figure from **'Abey** who wrote in numerous publications, including *al-Safa'*, *al-Mufid*, *al-Haris*, *Lubnan*, *al-Balagh*, *al-Muqtataf*, and *al-Ra'y al-'Am*. He also has a collection of **poetry** and a manuscript titled *History of the Nakadis*. His poetry is diverse, covering topics from love to nationalism, and his articles advocate sectarian and ethnic coexistence in the Middle East.

NAKADIYYA MASSACRE (Madhbahat al-Nakadiyyah). A known massacre of the **shaykhs** of the **Nakad family** that took place in 1795 by Emir **Bashir Shihabi**.

NASAB, PRINCESS (1547–1633). A **Ma'ni** princess; sister of Sayf al-Din al-Tanukhi, wife of Emir Qurqumaz, and mother of **Fakhr al-Din al-Ma'ni II**. She took charge of the Ma'ni principality after her husband was killed by the Ottomans. Princess Nasab was also an eloquent and persuasive public speaker. In one incident, she invited 30 Druze **shaykhs** in the **Shuf** and influenced their handlings of the Ottoman tax crisis. She instructed them to send only half the amount that the Ottoman governor of **Syria**, Hafiz Pasha, had demanded; the other half was to be postponed one year, during which she (at the time, age 70) would stay as a hostage in **Damascus**.

Princess Nasab was often referred to as "The Great Lady" (*al-Sitt al-Kabira*) and was instrumental in giving advice to Fakhr al-Din II, who considered his mother a blessing from God and therefore always sought her approval. Her wisdom and forgiveness in dealing with other residents of **Mount Lebanon** contributed to Fakhr al-Din's success, especially his policy of religious and sectarian tolerance. *See also* LEADERSHIP; WOMEN.

NASER, JAMAL 'ABD AL- (1918–1970). A popular **Arab nationalist** leader and president of **Egypt** (1952–1970) who advocated Arab solidarity and cooperation. He had strong political ties with a number of Druze personalities, including the Lebanese leader **Kamal Junblat** and the Syrian army general **Shawkat Shuqair**. *See also* ARAB NATIONALISM.

NASIR AL-DIN, SAMI IBN RASHID (1896–1963). A court officer, lawyer, and judge in the **Shuf** region who resigned at the beginning of the French Mandate. He is remembered as a nationalist poet who recited his poems on various occasions but often without recording them on paper. Consequently, much of his **poetry** was lost.

NASKH. *See* TAQAMUS.

NASRALLAH, 'ABBAS IBN 'ABDALLAH (1893–1974). A Lebanese from the **Shuf** region who migrated to the **United States** in 1910, served in the U.S. Army during World War I, and was stationed in **France** for nearly a year. He became active in the 1920s in the American Druze association **al-Bakourat al-Durziyya**, helped send funds to support the efforts of the **Great Revolt of 1925–1927**, and later, in the 1950s, joined forces with other members of the American Druze community to establish a committee for the Druze **Orphanage**. 'Abbas wrote many articles in various newspapers in defense of **Arab** causes and, one year before his death, published a collection of **poetry**, *Diwan 'Abbas*.

NASUT. The reflection of God, the Creator, into created beings. God's light manifest itself in the station (***maqam***) through illumination (*Ishraq*); the receiver's purity enables this to take place. In **Isma'ilism**, the *nasut* is contained in the body of the **imam**. In **Druzism**, on the other hand, it is restricted in its fullest to only eight manifestations. *See also* COSMOLOGY; LAHUT.

NATIONAL PARTY. *See* HNEIDI, FADLALLAH.

NATIQ (pl. *nutaqa'*). Proclaimer, spokesman, messenger, or prophet; the conveyor of a Divine Message. Drawing on **Isma'ili** teachings, the Druze **manuscripts** acknowledge seven spokesmen: **Adam**, **Noah**, **Abraham**, Moses, **Jesus**, **Muhammad**, and **Muhammad Ibn Isma'il**. *See also* BIBLE; 'IRFAN; QUR'AN; TAWHID.

NATUR. *See* ZAR'UN.

NATUR, SALMAN (1949–). A journalist and activist from **Daliyat al-Carmel**, **Israel**. In addition to authoring several books, he served as an editor to the *al-Itihad* newspaper and contributed many articles to several other publications.

NATUR, SAMIH (1946–). A poet and writer from **Daliyat al-Carmel**, **Israel**, who founded the magazine *al-'Amamah*, which deals with Druze communal affairs.

NAWFAL, SALIM (1865–1927). A Druze **shaykh** from al-Kfir, near **Hasbaya**, who was acknowledged by the Ottoman authorities for his mediation role in the **Damascus** region. In recognition of his activities, the Ottoman sultan awarded him a symbolic sword that was later bestowed on **Majid Arslan** by Nawfal's son.

NEW ERA. A title given to the period beginning with the emergence of the Druze **movement** in the early 11th century. Druzes believe that the New Era is still in progress and will come to an end with the **Judgment Day**. *See also* DRUZISM; NIDHARA.

NEW TESTAMENT. *See* BIBLE.

NIDHARA. A period of 21 years (996–1017) in which three *nudhur* (**al-Samiri**, **al-Qurashi**, and **al-Tamimi**) were appointed by the **Fatimi caliph al-Hakim** to preach *Tawhid* and prepare people for the **New Era**, or the final phase of *Tawhid*, which was declared by **Hamza Ibn 'Ali** in 1017.

NIMER, BANU. *See* TANUKH.

NIMER, NIMER (1941–). A writer and educator from **Hurfaysh**, **Israel**. He has contributed articles to various **Arabic** and Hebrew publications, including *al-Mirsad*, *al-Anba'*, *al-Mawkib*, *al-Itihad*, *'Al Hamishmar*, and *Bamerhav*.

NIQAB. A **women**'s head covering that is usually white and distinguishes the initiated (*'uqqal*) Druze women from the uninitiated (*juhhal*). The uninitiated Druze women usually wear a more revealing head cover, such as the *mandil*, or, if they live in urban areas and are younger, no cover at all. Different styles of the *niqab* can be found in different Druze communities in the Middle East. The *niqab* in Druze tradition usually reveals the face only, but more religious women stretch it to cover the lower half or more of their face.

NIYYA (Intentionality). *Niyya* is an important concept in Druze teachings. Its significance is twofold. First, one must be conscious of his or her intentions, making sure that they are pure and not in conflict with the principles of **Druzism**. Second, one must not fall into error and judge others, for only God knows what people's intentions are.

NIZARI. A branch of **Isma'ili Shi'is** who emerged in the late 11th century over a dispute regarding the succession of the Isma'ili **Fatimi** dynasty in **Egypt**. Nizar and his brother, al-Musta'li, fought each other to inherit their father's reign. Nizar was put to death, but his followers continued to support and advocate his legitimacy.

NOAH. A biblical figure who built the ark in order to save his family in the story Genesis (Genesis 6–10). In **Druzism**, he is considered to be the second spokesman (*natiq*) after **Abraham**.

NUDHUR (pl. of *nadhir*, meaning "warner"). Missionaries (*da'is*) who were sent by the **Fatimi caliph al-Hakim** three months after he took office in 996 to secretively organize and spread the good news of the coming **New Era** of *Tawhid*. They argued that in this era, *Tawhid* and the truth will be revealed to those who have been preparing themselves for this era. The three were **al-Samiri**, **al-Qurashi**, and **al-Tamimi**. They took turns holding the leading positions, each serving a period of seven years. In December 1016, they met with **Hamza Ibn 'Ali** and other missionaries in the **Ridan Mosque**. Subsequently, up until 1043, they served as luminaries (*hudud*) under Hamza.

NU'MAN III, AL- (585–613). The son of al-Mundhir IV, who was one of the **Lakhmi** kings in Hira. After his death, some **Tanukhi** and other Lakhmi tribes migrated and settled in **Ma'arat al-Nu'man** before they relocated to **Mount Lebanon** in the eighth century. *See also* ARSLAN; BUHTURI; MUNDHIR III AL-.

NUSAYRI, NUSAYRIS. *See* 'ALAWI, 'ALAWIS.

NUWAYHID, 'AJAJ (1896–1982). Writer, political activist, and lawyer who pursued public careers in **Palestine** and **Jordan** from the 1920s through the 1940s. Among the many positions that he held were secretary of the Supreme Muslim Council (1922–1932) and member of the Muslim Committee for the Defense of the Holy Places. He returned in 1959 to Ra's **al-Matn**, **Lebanon**, where he lived and authored many publications until his death.

– O –

'OBEID, 'ALI (?–1959). A poet from **Suwayda**, Syria, who participated in the **Great Revolt of 1925–1927**. He later settled in al-Azraq, **Jordan**.

'OBEID, ANIS (1934–   ). An American Druze cardiovascular specialist who graduated from the **American University of Beirut (AUB)** in 1957. After several years of service and training in **Lebanon** and the **United States**, he helped establish the Medical Center for Heart Diseases at Syracuse University and served as its chair for 10 years. He was given a number of awards, including the Community Involvement Award from the Arab Anti-Discrimination Committee (ADC) in 1993, and has served on a number of professional and community boards of directors, including the **American Druze Foundation (ADF)** and the **American Druze Society (ADS)**. 'Obeid is also a poet who has recited his **poetry** on numerous occasions and has recently published a collection of poems titled *Sada al-Sinin* [*The Echo of the Years*].

OCCULTATION (Ghayba). A state of concealment of the **imam** in **Shi'ism**. In the early Druze **movement**, it refers to the periods when **Hamza Ibn 'Ali** went into retreat, either on his own or with some of his associates. For example, between 1021 and 1043, he was in an undisclosed location but maintained direct contact with his subordinate **Baha' al-Din al-Samuqi** and instructed and approved his actions and writings. For the general community, he was in a state of occultation. Baha' al-Din joined Hamza and the other luminaries (*hudud*) in occultation in 1043; they will all return on the **Judgment Day**. *See also* HAKIM BI-AMRALLAH, AL-.

OCTOBER 1973 WAR. A war in which **Syria** and **Egypt** launched a surprise attack on **Israel** in an attempt to recover some or all of the territories captured by Israel in the **Six-Day War of 1967** (the **Golan Heights** from Syria and the Sinai Peninsula from Egypt). The pressure from the Soviet Union and the **United States** forced the two sides to abide by a cease-fire resolution that took effect on 22 October. In this war, Druzes fought on both sides, in the Syrian and Israeli armies. *See also* ARAB-ISRAELI WARS.

OLIPHANT, LAWRENCE (1829–1888). Traveler, lawyer, diplomat, and author of an important book on the city of Haifa. Oliphant built a home near Haifa, in the Druze town of **Daliyat al-Carmel**, where he lived for two years. In addition to his written account of the Druzes in Daliyat al-Carmel, Oliphant also joined the celebrations of the prophet Jethro **(Shu'ayb)** in **Hittin** near Tiberias in 1882 and wrote a personal account of the event.

ORGANIZATIONS. Many organizations were established by the Druze community and individual Druzes throughout the history of the sect. Among such organizations is an early one established in the **United States** in 1908 and named **al-Bakourat al-Durziyya** and known after 1946 as the **American Druze Society (ADS)**. Other organizations include the **American Druze Foundation (ADF)** and the Druze **Orphanage** in **Lebanon** and **Syria**. *See also* HASBAYA WOMEN'S ASSOCIATION; INSTITUTE OF DRUZE STUDIES (IDS); 'IRFAN TAWHID FOUNDATION (ITF).

ORPHANAGE, THE (BAYT AL-YATIM). A nonprofit social institution for public service founded in the 1960s by **'Arif al-Nakadi**. The Orphanage provides room and board as well as a special **educational** program to qualified students. There are two orphanages: one in **Leb-**

anon and one in **Syria**. The Orphanage has representatives in the **diaspora** who raise awareness and collect funds to further the institution's programs. *See also* ORGANIZATIONS.

OTTOMAN EMPIRE. A vast **Islamic** empire that rose to power in the 13th century in Anatolia and encompassed the entire Middle East and parts of Europe and North Africa by the 16th century. The founder was Osman I (d. 1326). In 1516, Sultan Selim (r. 1512–1520) conquered the **Arab** lands and was supported by the Druze prince of **Mount Lebanon**, **Fakhr al-Din al-Ma'ni I** (r. 1506–1544). The Ottomans subsequently promoted the Druze princes but at times fought them, as in the case of **Fakhr al-Din II** (r. 1590–1635). Fakhr al-Din was initially supported by the Ottoman Empire but was later defeated by their army. The Ottoman *millet* system recognized the Druzes as an independent religious community beginning in the 1890s. The empire was dissolved with the emergence of Turkish nationalism and the leadership of Ataturk in 1924. *See also* BUHTURI; COURT SYSTEM; SHIHABI.

– P –

PALESTINIANS. Druzes have lived among Palestinians since the emergence of their **movement** in the 11th century. The Druze **manuscripts** mention several Druze **shaykhs** from the land of Palestine and at times refer to them as the people of **Turab**. Some Druze settlements in Palestine were discontinued in the past few centuries as persecution of members of the sect intensified.

Those Druzes who lived in the **Galilee** and **Carmel** were referred to as Palestinians until 1948, when they became citizens of the state of **Israel**, especially in 1956, when compulsory service of Druze men in the **Israeli Defense Forces** (**IDF**) became mandatory.

The relationship between Palestinians and Druzes before the 1948 **War of Independence** leading to the creation of the state of Israel was at times friendly but with recurrent periods of antagonism. The period after 1948 and the subsequent enlistment of Druzes in the IDF (especially after 1956) have further contributed to tensions between Druzes and Palestinians.

In **Lebanon**, the Druzes under **Kamal Junblat** supported and at times collaborated with the Palestinians fully during the early years of the **Civil War of 1975–1990**. But during the **leadership** of **Walid Junblat** after 1977, the Palestinian militias' unpopular actions in Lebanon led Druzes to distance themselves from the Palestinians. *See also* ARAB-ISRAELI WARS.

PASHA, IBRAHIM. *See* IBRAHIM PASHA.

PEOPLE OF APOSTASY (Ahl al-Riddah). A term given to those individuals who joined the Druze **movement**, served as missionaries (*da'is*), departed from the movement, and began defaming the sect's teachings, attributing inauthentic ideas to its followers. In the process, they contributed greatly to the misconceptions and misunderstandings of **Druzism** and the Druze community. Examples of such individuals include **Darazi**, Ibn Ya'la, **Ibn al-Barbariya, Sahl, Lahiq, Sukayn**, and **Mus'ab**. *See also* APOSTATE.

PEOPLE OF INTERPRETATION (Ahl al-Ta'wil). A term used to refer to those who believe that scriptural verses have additional inner, **esoteric** meanings. The forefathers of Druzes were part of *Ahl al-Ta'wil* until they joined the *Tawhid* movement in the 11th century. *See also* PEOPLE OF REVELATION; PEOPLE OF UNITARIANISM.

PEOPLE OF QAF (Ahl al-Qaf). *See* QAF.

PEOPLE OF REVELATION (Ahl al-Tanzil). This term is general and applies to all mainstream traditions that advocate only **exoteric** meanings to scriptures. In **Islam**, the title refers to Sunnis. *See also* PEOPLE OF INTERPRETATION; PEOPLE OF UNITARIANISM.

PEOPLE OF UNITARIANISM (Ahl al-Tawhid). A term used with its derivative, *Muwwahhidun* (Unitarians), to refer to followers of *Tawhid*. They consider that the final interpretation is to be with God and therefore that the **exoteric** and **esoteric** meanings are essential for advancing in spirituality; some Druze **manuscripts** speak of "the esoteric of the esoteric" (*batin al-batin*) as a way of pointing to a higher level of interpretation of the scriptures. The Druze doctrine acknowledges that not all Druzes are *Muwwahhidun* and that not all *Muwwahhidun* are Druzes. *See also* PEOPLE OF INTERPRETATION; PEOPLE OF REVELATION.

PEOPLE'S PARTY (Hizb al-Sha'b). A Syrian **Arab nationalist** movement that joined forces with **Sultan al-Atrash** in the **Great Revolt of 1925–1927**. Its objective was to fight the French forces and eventually gain independence for **Syria** in particular and for the **Arab world** in general. *See also* SHAHBANDAR, 'ABD AL-RAHMAN.

PERSIAN, SALMAN THE. *See* FARISI, SALMAN AL-.

PHALANGES PARTY. *See* LEBANESE PHALANGES PARTY (LPP).

PHILIPPINES. A small minority of Druzes live in the Philippines. **Migration** of Druzes to the Philippines began in the early decades of the 20th century. Among those who have distinguished themselves is **Diana Taqiyyidin**, a concert pianist who lives today in the **United States**. *See also* DIASPORA.

PIKI'IN. *See* BUQAY'A, AL-.

PILGRIMAGE (Hajj). An **Islamic** pillar. **Muslims** are expected to visit the holy city of Mecca at least once in their lifetime (if they are able to comply). In past centuries, some Druzes were able to perform the pilgrimage, but in recent times pilgrimage is almost nonexistent among Druzes. The honorary title **Prince of Pilgrimage** (*Amir al-Hajj*) was given to the son of the Druze **Fakhr al-Din al-Ma'ni II** in the early 17th century.

PILLAR OF UNITARIANS. *See* RAJBAL (RAJ PAL) IBN SUMER.

POETRY. *See* LITERATURE.

POLITICS. Druze politics are often shaped by the reality of being a small minority in the countries where they live. They have always developed strategies to maximize their participation in the political system, whether through military advancement or through activism in sociopolitical movements. *See also* BA'TH PARTY; DUALISM; LEADERSHIP; MASHAYIKH AL-DIN; MASHAYIKH AL-ZAMAN.

POPE, THE. *See* VATICAN, THE.

PRINCE OF ELOQUENCE (Amir al-Bayan). A title given to the Lebanese Druze leader **Shakib Arslan** because of the many essays and speeches he wrote and delivered throughout the **Arab** and **Islamic** world on topics ranging from Islamic causes to Arab culture and politics.

PRINCE OF PILGRIMAGE (Amir al-Hajj). An honorary title given to the leader of the annual **pilgrimage (***hajj***)** to the holy city of Mecca. In the early 17th century, the title was awarded to the son of the Druze prince **Fakhr al-Din al-Ma'ni II.**

PRINCE OF THE SWORD AND THE PEN (Amir al-Sayf Wal-Qalam). A title given to the early 20th-century Druze leader **'Adil Arslan** for his heroic role in defending the **Arab** lands and for participating in the intellectual life of the Arabs through his eloquent writings.

PROGRESSIVE SOCIALIST PARTY (PSP) (al-Hizb al-Taqadumi al-Ishtiraki). A political party that was founded in 1949 by **Kamal Junblat** and is presently led by his son, **Walid Junblat.** The socialist and nationalist ideology of the party has appealed to and drawn participation mainly from Druzes but with some non-Druze Lebanese. The party's manifesto stipulates a united and secularist **Lebanon,** complete equal rights and opportunities to all Lebanese, and full participation in the Lebanese political system. *See also* CIVIL WAR OF 1958; CIVIL WAR OF 1975–1990; ISRAELI INVASION OF LEBANON; LEBANESE NATIONALIST MOVEMENT (LNM); MARONITES; WAR OF THE MOUNTAIN.

PROPHETS. Druzes venerate many prophets in the **Judeo-Christian–Islamic traditions** and have **visitation sites** for some of them. These prophets, Druzes believe, have come from God and fulfilled His command. Examples include **Jesus**, **Jethro**, and **Job**. *See also* BIBLE; COSMOLOGY; NATIQ; QUR'AN.

PYTHAGORAS. *See* 'IRFAN.

– Q –

QADDAH, 'ABDALLAH IBN MAYMUN AL-. Grandson of **Imam Isma'il Ibn Ja'far** (d. 765). He is considered by the **Isma'ilis** to be the legitimate successor in the line of **'Ali Ibn Abi Talib** and of the Prophet **Muhammad**. Al-Qaddah is known as the "second founder" of Isma'ili **Shi'ism**.

QAF. The 23rd letter of the **Arabic** alphabet. The Druze pronunciation of this letter tends to keep the hard "q" sound rather than softening it to a "g" or "k" sound used in most contemporary Arabic dialects. Because of the Druze pronunciation of this letter, some observers have referred to them as the people of *Qaf* (*Ahl al-Qaf*). However, this Druze "authentic" pronunciation of the "*qaf*" is also used by some non-Druze rural peoples. Moreover, some Druzes who live in urban communities soften the "q" as well.

QA'IM BI-AMR ALLAH, AL- (r. 934–946). The second **Fatimi caliph** and **imam**. He is considered to be one of the stations (*maqamat*) in the Druze **faith**.

QA'IM AL-QIYAMAH. A title given to the initiator or proclaimer of the **Judgment Day**. He will serve as the judge of humankind. *See also* HUDUD; QA'IM AL-ZAMAN.

QA'IM AL-ZAMAN. Literally, "Master of Time" or "Lord of the Ages." Title given to the expected **Shi'i** Madhi. In **Druzism**, the title often refers to the first luminary, **Hamza Ibn 'Ali**. *See also* HUDUD.

QA'IMAQAM. Acting governor of an administrative unit within a larger district. The title was given to the two governors appointed by the **Ottoman Empire** for **Mount Lebanon** during the period of 1841–1861. In that context, there were two *Qa'imaqamiyyas*, one Christian and the other Druze. At times, this title is also used to refer to the acting spiritual leader of certain Druze communities, *qa'ima-qam* **shaykh al-'aql**. The acting leader may subsequently be elected as the permanent head of the community. *See also* LEADERSHIP; MUTASSARRIFIYYA.

QA'IMAQAMIYYA. A system of government established in 1841 in **Mount Lebanon** with two governors, one Christian and the other Druze. This arrangement was made as the **Shihabi** Emirate was coming to an end with **Bashir Shihabi** (r. 1787–1840) being exiled; Bashir Shihabi III proved to be ineffective. *See also* MUTASSAR-RIFIYYA; QA'IMAQAM.

QANAWAT. A city located a few miles northeast of **Suwayda** in the **Jabal al-Duruz**, **Syria**. Qanawat is the home of the spiritual leaders of the al-**Hajari** family. It has also served as a meeting place of the Syrian Druze community during periods of political and military struggles, such as the **Great Revolt of 1925–1927**.

QARAFA, JAMI' AL-. A **mosque** that was built in 976 in **Cairo** and later became known as Jami' al-Awliya'. Some sources state that **Hamza Ibn 'Ali** and his associates convened and met the **Fatimi caliph al-Hakim** regularly in this mosque.

QARMATI, QARMATIS. Also referred to as Qaramitah, Caramithians, or Karmathians; a 10th-century sectarian **movement** within the **Isma'ili** tradition that is often confused with the Druze movement. The movement is traced to Hamdan Qarmat's teachings, which are **Shi'i** in orientation with some **gnostic** and other philosophical influences. Qarmat disappeared in 899, and the Qarmatis split from the Isma'ilis over a succession dispute. They occupied **Damascus**, Homs, and Hama between 902 and 906 until the **'Abbasi** defeated them. They were forced to flee and settle in Bahrain. The Qarmatis survived in Bahrain throughout most of the 11th century, but they were eventually absorbed into Isma'ili society.

The Qarmatis began a military campaign in 969 and conquered

much of southern **Syria**, but the **Fatimi** forces drove them out of the land permanently in 978.

QARNAYYIL. Also Qarnadila, meaning "Mountain of God"; an ancient city that dates back to the Phoenician era. Qarnayyil is also known by its residents as 'Alay al-Matn. It has two *majlises*, one of the A'wars and the other of the Hilals.

QASIM, NABIH AL- (1945–). A critic, educator, and writer from Ramah, **Israel**. In addition to writing several books, he also contributed articles to *al-Yawm*, *al-Anba'*, *al-Mirsad*, *al-Itihad*, *al-Ghad*, *al-Sharq*, and other publications.

QASIM, SAMIH AL- (1939–). Prominent poet and journalist who was born in al-Zarqa, **Jordan**, and whose **family** resettled in Ramah, **Israel**, which was the original home of his father. He wrote for communist publications in Israel, including *al-Ghad*, *al-Itihad*, and *Hadha al-'Alam*. More recently, he founded and became general editor of *Kull Al-'Arab* [*All the Arabs*], a newspaper published in Nazareth, Israel. Samih al-Qasim has also served as chairman of the general Union of Arab Writers in Israel. He has published over 40 collections of **poetry**, and some of his poems have been translated into other languages, and several have been set to **music**. Moreover, some of his works have been included in the curriculum of many schools, colleges, and universities around the world. *See also* LITERATURE.

QASSAM, YUSEF (1854–1954). A devout **ascetic shaykh** from Sahnaya, near **Damascus**. He memorized the entire **Qur'an** at age seven; joined the Druze spiritual institution in **Hasbaya, Khalawat al-Bayyada**, at the age of 21; and spent his life in **worship** and contemplation.

QAWAQJI, AL-. *See* SA'B, HAMAD.

QAYSI. An ancient northern Arabian tribe that competed with and fought against the southern Arabian tribe, the **Yamani**. The **Qaysi-**

Yamani tribal conflict found its way into Druze society. *See also* DUALISM; FAMILIES.

QAYSI-YAMANI. An ancient Arabian tribal conflict that had its base in many Arabian tribes and also among the early Druze tribes. The Qaysi-Yamani factions among the forefathers of the Druzes date back to the old south and north divisions of Arabia long before the emergence of their religious **movement**. This **dualism**, however, became more visible after the era of **Fakhr al-Din al-Ma'ni II**.

Nearly a century later, the conflict intensified, and the Qaysis defeated the Yamanis in the battle of **'Ayn Dara** in 1711. Some of the Yamani leaders were killed in that battle, and many surviving Yamanis fled and their homes and lands were confiscated. Once the Yamanis were gone, the **Shihabi emirs**, beginning with Melhim al-Shihabi (r. 1732–1754), adopted the strategy "divide and rule" and instigated a new dualism that provoked hostilities between the **Yazbakis** and the **Junblatis**.

The other important **family**, the **Arslanis**, on the other hand, have attempted to remain neutral, and in the 19th century they were the ones to mediate between the two factions. Later, however, some Arslanis were drawn into the conflict, and writers began reporting the conflict as Junblati-Arslani. In the 1990s and after various consultations between the present leaders of the two factions, **Walid Junblat** and **Talal Arslan**, the Druze community in **Lebanon** seems to have reduced the intensity of the conflict if not terminated it.

QIYAMA. *See* JUDGMENT DAY.

QRAYYA QBEA', BATTLE OF. Site of one of the major battles during the Lebanese **Civil War of 1975–1990** and, in particular, the **War of the Mountain**. The militias of the **Lebanese Phalanges Party (LPP)** were able to enter and control the **al-Matn** region. Forty of their vehicles reached al-Qrayya and began to congregate in Dayr al-Kahluniyya. The commander of the LPP militias, Ernst Jemayyel, was killed, and an engagement between the LPP militias and the Druze militias took place, and al-Qrayya Qbea' was heavily bombarded. A week later, the Druze forces succeeded in regaining control over the town.

QUEEN VICTORIA AWARD. *See* SALMAN, MERHI IBN SHAHIN.

QUR'AN, AL-. The **Islamic** scriptures as received by **Muhammad** between 610 and 632 through the angel Gabriel and later collected and compiled into one book in the 650s. The Druze **manuscripts** are replete with Quranic references; **Druzism** considers itself a hermeneutic of the Qur'an and the **Bible**.

Many Druze **shaykhs** have memorized the Qur'an and mastered the Quranic sciences, including **Shuja' Al-Din 'Abd Al-Rahman** (d. 1348), **Sitt Nafiseh** (15th c.), **Jabir al-Halabi** (d. 1640), and **Yusef Qassam** (d. 1954). Some Druze sages have argued that a Druze is not a true Unitarian (*Muwwahhid*) if he or she does not master the knowledge found in the Qur'an and the Bible. Nevertheless, most Druzes are not knowledgeable of both scriptures. *See also* EPISTLE OF WISDOM; HIKMAH.

QURASHI, ABU 'ABDALLAH MUHAMMAD, AL-. One of the five primary representations of the luminaries (*hudud*) during the establishment of the Druze **movement** in the 11th century. Earlier, between 996 and 1016, he was also one of the *nudhur* appointed by the **Fatimi caliph al-Hakim**. Al-Qurashi served as the chief *nadhir* for seven years and then joined the third *nadhir*, **al-Tamimi**. Along with the other luminaries, he met **Hamza Ibn 'Ali** in December 1016. Al-Qurashi is also known in the **manuscripts** as the Ambassador (*Safir al-Qudrah*). He departed from **Cairo** with Hamza and the other two luminaries, **al-Tamimi** and **al-Samiri**, leaving **Baha' al-Din al-Samuqi** in charge of the community until 1043.

– R –

RABI'A OF BASRA (?–801). The fourth daughter (Rabi'a means "fourth") of a poor, devout man in Basra during the early **'Abbasi** period. After the death of her parents, she was captured, sold into slavery, and then freed, spending the rest of her life as an **ascetic**. She was adopted into the Druze oral and written traditions as a **saint** and as a model of piety and dedication to the love and service of

God. Druzes believe that Rabi'a was one of the early true Unitarians, followers of *Tawhid* before the emergence of the Druze **movement** in the 11th century. *See also* ASCETICISM; WALIYY; WOMEN.

RADHILAH, RADHA'IL. *See* FADILAH.

RAJ'A. Literally, "return." It refers to the rebirth of the soul in a newly born body. *See also* TAQAMUS.

RAJBAL (RAJ PAL) IBN SUMER. An 11th-century spiritual leader from India who was also known in the Druze **manuscripts** as the "Wise Shaykh" and the "Pillar of Unitarians." He was in charge of the missionaries (*da'is*) in the Indian subcontinent. Rajbal corresponded with **Baha' al-Din al-Samuqi** during the propagation period of the Druze doctrine between 1021 and 1043.

RAMAT YUHANAN, BATTLE OF. Also known as the battle of Husha and Kasayer; a battle that took place during the Israeli **War of Independence** (1948) in which Druzes fought against the Jewish forces in **Palestine**. The battle also marks the end of Jewish-Druze fighting and the beginning of cooperation between the two communities. *See also* GALILEE; ISRAEL; ISRAELI DEFENSE FORCES (IDF).

RAMMAL, MUHAMMAD. An activist who became the secretary of the **Israeli** trade union, the Histadrut, for the region of **Galilee**. He has been involved in the community's affairs since the 1960s.

RASA'IL AL-HIKMAH. *See* EPISTLES OF WISDOM.

RASHID. *See* ABU LATIF.

RASKH. The belief that a person is reborn as a stone or a thing. It is not actually a part of the Druze belief system, but some authors have wrongly attributed it to Druzes. *See also* TAQAMUS.

RAYIS, KAMAL AL- (1931–1995). A medical doctor who worked for over three decades as the personal physician of the royal Kuwaiti family, al-Sabah.

RAYYAN, ABU 'ABD AL-QADIR AL-. A 15th-century devout **shaykh** from the village of al-Kunaysa who is remembered for his **ascetic** practices. He was one of the students of **al-Emir al-Sayyid al-Tanukhi**.

REFORM. *See* MOVEMENT, DRUZE.

REINCARNATION. *See* TAQAMUS.

REVOLT OF 1925–1927. *See* GREAT REVOLT OF 1925–1927.

RIDA. Contentment, satisfaction; the sixth act of **worship** in the Druze **faith**. *See also* DRUZISM.

RIDAN, ABU HASAN HANI (1886–1970). A devout **shaykh** and poet who wrote a number of works, including a collection of **poetry** and commentaries on the ***Epistles of Wisdom*** and its connection with the **Qur'an**. At times, he used the pen name "The Hiding Poet" (*al-Sha'ir al-Mustatir*). Although some of his poems are nationalistic or poems of praise to certain individuals, such as the three **Arslani** leaders **Shakib**, **'Adil**, and **Majid**, many poems are mystical and commemorate famous sages such as **al-Shaykh al-Fadil** (d. 1640) and Shaykh **Mahmoud Faraj** (d. 1953). *See also* LITERATURE.

RIDAN MOSQUE. An important meeting place for the leaders of the Druze **movement** in the early 11th century. It was also the residence of the first luminary, **Hamza Ibn 'Ali**. Symbolically, it is the place from which the **New Era**, the last cycle of *Tawhid*, was proclaimed. The Ridan Mosque is often referred to as the starting point (*al-Muntalaq*) of **Druzism** and the Druze movement.

RIDDAH, AHL AL-. *See* PEOPLE OF APOSTASY.

RIF, 'ABD AL-KARIM AL- (1886–1951). A title given to 'Abd al-Karim Mahmud 'Amer by **'Adil Arslan** after a victory in a battle during the **Great Revolt of 1925–1927**. Al-Rif's role in the battle, which later became known as "The Victory Battle," led to the demolition of 'Amer's home by the French forces. He managed to escape with others to **Jordan**, where he lived for the following 10 years.

RISALA (pl. *rasa'il*). Treatise, letter, or epistle in the primary Druze **manuscripts**. *See also* EPISTLES OF WISDOM.

– S –

SA'B. A large **family** that migrated from northern **Syria** and settled in **Mount Lebanon**, particularly in the city of **Shwayfat**. Relatives of the Sa'bs include the Khayr al-Dins of **Wadi al-Taym** and the Hajalis of **Jabal al-Duruz**. Other Druze families with the name Sa'b may not be related to the Sa'b of Shwayfat.

SA'B, 'AFIFAH (1900–1989). A journalist and educator from **Shwayfat** who contributed articles to numerous publications, including *al-Muqtataf*, *al-Ma'arif*, and *Sawt al-Mar'ah*. She was also active in the Lebanese and **Arab women**'s movements. In 1958, 'Afifah was granted the **Cedars of Lebanon** Award for her service.

SA'B, GHASSAN. A Druze civil engineer who graduated from the **American University of Beirut (AUB)** in 1966, migrated to the **United States**, and later became the chief executive officer of a construction corporation that established much of the infrastructure of Flint, Michigan, in the 1980s. Sa'b has also served as the chairman or board member of numerous institutions, including the University of Michigan at Flint, the Lebanese American University, the Flint Chamber of Commerce, the American Task Force for Lebanon, the **American Druze Foundation (ADF)**, and the **American Druze Society (ADS)**. He is a philanthropist and humanitarian who has contributed funds to a number of projects in the United States and abroad.

SA'B, HAMAD (1891–1941). A Lebanese Druze nationalist from Kahluniyya in the **Shuf, Lebanon**, who participated in the **Great Revolt of 1925–1927**. Later, he joined the forces of the famous military commander al-Qawaqji and participated in the **Arab Revolt of**

1936. He died in a battle in 1941 while assisting in the Iraqi revolt against the British forces. It is said that he was in Qawaqji's car when it was bombed and that he sacrificed his life in order to save Qawaqji.

SA'B, MAHMOUD KHALIL (1909–1976). A Lebanese writer and mayor of **Shwayfat**. Among many roles, he was appointed to oversee the institution of the Druze endowments (*waqf*). He also wrote an important book on **Mount Lebanon**.

SA'B, NAJIB (1946–   ). A writer, educator, and journalist from Abu Snan, **Israel**. He served in several public roles and specialized in adult **education**. His articles appeared in *Sada al-Tarbiyya, al-Mirsad, al-Usbu', al-Ikhwah*, and other periodicals.

SA'B, NAJLA (1908–1971). An activist in the Lebanese **women**'s **movement** who was elected president of the women's **organization** in 1939 and the women's union in 1940. She represented the Lebanese women's movement in **Cairo** in 1944; the **United Nations** Educational, Scientific, and Cultural Organization (UNESCO) in 1946; the United Nations Women's Rights Conference in 1948 and 1956; and the Red Cross in 1957 and 1963. She was given the **Cedars of Lebanon** Award in 1964 and again in 1967.

SABALAN. A **visitation site** in the town of **Hurfaysh, Israel**. Some believe that the Prophet Sabalan is Zevulun of the **Bible**, one of the sons of the patriarch Jacob. Others argue that he was one of the missionaries (*da'is*) who joined and worked at propagating the Druze **movement** in the early 11th century. *Eid al-Nabi Sabalan* (Holiday or Feast of Prophet Sabalan) was established in 1971.

SACRED SITES. There are two types of sacred sites: the first is sacred shrines (*maqamat*) and the other **visitation sites** (*mazarat*). Both terms are at times used interchangeably, and the latter may evolve into the former (a *mazar* becomes a *maqam* over time). *See also* JOB; KHIDR, AL-; SABALAN; SAMUQI, BAHA' AL-DIN AL-; SHU'AYB.

SACRED TRUSTS. *See* WAQF.

SAFARA (Ambassadorship). *See* QURASHI, ABU 'ABD AL-QADIR AL-.

SAFIR AL-QUDRAH. *See* QURASHI, ABU 'ABD AL-QADIR AL-.

SAHL. One of the early 11th-century members of the Druze **movement** who deviated from the teaching of the sect. He is considered to be an **apostate.** *See also* PEOPLE OF APOSTASY.

SA'ID. *See* ABU LATIF.

SAINT. *See* WALIYY.

SALADIN (r. 1171–1193). Also Salah al-Din. A legendary **Muslim Kurdish** warrior who overthrew the **Fatimi** dynasty in **Egypt** in 1171 and established the **Ayyubi** dynasty. The Ayyubis ruled from Egypt until 1250. Saladin supported the Druze **Buhturi** prince **Jamal al-Din Haji** in his struggle against the crusaders. Saladin's most decisive victory was the battle of **Hittin,** in which he defeated the crusaders in 1187 and proceeded to conquer Jerusalem.

SALALHA, MALIK HSAIN (1953–   ). Writer and poet who lives in **Bayt-Jann, Israel.** His articles have appeared in *al-Huda,* **al-'Amamah,** *al-Sharq, al-Mawakib,* and other publications. He is also known for his genealogical study of the various **families** residing in his town, Bayt-Jann.

SALHA, SITT. An 11th-century devout female member of the Druze **movement** and the daughter of a man by the name of Jum'a Kabbul, a follower of the Druze heretic **Sukayn.** She coincidentally met prince **Mi'dad Fawarisi** earlier that day and provided him with information that led to the killing of her own father as well as most of Sukayn's followers. She is revered in Druze tradition. *See also* WOMEN.

SALIM, NAYIF (1935–). A poet from the village of **al-Buqay'a, Israel,** who became active in the Communist Party of Israel in the 1960s and then the **Druze Initiative Committee** (*Lajnat al-Mubadarah al-Durziyya*) beginning in the 1970s. In addition to several **poetry** collections and compilations, he has contributed articles to various publications in **Arabic** and Hebrew, including *al-Jadid, al-Itihad, Zo Haderekh, al-Huda,* and others.

SALMAN. A **family** that descended from the Faraj of northern **Syria.** They migrated to **Mount Lebanon** and settled primarily in **Shwayfat** in 1252. It is believed that the forefather of the Salmans was named **'Aql** and that he moved and lived first in **'Alay** before moving to Shwayfat. Another Salman family lived in Kafr Salwan and was known as Al-Khadr. This family relocated to **'Ayn Dara** but resettled in Ramliyya after 1711.

SALMAN, MERHI IBN SHAHIN (1850–1932). A Druze from **Shwayfat** who worked for the British administration in Sudan as a translator. He was given the Queen Victoria Award for his dedicated work. Merhi returned to Shwayfat and, from 1887 to 1918, was selected several times as a mediator.

SALMAN, SHAHIN (1816–1870). A dedicated official who led a successful career under three of the **Arslan emirs:** Ahmad, **Amin,** and Muhammad. In 1860, he was selected in **Shwayfat** as a mediator and resolved many conflicts and feuds in the area. As a result, the Christians and Druzes of Shwayfat remained united in spite of the **Civil War of 1860**.

SALMAN THE PERSIAN. *See* FARISI, SALMAN AL-.

SAMIRI, ABU AL-KHAYR SALAMAH AL-. One of the major Druze luminaries (*hudud*) who is the representation of the fourth cosmic principle. He was also one of the three *nudhur* appointed by the **Fatimi caliph al-Hakim** in 996 to prepare spiritually fit individuals for the **New Era** of the *Tawhid* movement. After seven years as *nadhir*, he joined and worked under his successor, **al-Qurashi,** the second chief *nadhir*. Samiri's title in relation to **Hamza Ibn 'Ali** was "The Right Wing" (*al-Janah al-Ayman*).

SAMUQI, BAHA' AL-DIN AL-. The fifth luminary who was appointed by **Hamza Ibn 'Ali** in 1021 to succeed him as the head of the community while Hamza was absent. Baha' al-Din remained in this position until 1043, when the propagation of **Druzism** came to a close. In that year, Baha' al-Din left **Cairo** and is said to have joined Hamza Ibn 'Ali with the other luminaries (*hudud*) in an undisclosed location.

Baha' al-Din was born in **Samuqa** near **Aleppo** to a **family** known as Ta'i and is known in some historical sources as Abu al-Hasan al-Dayf, 'Ali Ibn Ahmad Ibn al-Dayf, or 'Ali Ibn al-Dayf. He was sent by the **Fatimi caliph al-Hakim** in 1015–1016 on a military mission to **Syria** in which he conquered Aleppo from the Hamdanis and became its governor. To distinguish him from the other luminaries, he was given a number of titles, including "The Left Wing" (*al-Janah al-Aysar*), that is, a helper to Hamza Ibn 'Ali during the period when **al-Tamimi** was the *hujjah* between Hamza and other luminaries and **al-Qurashi** the *Safara* (ambassadorship) between Hamza Ibn 'Ali and al-Hakim. Baha' al-Din is also known as al-Muqtana (the owned), *Lisan al-Mu'minin* (the believers' tongue), and *Sanad al-Muwahhidin* (the **Unitarians'** pillar).

Baha' al-Din has a number of honorary shrines and **visitation sites**, including one in the **Shuf** area in the district of **'Alay, Lebanon**, and a more recently constructed one in the town of **Bayt-Jann, Israel**. The one in 'Alay is known by two names: "The Shrine of the Noble" and "The Shrine of Shamleikh."

SAMURA'. A city in Iraq that was known in the **'Abassi** period as *Surra man Ra'a* (pleased is the one who saw or witnessed). Residents of the city were referred to as Samurri, Samiri, or Samurra'i. The fourth luminary in **Druzism**, **Salamah al-Samiri**, is originally from Samura'.

SARAH, SITT. An early 11th-century devout female and the daughter of Abi al-Hasan Taqi al-Din Ibn Ahmad al-Ta'i, brother of **Baha' al-Din al-Samuqi**. She was an important missionary who was appointed by Baha' al-Din to lead a mission to **Wadi al-Taym**. Her mission was to persuade one major **apostate** known as **Sukayn** and his followers to come back to the *Tawhid* movement. Her predecessor, the famous missionary **'Ammar al-Maghribi**, was killed by Sukayn's followers.

Some authors have argued that Baha' al-Din wanted to stress gender equality and to show not only that **women** could not only be leaders of men but also that, in certain circumstances, they could succeed where men failed. The Druze tradition elevates Sarah to a high spiritual status in the **faith**.

SARIYY AL-DIN, HUSAYN IBN RASHID (1892–1972). A prominent medical doctor who was trained in **Great Britain**, appointed to the **American University of Beirut (AUB)**, moved to **Jabal al-Duruz**, and became the general director of health services there. Later, he returned to the AUB and was subsequently appointed as the general doctor of the City of **Beirut**, where he established the Center for the Health of Mothers and Children. He was granted the **Cedars of Lebanon** Award posthumously.

SATAN (Iblis). Devil, adversary. In the Druze doctrine, the adversary (*didd*) and his helpers are perceived as agents of Satan. These agents are represented in each **cycle** throughout human history. In the present cycle, the **Cycle of Disclosure** (*Dawr Kashf*), **Darazi** is often referred to as the adversary. *See also* PEOPLE OF APOSTASY.

SAWWAF, SAWWAFS. A **family** that migrated from northern **Syria** at the beginning of the ninth century to join the **Tanukhis** and help guard the Lebanese coastal areas at the request of the **'Abbasi caliph** Haroun al-Rashid. They are part of the **Yamanis** who lost the struggle against the **Qaysis** in 1711, and those who survived fled and subsequently adopted different names.

SAYIS. A **shaykh** responsible for a **sacred site** or for the **worship** hall, *khalwa* or *majlis*. His responsibilities include opening and closing the building before and after congregations or other events and at times also the maintenance of the site and its surrounding.

SAYYID AL-HADIN. *See* MASTER OF GUIDES.

SCHOOL OF REASON. *See* 'AQL.

SELJUK, SELJUKS. A Turkish Sunni dynasty that established itself in Persia in the 11th century and then expanded and controlled some parts of Iraq and **Syria**. When the Seljuks conquered the Druze region during the rule of Prince Zahr al-Dawlah, the son of **Buhtur**, they acknowledged the **Buhturi** principality and helped expand its territory to include other towns such as Qunaitrah in Syria. *See also* AYYUBIS; FATIMIS; MONGOLS.

SEVENERS. *See* ISMA'ILI.

SGHAYYAR, AL-. *See* ABU AL-HUSN.

SGHAYYAR, SA'ID AL- (1921–). A **Syrian** Druze who migrated to South America and was active in the Druze community there, strengthening its connection with the homeland through publications and public forums. Among his published works is the book *Banu Ma'ruf* (*Sons of Mercy* or *Sons of Beneficence*).

SHA'AR, FANDI IBN FARIS AL- (1909–). A Lebanese literary figure, educator, translator, and social activist who was born in 'Inab. After a teaching career, he migrated to Saudi Arabia and then to Kuwait, where he worked as an accountant for 14 years in the Ministry of Health.

Later, he returned to **Lebanon** to teach and write. Among his important translations into **Arabic** are George Orwell's *1984*, Jonathan Randal's *Going All the Way*, and Charles Churchill's *Between Maronites and Druzes*. He was given several honors for his achievements, including the 1992 Lebanese Ministry of Culture Award.

SHA'AR, SAMIR IBN HUSAYN AL- (1934–1972). A medical engineer who advanced the study of artificial body organs, including the heart. One of his inventions is the "Saar Actuator Artificial Heart Controller." He himself suffered from kidney failure, which eventually took his life. He was posthumously honored for his achievements by the **United Nations** Educational, Scientific, and Cultural Organization (UNESCO).

SHAFLIN, BUSTAN UM HAMAD. An activist Druze **woman** known for encouraging the rebels against the French forces. She is also known for her refusal to take revenge on a French captive during the **Great Revolt of 1925–1927**. There is a school named after her in the town of Salkhad, **Syria**.

SHAHBANDAR, 'ABD AL-RAHMAN (1880–1940). A notable **Syrian** nationalist who strongly opposed compromise with the French authorities in the 1920s. He organized the Iron Hand Society in 1921, which opposed the French and instigated many confrontations. Shahbandar was instrumental in helping the **Great Revolt of 1925–1927** in **Jabal al-Duruz** to spread to the rest of Syria. In cooperation with **Sultan al-Atrash**, he fought for keeping the provisional government. He fled to Transjordan in 1927 and later worked to form the People's Party, Syria's first nationalist party. He was assassinated in June 1940, and his murderers fled to Iraq.

SHA'IR AL-MUSTATIR AL- (HIDING POET). *See* RIDAN, ABU HASAN HANI.

SHAMLIKH. *See* SAMUQI, BAHA'AL-DIN AL-.

SHAMS. A **family** that moved from northern **Syria** to the town of al-Majdal in 1251 and later resettled in Kawkaba and **Hasbaya**. Al-Majdal took their family name and became **Majdal Shams**. About 300 years ago, some of the Shams family members relocated to al-**Shuf**, **Lebanon**.

SHAMS, AMIN (1906–1977). A distinguished judge in the Druze **court system** in **Lebanon**. He was granted the **Cedars of Lebanon** Award for his contribution to the well-being of the community.

SHARARA, BANU. *See* TANUKH.

SHARI'A. Islamic code of law compiled under four Sunni schools known as Maliki, Shafi'i, Hanbali, and Hanafi (named after their founders, the **imams** Malik, al-Shafi'i, Ibn Hanbal, and Abu Hanifa). The **Shi'i Twelvers** adhere to other schools such as the Usuli and the

Akhbari. The Druze legal code draws on all Islamic schools but is based mainly on the Sunni Hanafi school. *See also* COURT SYSTEM.

SHASHIYA. A tax levied in the early 1780s by Emir Yusef Shihabi on religious individuals who wore headgear. The Druze *shaykh al-'aql*, **Yusef Abu Shaqra**, led a campaign and a massive protest. The tax was eventually removed, but the **shaykh** was later poisoned by the **emir**.

SHA'WANEH. Also Sha'wana. A mythical saintly **woman** in the monotheist tradition before the emergence of the Druze **movement**. She has **sacred sites** in the Middle East, including the one in the **Bekáa** Valley, east of the Baruk Mountain in **Lebanon**. Sha'waneh is one of the devout spiritual figures who are venerated in the Druze tradition. *See also* RABI'A OF BASRA.

SHAWQI, AHMAD (?–1933). An **Egyptian** poet and literary figure who praised the Druzes in his **poetry** during the **Great Revolt of 1925–1927**. He described the Druzes as "protectors" of the **Arab** lands, as "good hosts," and as "a spring of purity and gentleness." He befriended a number of Druze leaders, including **Shakib Arslan**, who has written a book on his friendship with Shawqi.

SHAYKH, SHAYKHS (Sheikh, pl. *shuyukh* or *mashayikh*). This term is used in Druze circles to refer to a member of the initiated (*'uqqal*). It is also a title for the political leader of certain **families** such as the **Junblatis**. *See also* SHAYKH AL-'AQL; SHAYKH AL-MAS-HAYIKH.

SHAYKH AL-'AQL. The spiritual leader of a Druze community. The position is similar to and a continuation of the role of the **imam** of the community. The position requires that the elected *shaykh al-'aql* have two qualifications, namely, to be capable of organizing and directing the community spiritually and to have the highest moral character and behavior.

The first **shaykh** (referred to at the time as *shaykh al-mashayikh*) was perhaps Prince **Mi'dad al-Fawarisi**, who was mentioned in the Druze **manuscripts**. In recent centuries, the position has at times been politicized and factionalized in some communities. **Lebanese** *shaykh al-'aqls* include **Isma'il Ibn Sa'b Abu Hamzeh** (1778–1798) and **Husayn Hamady** (1915–1946), and **Syrian** *shaykh al-'aqls* include Husayn Jarbu'. *See also* LEADERSHIP.

SHAYKH AL-FADIL, AL- (1597–1640). Meaning "The Virtuous Shaykh," this title was given to Shaykh Muhammad Abu Hilal, a Druze sage known for his **ascetic** lifestyle and spiritual **leadership**. He grew up as an orphan and worked for a landowner **shaykh** in exchange for lessons in reading and writing. Then he traveled to **Damascus** for 12 years of study of the **Qur'an**, Hadith, and jurisprudence. He has a **sacred site** in 'Ayn 'Ata, between **Hasbaya** and Rashaya. Al-Shaykh al-Fadil is remembered for the stories about his exemplary life and for his spiritual and mystical **poetry**.

SHAYKH AL-ISLAM. A title given to the chief legal figure and head of the learned theologians, the Ulema. Based on his excellence in the Quranic sciences, the Druze **shaykh Jabir al-Halabi** (d. 1640) was granted this title in the district of **Aleppo** in the early 17th century after a contest with leading theologians organized by the Ottoman governor.

SHAYKH AL-MASHAYIKH. A term used to refer to the *shaykh al-'aql* often in the early period of the Druze community. The first *shaykh al-mashayikh* was **Mi'dad al-Fawarisi**. The term has also been used to refer to the distinguished figure among the political leaders.

SHAYKH AL-SAFI, AL-. A prominent 16th-century **shaykh** from 'Ayn Hirsha whose actual name is al-Shaykh Abu Safi Muhammad Abu Turabah. He lived a life of **asceticism** and piety and became a model for subsequent shaykhs. He was a disciple of **al-Shaykh al-Fadil**.

SHAYKH AL-TAHIR, AL-. *See* SIBAT, MUHAMMAD IBN IBRAHIM.

SHI'I, SHI'IS. A branch of **Islam**; followers or supporters of **'Ali Ibn Abi Talib** (Shi'at 'Ali, the party of 'Ali). Later, Shi'is split into three groups: Zaydis (Fivers), **Isma'ilis** (Seveners), and Ja'faris (**Twelvers**). The Druzes broke away from the Isma'ilis in the 11th century. Relations between Shi'is and Druzes have fluctuated over the history of the sect and have been often influenced by the politics of the regions in which they live.

SHIHABI, SHIHABIS (r. 1697–1842). A Lebanese princely **family** that ruled **Mount Lebanon** after the end of the **leadership** of the **Ma'ni** princedom (r. 1508–1697). During the Shihabi era, the Druze **Qaysi-Yamani** conflict intensified, leading to the emergence of the **Maronites** as the strongest community in **Lebanon**. The Shihabis were originally Druzes and/or **Sunnis** but converted to Maronite Christianity in the mid-18th century.

SHIHABI, BASHIR, II (1767–1840). A prince of **Lebanon** who was born in **Kisrawan** and raised in **Beirut**. Bashir Shihabi built his mansion in **Bayt al-Din**. Some historians say that he was born a Sunni or Druze and lived his life as a **Maronite**. The Druze **Nakadis** attempted to overthrow him, but in retaliation he massacred their **shaykhs** in 1795. As an opponent of Shaykh **Bashir Junblat**, he fought Junblat and defeated him in the battle of al-**Simqaniya**.

In the 1830s, Bashir II cooperated with **Ibrahim Pasha** of **Egypt** and assisted him in subduing the Druzes. Bashir was exiled in 1840 after a widespread revolt against his rule erupted in **Mount Lebanon**.

SHIRWAL. Loose-fitting trousers, traditionally worn by Druze men. Because of the influence of modern dress, the *shirwal* has become rare except in rural mountainous regions. *See also* NIQAB.

SHISHAKLI, ADIB AL- (1909–1964). Ruler of **Syria** who ordered an attack in 1954 on the Druzes of **Jabal al-Duruz**. He was then forced to leave office during a military coup and to depart to **Lebanon** and from there to South America, where he settled in **Brazil**. Subsequently, Shishakli was pursued for 10 years and was assassinated in 1964 by **Nawaf Ghazala**, who was avenging the death of members of his **family**.

SHRINES. *See* SACRED SITES.

SHU'AYB. Also Jethro; a biblical figure, father-in-law of Moses, and prophet of the Midianites, inhabitants of the land of Midian (the southern part of present-day **Jordan** and **Israel**). He is known in the **Qur'an** and among Druzes as Shu'ayb. His tomb and shrine are in **Hittin**, near Tiberias, overlooking the Sea of **Galilee**, Israel. The site was mentioned by historians as early as the 12th century.

The site was renovated and expanded by Druzes in the 1880s at the initiative of the spiritual leader from the town of Julis, Shaykh **Muhanna Tarif** (d. 1889), who formed a committee to solicit funds for the renovation project. The site was further renovated, and additional buildings were added during the British Mandate as well as after the emergence of the state of Israel in 1948. The shrine of Jethro is still considered to be the largest and most important among Israeli Druzes today if not among all Druzes. An annual festival and holiday, *Eid al-Nabi Shu'ayb*, is celebrated by Druzes on 25 April, and the site is continuously frequented year-round.

There is also a **visitation site** and symbolic tomb for Prophet Shu'-ayb in **Jordan** in a valley named after him, *Wadi Shu'ayb*. He is said to have spent some time in this valley on his journey north. The site in Jordan is visited by different religious communities in that region and not only by the Druzes.

SHUF, AL-. Subdistrict of **Mount Lebanon** southeast of **Beirut**. It is the largest communal center of Lebanese Druzes and the seat of power for both the **Arslanis** and the **Junblatis**.

SHUF POET. *See* ABU GHANIM, FUAD IBN SULAYMAN.

SHUF TECHNICAL INSTITUTE. A technical college established by the present Lebanese *shaykh al-'aql* **Bahjat Ghayth**.

SHUJA'. One of the **families** that migrated with the **Tanukhis** to **Lebanon** in the middle of the eighth century and settled in Salima, Zar'un, and other areas. It is related to many other family branches, including the Qabani, Abi Rashid, Farhoud, and al-Basha.

SHUQAIR, SHAWKAT (1912–1982). A commander in the **Lebanese army** from Arsun who joined the **Syrian** army in 1949 and became its general commander from 1953 until he retired in 1956. He was a personal friend of **Jamal 'Abd al-Naser** of **Egypt**. He was the recipient of many awards and honors for his military exploits from **Lebanon**, Syria, **Jordan**, and Egypt.

SHUYUKH AL-BUSTAN. *See* DAMASCUS.

SHWAYFAT. An old Druze town in the **Shuf, Lebanon**, and the seat of the **Arslani** faction. It was settled in the eighth century when the Arslani prince Mas'ud Ibn Arslan moved there with his **family** and other followers.

SIBAT. Known also as Shbat. This **family** is originally a branch of al-Faqih from **'Ayha**. Some were referred to in the Druze **manuscripts** as the family of **Sulayman,** with important figures such as Shaykh **Muhammad Ibn Ibrahim Sibat**.

SIBAT, MUHAMMAD IBN IBRAHIM (?–1041). One of the early **shaykhs** in the Druze **movement** known as *al-Shaykh al-Tahir* Abi al-Ma'ali. He was mentioned in the correspondence of **Baha' al-Din al-Samuqi** several times and is considered one of the most pious shaykhs in his region. He has a **visitation site** in **'Ayha, Lebanon**.

SIDQ AL-LISAN. *See* TRUTHFULNESS.

SIJIL AL-ARSLANI, AL-. An important **manuscript** that was finally published in 1999. It chronicles the **Arslani** princely **family** from 758 to the present. The text also sheds light on historical events in **Lebanon** in general.

SIJIL AL-MU'ALAQ, AL-. A document issued by the **Fatimi caliph** and **imam al-Hakim**, calling on believers to be aware of the Oneness of God and the Prophethood of **Muhammad** and reiterating al-Hakim's role as caliph. It is included in the Druze manuscript known as the *Epistles of Wisdom* (*Rasa'il al-Hikma*).

SILMAN, JIMMIE, JR. (1927–   ). An American Druze whose family came to the **United States** at the beginning of the 20th century. After serving in the U.S. Navy, he launched a television career as a producer and director in 1951. He served as program director for the *Washington Post* and the *Newsweek* CBS station in Washington, D.C., and also taught advanced television production at the American University in Washington. His contributions were acknowledged with two Emmys.

SILMIYYA. A town in **Syria** where the **Isma'ili imam** Sa'id al-Khayr, known as **Ubaydallah**, resided until he escaped to North Africa. He then founded the **Fatimi** state in 909.

SIMQANIYA. A historic village located in the **Shuf** region and site of the 1825 battle in which Emir **Bashir Shihabi II** defeated Shaykh **Bashir Junblat** and his predominantly Druze army. It is also where the palace of Mahmud Harmush is located. *See also* 'IRFAN TAWHID FOUNDATION (ITF).

SINLESSNESS. *See* WORSHIP.

SIQILI, BURJUWAN. A 10th-century personal assistant and servant under **al-'Aziz**, the fifth **Fatimi caliph**. When al-'Aziz passed away in 996, it was Siqili who called on **al-Hakim** and placed the Fatimi crown on his head, proclaiming him the next caliph and **imam**.

SITR. A term that means "concealment" or "hiding" one's doctrine to protect it from misunderstandings. It is also used in concealing the identities of the **imams** in order to protect them from any harm. *Sitr* has often been attributed to the Druzes, though their political behavior at times indicates otherwise. *See also* CYCLE OF CONCEALMENT; CYCLE OF DISCLOSURE; TAQIYYA.

SITT (LADY) FAKHARA. *See* EL B'AYNI, SITT FAKHARA.

SITT AL-MULK. The guardian of **al-Zahir**, the seventh **Fatimi caliph**. Al-Zahir was 16 years old in 1021 when he took office after the mysterious disappearance of **al-Hakim**. As guardian, Sitt al-Mulk influenced the affairs of the Fatimi state affairs for several years.

SIX-DAY WAR (1967). In mid-May 1967, President **Jamal 'Abd al-Naser** of **Egypt** mobilized the Egyptian army, moved troops close to the **Israeli** border, insisted that the **United Nations** Emergency Force (UNEF) be removed, and closed the Strait of Tiran, preventing free passage of Israeli ships. **Jordan** and **Syria** then concluded a defense pact with Egypt. Shortly thereafter, on 5 June, the Israeli air force launched a surprise attack and destroyed the major military airports of Syria, Jordan, and Egypt, rendering the air power of these three countries almost defunct. This offensive was followed by six days of massive Israeli ground troop infiltration, resulting in the capture and occupation of the Sinai and Gaza Strip from Egypt, the West Bank from Jordan, and the **Golan Heights** from Syria. The Golan Heights houses a community of four Druze villages. The residents of these villages were cut off from their relatives and to this day remain under Israeli occupation. After diplomatic negotiations between Israelis and **Palestinians** in the 1990s, some parts of the West Bank and Gaza Strip are being handed back to the Palestinian Authority, while the Syrian Israeli negotiations have not yet produced a lasting agreement but have improved the situation for Druzes. For example, in recent years some Golani and Syrian Druzes have been allowed to visit each other, and Syria and Israel have permitted the marketing of Golani apples in **Damascus** and the exchange of Druze brides. *See also* ARAB-ISRAELI WARS.

SLEEM. An ancient Druze **family** that originated in the **Arab** tribe, Sleem. Members of the Sleem family came to the **Shuf** from **Aleppo** with the **Junblatis** at the beginning of the 17th century.

SLEEM, AS'AD IBN HASAN IBN SULAYMAN (1850–1923). A medical doctor from **'Abey** who graduated from the **American University of Beirut (AUB)** in 1881, traveled to Istanbul for further training, and then worked in the British Hospital in Gaza. He was innovative in a number of procedures, introduced new medicines, and authored numerous articles in various publications, such as *al-Muqtataf*, *al-Tabib*, and *Lubnan*.

SLEEM, DAWUD IBN HASAN (?–1913). A surgeon who graduated from the **American University of Beirut (AUB)** in 1884 and worked there until his departure to **Canada**. In Canada, he became known for having introduced a number of inventions in the field of electricity.

SLEEM, FOAD. Present representative of the Druze **Orphanage** and other Lebanese charities in North America. He is active in the **American Druze Society (ADS)**.

SLEEM, FOAD IBN YUSEF HASAN (1893–1925). A military commander who fought in the **Great Revolt of 1925–1927** under **Zayd al-Atrash** in Iqlim al-Billan and **Wadi al-Taym**. He initially gained control over **Hasbaya** and Rashayya, but the French authorities feared that the revolt would spill over to **Mount Lebanon**. Therefore, they directed heavy bombardment against the area from three major divisions. Foad Sleem died in battle and was buried near Shita. The place became known as *Tal Foad* (the Hill of Foad).

SLEEM, HASAN IBN SULAYMAN (?–1881). The first to be responsible for the endowments (*waqf*) of the **Dawudiyya School** in 1862. He worked as an assistant surgeon and raised his son, **Dawud Sleem**, to be a surgeon. *See also* DAWUD PASHA.

SLEEM, NASRI IBN YUSEF IBN HASAN (1903–1981). A military commander who fought in the **Great Revolt of 1925–1927** and later joined the Jordanian army, where he served until he became ill. He then retired and returned to **Lebanon** in 1944. But subsequently, he visited **Jordan** and rejoined the army as a consultant for the following 18 years.

SLEEM, SAMI IBN AS'AD IBN HASAN (?–1953). A journalist, educator, and literary figure who established the journal *al-Dhikra* and the newspapers *Sada al-Sahil* and *Minbar al-'Arab*. He also participated in the **Great Revolt of 1925–1927**.

SLEEM, YUSEF IBN HASAN (d. 1918). A medical doctor who is known for having considerably reduced the rate of death during the

1917 cholera epidemic. As a result, he was recognized and honored by the central government.

SONS OF MERCY. *See* BANU MA'RUF.

SOULS. *See* TAQAMUS.

SOUTH AMERICA. Druzes migrated to South and Central America at the end of the 19th century. The second wave took place in the beginning of the 20th century. Large Druze communities can be found in various countries, including **Argentina**, **Brazil**, **Uruguay**, and **Venezuela**.

SPOKESMAN. *See* NATIQ.

STARTING POINT (al-Muntalaq). *See* RIDAN MOSQUE.

STATION. *See* MAQAM.

SUFISM. The **Islamic** mystical tradition. **Muslim** mystics are known as *sufis*. The title *sufi* was given to devout persons who wore wool garments as early as the seventh century. The wool has symbolized the **ascetic** lifestyle of the wearers and their interest in the hereafter rather than in the comforts of this world. Some forms of sufism are oriented toward the **esoteric** dimension of the Quranic and other scriptural sources.

Because it has the two important characteristics of asceticism and esotericism, **Druzism** is often considered to be a sufi tradition. The devout Druze **shaykhs** usually wear wool clothes, and the most advanced few among them wear the distinguished striped wool garment known as *'abba*. The *'abba* is worn over a black wool shirt and black wool trousers, which is much wider and bulkier than the shaykh's waist, known as the *shirwal*. They eat small quantities of food and speak very little.

SUKAYN. An 11th-century religious activist who is also known in some sources as Mas'ud al-Kurdi. He became one of the early missionaries (*da'is*) who was appreciated by **Baha' al-Din al-Samuqi**.

Sukayn began spreading a false rumor that Baha' al-Din had been promoted to the position of **imam** and he himself to Baha' al-Din's position. With the cooperation with other **apostates**, he succeeded in spreading ideas that were erroneously attributed to the Druze doctrine. *See also* PEOPLE OF APOSTASY.

SULAYMAN. A general title given to the **shaykhs** who lived in **Wadi al-Taym** at the beginning of the 11th century and joined the ranks of the Druze **movement**. They included the shaykhs Abu Madi, Abu 'Ali Wahb, and **Muhammad Ibn Ibrahim Sibat**.

SUNNIS. *See* ISLAM.

SUWAYDA, AL-. The largest Druze city in the Middle East with a population of nearly 50,000. It is located in **Jabal al-Duruz** in southern **Syria**. It is also the administrative capital of Suwayda province.

SYRIA. Ever since the emergence of the Druze **movement** in the 11th century, large Druze centers have been established in various parts of Syria; from there, some Druzes migrated to **Mount Lebanon**. Additional Druzes settled in Syria at the end of the 17th century, but a large **migration** took place after the 1711 **'Ayn Dara** battle between the **Qaysis** and the **Yamanis**. The latter were defeated, and many of them left Mount Lebanon and settled in Syria. Another wave of Druze migration to Syria took place during and after the **Civil War of 1840–1860** in Mount Lebanon.

In the 1920s, the Druzes received worldwide attention for their part in leading the **Great Revolt of 1925–1927** against the French forces. The leader of that revolt, **Sultan al-Atrash**, who was from one of the largest Druze clans of that region, is considered to be a nationalist hero. In February 1942, **Jabal al-Duruz** was reunited to the rest of Syria, and in July 1943, national elections took place, resulting in a victory for the National Party. **France** withdrew its troops from Syria in 1946, and a year later the **Ba'th Party** was founded. Under the **leadership** of **Hafiz al-Asad** beginning in November 1970 and especially after February 1971, when he became president of Syria, the party has become and still remains the governing force under the leadership of his son, **Bashshar al-Asad**.

Druzes in Syria have remained loyal to the party and devout supporters of the Asad regimes. Today, they live mainly in **Hawran** and **al-Suwayda** provinces (see map 3). This predominantly Druze area is often referred to as **Jabal al-Duruz** or **Jabal al-'Arab** (The Druze or Arab Mountain). But other Syrian Druze areas include the **Golan Heights,** which has been occupied by **Israel** since the **Six-Day War** (June 1967). The district of **Aleppo** is also known for its Druze presence, especially in previous centuries. For example, the large Halabi family is originally from Aleppo (*Halab*). A smaller number of Druzes also live in **Damascus** or in other parts of Syria. *See also* ASMAHAN; ATRASH, FARID AL-; ATRASH, SULTAN AL-; BALLAN, FAHD; HALABI, JABIR IBN MUHAMMAD AL-.

SYRIAN-PALESTINE CONGRESS. A political organization established by Syrian exiles in **Cairo** in June 1921. One of its factions was headed by **Shakib Arslan** and Rashid Rida and placed greater emphasis on Islamic unity. Another group included **'Adil Arslan**, who advocated **Arab nationalism** and pan-Arab ideologies.

– T –

TAFISH, KHALIL. *See* TARIF, MUHANNA.

TAGHLIB. *See* NAKAD.

TA'I, BAHA' AL-DIN. *See* SAMUQI, BAHA' AL-DIN AL-.

TA'I, SARAH. *See* SARAH, SITT.

TA'IF, AGREEMENT OF. A meeting of Lebanese representatives in 1989 in Ta'if, Saudi Arabia, to develop a program for reconstructing **Lebanon** after the **Civil War of 1975–1990**. The resulting agreement dealt with justice and equality for all Lebanese; it provided a program for the end of political sectarianism in Lebanon. In the Druze view, the agreement was meant to abolish sectarianism and sectarian sentiments and to improve the rights and benefits of the smaller political and religious groups, including the Druzes. *See also* CIVIL WAR OF 1975–1990.

TAJASUD. *See* TAJSID.

TAJALI. Theophony; manifestation of God's Light in the Station (*maqam*). A belief that God's splendor illuminates a station that is most advanced spiritually. This is a belief that Druzes adopted from previous traditions and made central to their doctrine. There are eight stations described in the Druze doctrine.

TAJRID. A belief that God is Unique and One and is stripped of all attributes. *See also* FAITH; TAWHID.

TAJSID. From *Jasad*, meaning "body." A belief that God becomes human in a body. Although this belief is often attributed to Druzes, it is not a part of the belief system of **Druzism**.

TALAQ. Divorce. It is permitted under Druze law but only under stricter conditions than in Islamic law (**Shari'a**). For example, unlike **Islamic** law, remarrying one whom one has divorced or having any communication with him or her is prohibited in **Druzism**. *See also* COURT SYSTEM.

TAL FOAD. *See* SLEEM, FOAD.

TALHUQ, SA'ID IBN FA'UR (1827–1903). An attorney trained in Istanbul who became the head of the **B'abda** court. He approached the *mutassarrif*, **Dawwud Pasha**, in 1862 and expressed the need to establish a Druze school. A school was established and named after Dawwud Pasha, the Dawudiyya.

TALI, AL-. The Follower; the fifth luminary (*hadd*, pl. *hudud*) and cosmic principle. During the emergence of the Druze **movement** in the 11th century, he was represented by **Baha' al-Din al-Samuqi**. *See also* COSMOLOGY.

TALI', RASHID (1876–1926). An important Druze **Arab nationalist** who served in many important positions in **Syria**, **Jordan**, and **Leb-**

anon. For example, King 'Abdallah of Jordan asked him to form an **Arab** government in Jordan. His subsequent conflict with the British authorities forced him to leave Jordan for Jerusalem and then for **Egypt**. He also participated in the **Great Revolt of 1925–1927**.

TA'LIH. The act of believing that a person is perceived as being God. This term is erroneously attributed to Druzes as well as the deification of the **Fatimi caliph al-Hakim**.

TAMIMI, ISMA'IL IBN MUHAMMAD AL-. One of the early leaders of the Druze **movement** in the first half of the 11th century. He is considered to be the embodiment of the second—the **Universal Soul** (*al-Nafs al-Kuliyya*)—of the five main luminaries (*hudud*) in **Druzism**. Al-Tamimi was also one of the three primary figures known as warners (*nudhur*) during the preparation phase of Druzism, between 996 and 1017. In addition, he served as the *hujjah* between **Hamza Ibn 'Ali** and the other luminaries.

TANASUKH. *See* TAQAMUS.

TA'NIS. The act of believing that God has the characteristics of humans or is perceived to be human. Though this phenomenon is erroneously attributed to Druzes, it is not a part of the Druze doctrine.

TANTUR. A decorative horn that was usually worn on the head by **Maronite** and Druze **women** until the mid-19th century. *See also* NIQAB; SHIRWAL.

TANUKH, TANUKHI, TANUKHIS. A large early Arabian tribe. Initially, some Tanukhi clans migrated north and settled in Iraq, where they founded the Tanukhi state. They ruled for nearly 130 years until the Lakhmis became the dominant force in that region. When Khalid Ibn al-Walid conquered the Hira region in 632, there were three Tanukhi kings, 16 Lakhmis, and five others. After that year, some branches of the Tanukhis and Lakhmis began migrating to northern **Syria**. Tanukhi leaders joined the **Islamic** forces and fought with Khalid in the battle of **Ajnadayn** (634).

Later, during the **'Abbasi** dynasty, additional Tanukhi clans relocated first to northern Syria, some to **Jabal al-A'la**, and others to **Ma'arat al-Nu'man**, **Aleppo**, and **Damascus**. The Tanukhi settlements in **Mount Lebanon** were established in different stages, one of which was in the middle of the eighth century. But at the beginning of the ninth century, other Tanukhis moved to the Lebanese Mountains. The **families** that migrated with the Emir Tanukh from northern **Syria** to Mount Lebanon at the beginning of the ninth century include Banu 'Atir, **Abu Hamzeh**, **Banu 'Abdallah**, Banu Firas, Banu Sharara, Banu 'Azayim, Banu Hilal, Banu Khadr, and Banu Nimer. One of the important early Tanukhi branches was the **Buhturis**, cousins of the **Arslanis** and the first important Druze princedom.

TANUKHI, 'ALI IBN 'ALAM AL-DIN. A **Tanukhi** prince, an enemy of the **Ma'nis**, and a friend of the Ottomans. He murdered all his cousins for their cooperation with the Ma'nis, and with this act, the Tanukhi-**Buhturi** line of princes was extinguished.

TANUKHI, AL-EMIR AL-SAYYID JAMAL AL-DIN 'ABDAL-LAH (1417–1479). A prominent theologian, commentator, and reformer. He was the son of the **emir** 'Alam al-Din Sulaiman from **'Abey**. He had four children, three of whom died at a young age and the fourth, **Sayf al-Din 'Abd al-Khaliq Tanukhi**, on his wedding day.

Al-Sayyid Jamal al-Din became famous for his **asceticism**, religious and spiritual insights, and strict ethical code. His moral directives were not appreciated by his contemporaries, leading him to a self-imposed 12-year period of exile in **Damascus**. There he was also a challenge or a threat to other religious figures as a result of his practices. Later, a mission of **shaykhs** from **Mount Lebanon** visited him in Damascus and asked him to come back to 'Abey and teach his reforms.

He excelled in Quranic sciences and in the prophetic traditions as well as in other **literatures**, histories, and linguistics. He wrote commentaries on the Druze scriptural sources. Some of his works have survived, but others were lost during invasions or internal wars in Mount Lebanon.

Al-Sayyid's position and his commentaries are central in Druze society, but his teachings that link Druzism to **monotheism** and stress the need for Druzes to study the **Qur'an** and the **Bible** seem to fall on deaf ears in most Druze communities except among the advanced in spirituality. *See also* MASHAYIKH AL-DIN; WALIYY.

TANUKHI, JAMAL AL-DIN HAJI IBN NAJM (1236–1298). *See* HAJI, JAMAL AL-DIN.

TANUKHI, NAHID AL-DAWLAH (?–1157). *See* ARSLAN, NAHID AL-DIN BUHTUR.

TANUKHI, NAJM AL-DIN MUHAMMAD (?–1305). Son of the famous **emir** of **Mount Lebanon Jamal al-Din Haji**. He fought against the **Mamluks** but was defeated in 1279.

TANUKHI, NASIR AL-DIN MUHAMMAD. An important **shaykh** who advocated the study of the **Qur'an** and its sciences as well as the commentaries of **al-Emir al-Sayyid al-Tanukhi**. His example earned him **leadership** among the initiated (**'uqqal**) but also led to his murder by jealous rivals.

TANUKHI, SALIH IBN YAHYA. *See* IBN YAHYA, SALIH.

TANUKHI, SAYF AL-DIN 'ABD AL-KHALIQ. Son of **al-Sayyid Jamal al-Din Tanukhi** (d. 1479). His name is 'Abd al-Khaliq, and his nickname is Sayf al-Din. He is referred to as the second 'Abd al-Khaliq, the first 'Abd al-Khaliq having died at an early age. He gained spiritual knowledge from his father and was exposed to learned men during the 12 years of living with his father, who was in self-imposed exile in **Damascus**. After returning to **'Abey**, he continued the path of his father, but he was not to live long and died suddenly on the day of his wedding.

TANUKHI, SAYF AL-DIN YAHYA (1390–1455). A Tanukhi prince and poet who lived during the time of **al-Sayyid al-Tanukhi**. He was also a wealthy landowner who became an **ascetic**. He is often compared with the famous prince turned ascetic **Ibrahim Ibn Adham** (d. 875), since both gave up their wealth to lead a contemplative, spiritual lifestyle. Initially, Sayf al-Din excelled in romantic **poetry** until he became an ascetic and turned to mystical poetry.

TANUKHI, YAHYA (?–1633). One of the devout **emirs** whose greatness was appreciated by the community and highly praised by his contemporary **al-Shaykh al-Fadil**. Emir Yahya was murdered by **'Ali 'Alam al-Din**.

TANZIH. The act of believing that God is Unique, Pure, and One; the process of stripping all associations and things from Him.

TANZIL. Revelation; the first stage of belief or the **exoteric**. It reflects the literal message of the scriptures. The other two stages are *ta'wil* and *Tawhid*. *See also* ESOTERIC; IMAN; IHSAN.

TAQAMUS. The Druze term for reincarnation, transmigration of souls, or metempsychosis. It is derived from *qamis*, meaning "shirt," and implies that the body is the shirt for the soul. Druzes believe that when the body dies, the soul instantly enters a newly born body, for it cannot exist without a body. A second distinction is that Druzes believe that *taqamus* takes place only among humans, that humans do not degenerate into animals, plants, or things through **maskh**, *faskh*, or **raskh**, respectively.

Moreover, the Druze teachings instruct that in a multiplicity of lives, the soul experiences all possible manifestations—being poor, rich, healthy, ill, and so on—and that at the end of times, the soul is judged according to its cumulative record of good and bad deeds.

TAQDIS (Veneration). The concept of *taqdis* in **Druzism** takes second place after that of *Tawhid*. Druzes believe that in order to understand God and be devoted to Him, one must be dedicated to the intermediaries, including *hudud*, **prophets**, and **sages**. *See also* FAITH; WALIYY; WORSHIP.

TAQI AL-DIN, HALIM (1922–1983). A faculty member at the Lebanese University between 1960 and 1981. He was appointed the head of the Lebanese Druze Supreme Court. Shaykh Halim was assassinated in his home during the **Civil War of 1975–1990**.

TAQI AL-DIN, SA'ID (1904–1960). A literary figure and political activist who was born in **B'aqlin** and educated at the **American University of Beirut (AUB)**. He was a member of the **Syrian** Nationalist Party but was accused of planning a coup against the Syrian regime. In order to escape the death sentence, he traveled to **Mexico** and then to Colombia, where he died of natural causes. Sa'id has published numerous stories and essays on a variety of topics, especially life in **Lebanon**. *See also* LITERATURE.

TAQI AL-DIN, ZAYN AL-DIN 'ABD AL-GHAFFAR (?–1557). A Druze sage, originally from **B'aqlin,** who has written commentaries on the Druze scriptures. He is often considered one of the great learned Druze men after **al-Sayyid al-Tanukhi**. His teachings were met with resistance, and he had to move and live in seclusion for seven years. He was killed by one of his opponents and was buried in **Kafr Matta**, where he has a **visitation site** today.

TAQIYYA. Prudent dissimulation. Some early **Shi'i** groups have practiced outward adoption of other **faiths** while maintaining their own beliefs in order to avoid persecution. This practice was at times attributed to the Druzes, and to some extent Druzes may indeed have initially been impacted by it. However, certain stances that Druzes have taken in recent centuries indicate that they did not subscribe to *taqiyya* and preferred to assert their Druzeness. *See also* CYCLE OF CONCEALMENT.

TAQIYYIDIN, DIANA. Also Taqi al-Din Diana; a contemporary concert pianist who has taught at the **American University of Beirut (AUB)**. She was born to a Druze **family** in the **Philippines**. During the **Civil War of 1975–1990**, she settled in the **United States**. *See also* MUSIC.

TARIF. A prominent Druze **family** from the town of Julis, **Israel**. In recent centuries, the family is known for having provided the spiritual **leadership** of the Druzes in the **Galilee** and **Carmel** Mountain regions. Some members of the Tarif family also rose in the political and legal leadership of the community. *See also* TARIF, AMIN; TARIF, MUHAMMAD; TARIF, SALIH.

TARIF, AMIN (?–1993). The spiritual leader of the Druze community in **Palestine/Israel** between 1928 and 1993. His death initiated a heated debate regarding the issue of succession, as the Tarif **shaykhs** have been the spiritual leaders since 1753. This debate led to the selection of his son-in-law, **Muwwafaq Tarif**, to the position of spiritual leader.

Amin Tarif was a devout shaykh who was the son of **Muhammad Tarif** (d. 1928), the former spiritual leader of the community. In his youth, he went to **Khalawat al-Bayyada, Lebanon**, where he studied and contemplated the precepts of the *Tawhid* **faith**. He was revered by both the initiated and the uninitiated (*'uqqal* and *juhhal*) in the community.

Shaykh Amin is also remembered as a dedicated spiritual and community leader. For example, he conducted regular visits to all Druze villages to consult with shaykhs there and to revive the practices and teachings of **al-Emir al-Sayyid al-Tanukhi**. He encouraged the building of congregational **worship** places (*khalwas*) and the appointment of a person responsible (*sayis*) for each local *khalwa*. When Israel was established in 1948, his activism and behavior led the state to recognize his religious and spiritual **leadership**, his place in the community, and the community as independent in its **court system**. Unlike the spiritual leaders, the political leaders were regularly unable to draw as much support and popularity among members of the community. Shaykh Amin Tarif's tomb has become a **visitation site** in his town of Julis.

TARIF, MUHAMMAD (?–1928). A spiritual leader of the Druze community in **Palestine** between 1889 and 1928. He was the son of **Muhanna Tarif** (d. 1889) and the father of **Amin Tarif** (d. 1993); both served as the spiritual leaders of the community in Palestine/**Israel** in their time. Shaykh Muhammad was also granted the position of judge (*qadi*) of the Druze sect in Palestine by the Ottoman sultan in 1909.

TARIF, MUHANNA (d. 1889). The spiritual leader of the Druze community in **Palestine** at the end of the 19th century. He is remembered for having appointed a committee of **shaykhs** in the 1880s to solicit funds and for the subsequent renovation of the Jethro/**Shu'ayb** tomb in **Hittin,** near Tiberias in present-day **Israel**. The members of this mission were Shaykh Khalil Tafish and Shaykh Muhammad al-Farisi from **Hurfaysh**, Shaykh Muhammad Farhud from Ramah, and Shaykh Salman Hamud from Yarka.

TARIF, MUWWAFAQ. The present spiritual leader of the Druze community in **Israel**. He is the son-in-law of the previous spiritual leader **Amin Tarif**. After a heated debate in the community, Shaykh Muwwafaq was selected for the post.

TARIF, SALIH. The first Druze in **Israel** to hold the portfolio of a minister and to serve as chairman of the Israeli Parliament, the **Knesset**. He is a longtime Labor Party member. In January 2003, however, he was not elected to the 16th Knesset as a result of the Labor Party's loss of several seats.

TARIQA. Pathway, a mystical order; the path of allegorical interpretation, the inner meaning of the *Shari'a*. Some observers have referred to **Druzism** as a *tariqa* because of its similarity with **Sufism** and its hermeneutic of the **Qur'an** and Shari'a.

TASLIM. Obedience and submission to God; the Druze's seventh act of **worship**.

TAWBIKH. A reprimanding message or letter sent to a missionary (*da'i*) or member of the Druze **movement** who has deviated from the teachings of the movement. Such letters were sent to the **People of Apostasy** (*Ahl al-Ridda*), including **Darazi**, **Lahiq**, and **Sukayn**. The *Tawbikh* serves also as a last attempt to dissuade its recipient from apostasy.

TAWHID. Often translated as Unitarianism or Unification; the doctrine of or belief in the Unity and Oneness of God. In a spiritual sense, it is the ability to disassociate God from anything that can be imagined or thought.

Druzes believe that *Tawhid* was present in the early traditions, reappeared in **Islam**, was refined in **Shi'ism** and then **Isma'ilism**, but was represented in its final stage in the early 11th century in **Druz-**

ism. The Druze sources are replete with descriptions of *Tawhid*. Thus, Druzism is only one medium through which *Tawhid* is expressed. *See also* CYCLE OF CONCEALMENT; CYCLE OF DISCLOSURE; FAITH; PEOPLE OF INTERPRETATION; PEOPLE OF UNITARIANISM.

TA'WIL. The inner meaning of revelation (*tanzil*). Its supreme purpose is to bring the meaning of the revealed closer to the mind of the believer. The **imams** in **Shi'ism** were in charge of the *ta'wil*. *Ta'wil* is often referred to as the second stage to spiritual understanding and advancement (after *tanzil*). A third phase is that of *Tawhid*.

TAYAMINA, AL-. Those from **Wadi al-Taym**. Many Druzes sought refuge and settled in Wadi al-Taym during the early establishment period of **Druzism**. A term used by some sources to refer to the Druzes in the first few centuries after the emergence of their **movement**.

THAUMATURGIES (Karamat). Wonders, miracles. Many Druze **shaykhs** attained a high rank in spiritual practices and insights and are said to be able to predict the future, perform miracles, and have an impact on their surroundings. Examples include **Jabir al-Halabi**, **Salih Jaramani**, and **Salih 'Amer**.

THEOPHONY. *See* TAJALI.

TIME. Time is perceived in **Druzism** as representing two phases: the **Cycle of Concealment** (*Dawr Sitr*) and the **Cycle of Disclosure** (*Dawr Kashf*). The Cycle of Disclosure was initiated in the 11th century; it indicates the nearness of the **Judgment Day**.

TLAS, MUSTAFA (1932–). A **Syrian** Sunni officer who participated in the 23 February 1966 coup of the neo-**Ba'th Party** in Syria and professed loyalty to the armed forces of **Hafiz al-Asad**. He was appointed minister of defense in 1972. Before his military career, he was a schoolteacher assigned to the Druze province of **Suwayda** in **Jabal al-Duruz** and was befriended by **Sultan al-Atrash**. As a result of his early experiences in Suwayda, he has remained a loyal friend of the Druzes.

TRANSMIGRATION OF SOULS. *See* TAQAMUS.

TRUE MESSIAH (al-Masih al-Haq). *See* JESUS.

TRUTHFULNESS (Sidq al-Lisan). Literally, "speaking the truth"; the first and most important **commandment** in **Druzism**. The Druze doctrine asserts that all religious and spiritual commandments and directives are rooted in the principle of truthfulness; without truthfulness, one cannot fulfill the other commandments. *See also* FAITH; WORSHIP.

TWELVERS. The largest of the **Shi'i** groups who descended from **'Ali Ibn Abi Talib** and **Fatima**. They believe that the 12th **imam**, the awaited one, will return once again as the Messiah or *Mahdi*. Cooperation between Twelvers and Druzes has existed throughout the history of the sect but especially in the recent Lebanese setting.

TUDELLA, BENJAMIN DE. A Jewish-Spanish traveler who visited the coasts of Greater **Syria** (Bilad al-Sham) between 1165 and 1173. He recorded his experiences and observations, some of which included accounts of the Druzes in that region. He is perhaps the first Western traveler to mention Druzes in his writings.

TURAB. A title given to members of the Druze **movement** who lived in Palestine during the emergence of the Druze movement in the early 11th century. Meaning "earth," the name came to symbolize a down-to-earth, **ascetic** community that emphasized spirituality and interest in the hereafter. The Turab **shaykhs** who are mentioned in the Druze **manuscripts** include **Ghana'im Abu Al-Saraya** from Yarka near **Acre**. Abu al-Saraya, Abu 'Arus, **Abu 'Abdallah**, and others were described as "the Pure" (*al-Tahara*). They led an ascetic lifestyle and were committed to the **worship** of God and to serving the community. *See also* CARMEL; GALILEE; ISRAEL.

–U–

UBAYDALLAH (r. 909–934). Founder and first **caliph** of the **Fatimi** state. He migrated from **Silmiyya** in **Syria** and settled in North Africa. In **Druzism**, he does not hold a central place. *See also* IMAM.

UMARA' (sing. *amir, emir*). Princes; a term often used with several Druze princely **families**, such as the **Tanukhis, Buhturis, Ma'nis**, and **Arslanis**.

UMAYYA, UMAYYAS (r. 661–750). An **Islamic** dynasty that ruled the Islamic lands after the Rightly Guided caliphs (r. 632–661) and was overthrown by the **'Abbasis** (r. 750–1258). Several Umayya **caliph**s supported the Druze ancestors because their princes joined the Islamic armies and served as a buffer, protecting the Islamic lands from the **Byzantine**'s recurring infiltrations. *See also* TANUKH.

UNCLE JACK'S CONTEST. *See* HAMADY, JACK.

UNCLE NAFE. *See* KATTER, NAFE.

UNINITIATED. *See* JUHHAL.

UNION OF ARAB WRITERS. *See* QASIM, SAMIH AL-.

UNITARIANISM. *See* TAWHID.

UNITED NATIONS (UN). Druze-related issues have been discussed in the UN, including one regarding the **Israeli** decision to annex the **Golan Heights** in December 1981. After a debate, the assembly pronounced the annexation to be "null and void" three days later.

Throughout the history of the UN, several Druze diplomats have participated in its sessions. For example, it is often said that the Syrian lawyer and diplomat **Farid Zayn Al-Din** was among those who helped draft the UN Charter.

UNITED STATES. The Druze presence in the United States can be traced to the last three decades of the 19th century. Like other Middle

Easterners, some Druzes migrated to the New World in order to escape being drafted into the Ottoman army. Some simply were attracted to opportunities in the Americas. A majority of Druze migrants found employment in South America, but others entered the United States and **Canada**. Druzes in the United States are scattered throughout almost all states, but the largest concentration is in California, which has over 7,000 of the total 25,000 to 30,000 American Druzes. *See also* AMERICAN DRUZE SOCIETY (ADS).

UNIVERSAL INTELLECT (Al-'Aql al-Kulli). The cause of causes, the first luminary cosmic principle (*hadd*, pl. *hudud*), and the first created being (*al-Mubda' al-Awwal*). He was represented in the Druze **movement** in the 11th century by **Hamza Ibn 'Ali**, the author of many Druze epistles. *See also* 'AQL; CYCLE; DRUZISM; HUDUD; HUDUD 'ULWIYYA.

UNIVERSAL SOUL. The second luminary and cosmic principle; assistant to the **Universal Intellect**. *See also* COSMOLOGY; HUDUD; HUDUD 'ULWIYYA.

UPDATE, THE IDS. The newsletter of the **Institute of Druze Studies (IDS)**. It is published occasionally and reports academic and research activities related to Druzes and Druze studies.

'UQAYLI, YOSEF AL-. A Druze sage from the town of **Simqaniyya** in the **Shuf, Lebanon**. He is well known for his commentary on Druze scriptures.

'UQQAL, 'AQILAT (sing. *'aqil* and *'aqila*, "initiated"). The religious class in Druze society. They are a small minority, compared to the *juhhal*, or uninitiated. The *'uqqal* have an influential role that impacts the rest of Druze society. The process of becoming initiated is arduous, and that is probably why they have remained a minority throughout the history of the sect.

Individual Druzes need to have an inner readiness and motivation to join the ranks of the *'uqqal*. They are expected to change their lifestyle, adopt new clothing, and express their interest in joining the religious group. Once a person is permitted as *'aqil* or *'aqila*, they have to conform with the strict regulations placed on their lifestyle. If the person falls into error or commits the slightest misbehavior, he or she is dismissed permanently or banned from attending religious gatherings in the *majlis* or *khalwa* for a certain period of time. *See also* 'AQL; DRUZISM; FAITH; MASHAYIKH AL-DIN; SHAYKH; WALIYY; WORSHIP.

URUGUAY. A Druze community has existed in Uruguay since the last decades of the 19th century, when **Syrian-Lebanese migration** to the Americas was initiated. Prominent Druzes there include **Husayn Ibn Najm Abu Izziddin** (d. 1927), who served as a parliament member and a consul general. *See also* SOUTH AMERICA.

– V –

VATICAN, THE. Relations between the Druzes and the Vatican have fluctuated over the years based on the **politics** in the Druze areas and the policies of the Vatican. When civil wars raged and disrupted the region and Druzes fought against Christians (mostly **Maronites**), the Vatican expressed its displeasure and disapproval toward Druze leaders and naturally aided Christian groups. At the same time, Druzes have complained to the Vatican about the actions of the Maronites. In times of peace, however, Druze leaders have received letters from the various popes in regard to the churches in the Druze-inhabited areas, such as the 1791 letter from Pope Pius VI thanking **Bashir Junblat** for allowing the Maronites to build more churches. *See also* CIVIL WAR OF 1975–1990.

VENEZUELA. Druzes in Venezuela have been present since the first wave of Middle Eastern **migration** to the Americas, in the last part of the 19th century. *See also* SOUTH AMERICA.

VICTORY BATTLE. *See* RIF, 'ABD AL-KARIM AL-.

VISITATION SITE (*mazar*, pl. *mazarat*). A **sacred site** where a shrine is built in memory of one of the **prophets**, **saints**, or devout **shaykhs**. Such sites vary in size from one small room with little space around it to a large building or several buildings with trees and other plantations surrounding them. There are many visitation sites in the Middle East that are important for Druzes. Examples of sites for prophets include **Jethro**, **Job**, and **al-Khidr**; for saints, **John**, **Baha' al-Din al-Samuqi**, **al-Emir al-Sayyid**, and **Abu Husayn Mahmoud Faraj**; and for shaykhs, **Ahmad Amin al-Din** and **Salih 'Amer**.

VOLNEY, CONSTANTIN (1757–?). A French traveler who visited **Syria**, **Lebanon**, and **Palestine** in 1784. He spent three years in the area and wrote a travel account in which he included a discussion of the Druzes.

– W –

WADI AL-QARN, BATTLE OF. A battle between the **Ma'ni-Qaysi** faction and the **Yamani-'Alam al-Din**. The latter attempted to take control of the Ma'ni territories in 1650. The Yamani-'Alam al-Din's leader, **'Ali 'Alam al-Din**, was injured in this battle.

WADI SHU'AYB. *See* SHU'AYB.

WADI AL-TAYM. A valley located in southeastern **Lebanon** in which the Druze **faith** was propagated at the beginning of the 11th century. It has remained a Druze stronghold with surrounding towns of Greek Orthodox Christians and **Shi'i Muslims**. Some early sources refer to the Druzes as **Tayamina** after Wadi al-Taym.

WAHBEH, MJALEH (1954–   ). An army colonel, politician, and diplomat who was born in **Bayt-Jann, Israel**. He has served in a number of posts in the Israeli government, including assistant on **Arab** affairs to Prime Minister Ariel Sharon. He was elected a member of the Israeli **Knesset** in January 2003 with the Likkud Party.

WAHHAB, SHAKIB (1888–?). A **Lebanese army** officer who fought in the **Great Revolt of 1925–1927**. In the 1940s, he led a battalion against the Zionist forces in **Palestine**. One of his engagements was the battle of **Ramat Yuhanan**, near the villages of Husha and Kasayer. The lack of military reinforcements from **Damascus** caused the battalion to disintegrate slowly and forced Shakib Wahhab to return to **Lebanon**.

WAHID, AL-. The One who transcends numbers; one of the names or attributes of God. Only through contemplation may the One be fathomed by the human mind, which is only a tool that prepares the individual for a state of understanding of the One. In other words, the mind helps to put the seeker on the road to the One. The doctrine of contemplation, meditation, and **worship** of the One is at the core of the Druze doctrine. *See also* DRUZISM; FAITH; MONOTHEISM; TAWHID.

WALAYA. Allegiance, the seventh pillar of **Islam** according to some **Muslim** groups. In **Druzism**, it is the seventh act of **worship**, instructing loyalty, and devotion to the luminaries (*hudud*). *See also* FAITH; MONOTHEISM; TAWHID.

WALIYY (pl. *awliya'*). Saint; a revered religious person who has advanced in religiosity and spirituality. Many saints are revered in the Druze tradition, including **Mi'dad al-Fawarisi, Ibrahim Ibn Adham, 'Ammar al-Maghribi, Rabi'a of Basra, al-Shaykh al-Fadil**, and **al-Emir al-Sayyid al-Tanukhi**.

WALIYY AL-'AHD. Heir designate; designated successor of a **caliph**. In **Druzism**, at times the concept has been used in certain regions in reference to the future spiritual or political leaders. *See also* LEADERSHIP.

WALIYY AL-ZAMAN. *See* HAMZA IBN 'ALI.

WAQ'AT AL-JAMI' (Battle or Incident of The Mosque). It took place in 1019 at the **Ridan Mosque** in **Cairo**, where **Hamza Ibn 'Ali** and his close associates were convening. A large crowd had initially attacked **Darazi** for his heretical teachings, but he redirected the crowd to the Ridan Mosque, saying that he had been following Hamza's instructions. Hamza dismissed Darazi several months earlier because of his deviation from the authentic teachings of **Druzism**.

Druzes consider this to be the first battle in their communal history, and they often praise Hamza's heroic acts, for his small number of followers withstood a large crowd of attackers. Darazi was killed or executed after this incident. *See also* APOSTATE; MIHNA; PEOPLE OF APOSTASY.

WAQF (pl. *awqaf*, "endowments"). Also referred to as Sacred Trusts. Each Druze community, small or large, has a foundation that establishes charities and collects donations and lands for the well-being of the community. A committee of influential persons often manages the **organization**. The committee distributes funds to needy **families** and allocates resources to general communal projects. These endowments are not usually large, but extensive efforts go into managing them.

WAR OF INDEPENDENCE (1948). A war between the **Arab** and the Jewish forces over the control of **Palestine**, resulting in the independence of the state of **Israel**. The war created new conditions for the Druze communities in the region; contact between these communities was halted as a result of the Arab-Israeli conflict. *See also* ARAB REVOLT.

WAR OF THE MOUNTAIN (1983–1985) (Harb Al-Jabal). A confrontation between the Druzes and the **Lebanese forces**, leading to a series of battles over the control of **Mount Lebanon** during the Lebanese **Civil War of 1975–1990**. At the time of their 1982 invasion, the **Israelis** intended (among other objectives) to enable the Lebanese forces to take over the **Shuf** Mountains, where a large Druze population resided. The Druzes, under the **leadership** of **Walid Junblat**, regrouped and eventually regained previously lost towns.

The War of the Mountain reaffirmed the role of the Druzes in Mount Lebanon and also raised Walid Junblat's prestige as the predominant leader of the Druze community in the eyes of both Druzes and outsiders. In this war, many Christians and Druzes were displaced, and Christians were unable to return until much later when the civil war ended. *See also* LEBANESE PHALANGES PARTY (LPP); MARONITES.

WISE SHAYKH, THE. *See* RAJBAL (RAJ PAL) IBN SUMER.

WOMEN. The place and rights of women in the Druze tradition can be attributed to the reforms that were made during the emergence of the **movement** in the 11th century. Among these are the rights of women to **inheritance**, to initiate divorce, and to decision making in the household. Despite these reforms, social restrictions on how women conduct their daily affairs are still apparent in the Druze community, especially in rural or conservative settings. For example, a woman must not travel outside her hometown without being accompanied by a relative. In recent decades, many women have been active in national and regional women movements and rose to prominence in the community, including **Nazira Zayn al-Din**, **'Afifah Sa'b**, and **Najla Sa'b**. *See also* ARSLAN, HBOUS; HASBAYA WOMEN'S ASSOCIATION; JUNBLAT, SITT NAZIRA; MLA'EB, SA'DA; NASAB, PRINCESS; NIQAB; RABI'A OF BASRA; SALHA, SITT; SARAH, SITT.

WORD, THE. *See* HUDUD 'ULWIYYA.

WORSHIP. Druze society consists of the initiated (*'uqqal*) and the uninitiated (*juhhal*). Religious services usually take place on Thursday evenings and are structured into two sessions, open and closed. The initial open session is very general, and both *juhhal* and *'uqqal* are permitted to attend. Once the open session ends, the *juhhal* are expected or instructed to leave the worship hall, *majlis* or *khalwa*. Only initiated members in good standing are allowed to remain in the room during this closed session. While in the open session general questions about **faith** and practice are raised and discussed, during the closed session spiritual readings and mystical insights are meditated and pondered on.

Druze acts of worship reflect an interpretation of the biblical teachings and commandments and the pillars of **Islam**. They include, first of all, the principle of **truthfulness** (*sidq al-lisan*); this is the core of the Druze belief system and implies that if one masters it in regard to worship and to dealing with others, everything else will follow smoothly in whatever one engages in. Truthfulness is directly linked to intentionality (*niyya*); one's intentions must be pure. The second act of worship is **brotherliness** (*hifz al-ikhwan*); this means, literally, protecting one's fellow humans at all times and in all places. The third act of worship is renouncing vanities of all types. *See also* DRUZISM.

–Y–

YAHYA (John, ?–30). Son of Zakariyya and Elizabeth in the **Bible**. He is an important figure in **Druzism** and the Druze tradition. Yahya has a sacred shrine in **Lebanon**.

YA'LA, HASAN IBN. An 11th-century member of the Druze **movement**. He later deviated from the teachings of **Druzism** and joined the Druze **apostates**. *See also* APOSTATE; DARAZI, MUHAMMAD AL-; PEOPLE OF APOSTASY; SUKAYN.

YAMANIS. Ancient southern Arabian tribe that was in conflict with the northern Arabian tribes known as the **Qaysis**. The rivalry was carried into the Druze tribal competition and has always divided the Druze community into two competing factions. The competition has sometimes turned into a bloody confrontation, as in the battle of **'Ayn Dara** in 1711. *See also* DUALISM; QAYSI-YAMANI; YAZBAKI LIBERATION FRONT.

YATIM, BAYT AL-. *See* ORPHANAGE.

YAWM AL-DIN. *See* JUDGMENT DAY.

YAWM AL-QIYAMAH. *See* JUDGMENT DAY.

YAZBAKI, YAZBAKIS. A confederation of Druze **families** that opposed the **Junblati**-affiliated clans. After the **Yamanis** were defeated in **'Ayn Dara** in 1711 by the northern **Qaysi** tribes, Yazbaki-Junblati **dualism** replaced the old **Qaysi-Yamani** tribal competition. *See also* YAZBAKI LIBERATION FRONT.

YAZBAKI-JUNBLATI. *See* QAYSI-YAMANI.

YAZBAKI LIBERATION FRONT (Jabhat al-Tahrir al-Yazbaki-yya). Founded in East Beirut during the **Civil War of 1975–1990** by Farid Hamadeh, who opposed the **Junblati** power of **Walid Junblat** and befriended the **Lebanese forces**. He had hoped to revive the old **Yazbaki-Junblati** communal conflict. *See also* QAYSI-YAMANI.

YOUNG DRUZE PROFESSIONALS (YDP). A Druze association of young professionals that was initially established in 1997 in **Lebanon**. The association's objectives include helping its members find jobs as well as assisting Druze students in their **educational** programs. Similar associations were established in the **United States** and in Sydney, **Australia**. Attempts are being made to unite or link the various associations of the YDP and establish additional branches around the world. *See also* AMERICAN DRUZE SOCIETY (ADS); AMERICAN DRUZE YOUTH (ADY).

– Z –

ZAGHLUL, SA'D (d. 1927). An **Egyptian** statesman who befriended several Druze **Arab nationalists**. Among his often-recited letters is one sent to **Sultan al-Atrash** during the **Great Revolt of 1925–1927** in which he congratulated Sultan as a leader of chivalry and honor. Zaghlul was also a close friend of **Shakib Arslan** and other Druzes who were actively working for **Arab** and **Islamic** causes.

ZAHIR. *See* EXOTERIC.

ZAHIR LE I'ZAZ DIN ALLAH, AL- (r. 1021–1036). The seventh **Fatimi caliph** after **al-Hakim**. He persecuted members of the Druze **movement** immediately after he took office. The period of persecution between 1021 and 1026 by him and his governors is known in the Druze **manuscripts** as **Mihnat Antakia**. *See also* MIHNA; SAMUQI, BAHA' AL-DIN AL-.

ZAJAL. Popular **Arabic poetry** composed primarily in colloquial Arabic. Though it rhymes, it does not conform to meters. *Zajal* evolved gradually and was influenced by the local and geographical setting of the villages and towns. Druze poets who became prominent *zajals* include **Tali' Hamdan** and **Fuad Abu Ghanim**. *See also* LITERATURE.

ZAKI, MUHAMMAD IBN HAMID ABU 'ALI (1800–1862). One of the Druzes who was arrested by the Ottomans after the violent events between **Maronites** and Druzes in **Mount Lebanon** in 1860. He is known for his high rank in piety and spirituality and has a **visitation site** that was reconstructed in the 1980s.

ZAKI, SULAIMAN IBN 'IBADA (?–1925). A judge from the region of Rashaya and member of a **family** of judges. He was killed very early in the **Great Revolt of 1925–1927**.

ZARQA', AL-. *See* JORDAN.

ZAR'UN. A 900-year-old small Lebanese village with over 1,100 residents consisting of two major **families**, Daw and Zayd. An older family, Karami, is perhaps now extinct, though there is a **visitation site** (*mazar*) of the revered **Sitt um Muhammad Karami**. The Syrian Zar'uni and the Israeli **Natur** families have been traced to Zar'un. They left the village after the **Civil War of 1860**.

ZAWZANI, HAMZA IBN 'ALI. *See* HAMZA IBN 'ALI.

ZAYD. *See* ZAR'UN.

ZAYN AL-DIN. A **family** that is related to the al-Khatib family and resides in the **Shuf** and other regions. Some came from Jaramana.

ZAYN AL-DIN, FARID IBN MUHAMMAD IBN HASAN (1907–1973). A prominent **Syrian** lawyer and diplomat. Among other roles, he was a representative of Syria at the **United Nations** and in the Soviet Union. He has written several books on national movements in Europe as well as on other subjects. It is often said that he was among those who participated in drafting the UN Charter.

ZAYN AL-DIN, NAZIRA BINT SA'ID (1907–1976). A prominent early Druze feminist who was born to a **family** that moved from Istanbul to **Aleppo**, Jerusalem, and finally to **Beirut** because of her father's demanding legal career. She was a graduate of the Seminary in Nazareth and worked for the emancipation of **women** through participation in the establishment of women's **organizations** in the **Arab** and **Islamic** world as well as on the international level. She was one of the pioneers in writing a book about the veil (1928) and another on women and the clergy (1929).

ZAYTUN, SALIM IBN MAHMUD (?–1915). A prominent medical doctor who served in the British forces and then in the Ottoman army. He migrated to **Australia**, where he lived until he died in 1915.

ZAYTUNA. A **family** that came with the **Tanukhis** to the Lebanese Mountains. Some say that they were known as 'Abd al-Satir and can be found in B'albek. Others became known as Zaytun or Zeitoun and can be found in both **Lebanon** and **Syria**.

ZEVULUN. *See* SABALAN.

ZOZANI, HAMZA IBN 'ALI. *See* HAMZA IBN 'ALI.

ZUHAYRI. An ancient **family** that migrated to **Wadi al-Taym** at the beginning of the 12th century and settled in Tayrush and Mghal. It eventually relocated to **'Ayn Dara**. During the battle of 'Ayn Dara in 1711, the family dispersed to different locations. 'Ala' al-Dins of **Beirut** are said to also be Zuhayris.

Appendix A
The Fatimids

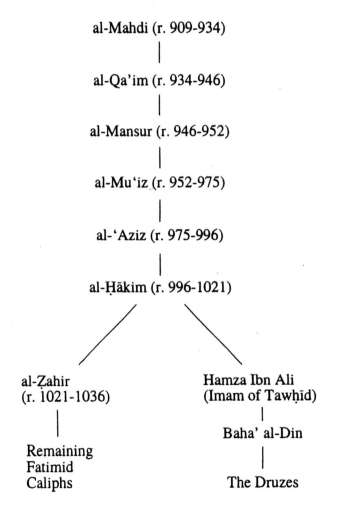

al-Mahdi (r. 909-934)

al-Qa'im (r. 934-946)

al-Mansur (r. 946-952)

al-Mu'iz (r. 952-975)

al-'Aziz (r. 975-996)

al-Ḥākim (r. 996-1021)

al-Ẓahir
(r. 1021-1036)

Remaining
Fatimid
Caliphs

Hamza Ibn Ali
(Imam of Tawḥīd)

Baha' al-Din

The Druzes

Appendix B

The Buhturis

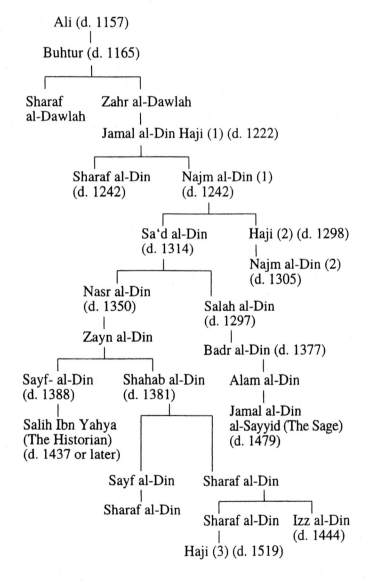

Appendix C

The Ma'nis

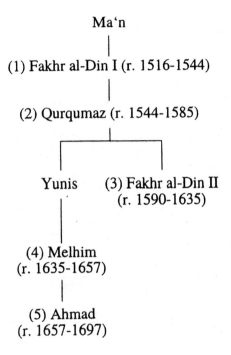

Ma'n
|
(1) Fakhr al-Din I (r. 1516-1544)
|
(2) Qurqumaz (r. 1544-1585)

Yunis   (3) Fakhr al-Din II
| (r. 1590-1635)

(4) Melhim
(r. 1635-1657)
|
(5) Ahmad
(r. 1657-1697)

Appendix D

The Shihabis

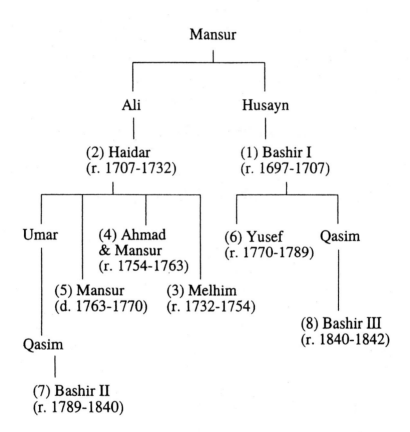

Mansur

Ali   Husayn

(2) Haidar
(r. 1707-1732)

(1) Bashir I
(r. 1697-1707)

Umar   (4) Ahmad
& Mansur
(r. 1754-1763)

(6) Yusef
(r. 1770-1789)   Qasim

(5) Mansur
(d. 1763-1770)   (3) Melhim
(r. 1732-1754)

(8) Bashir III
(r. 1840-1842)

Qasim

(7) Bashir II
(r. 1789-1840)

Bibliography

CONTENTS

INTRODUCTION

This selected bibliography incorporates entries for readily (and some scarcely) available writings on the Druzes. The objective here is to provide both the general reader and the specialist with a wide range of selected sources. Publications on the Druzes composed during periods of turmoil or external powers' involvement in the Middle East must be read with caution and not be taken at face value. Moreover, some biased references, whether for or against the Druzes, are included in this edition with the hope that any serious study of this community must investigate the diverse sources as well as the political, religious, historical, and economic circumstances of those regions inhabited by Druzes.

The bibliography includes a selection of Druze manuscripts that the reader may find useful. Most of these manuscripts are scattered in libraries and special collections around the world. Although many of them are not readily available, they are listed here, as their titles may shed light on the nature of the Druze doctrine and Druze studies in general.

Works by and about the prominent 20th-century leaders Shakib Arslan (d. 1946), Kamal Junblat (d. 1977), and Sultan al-Atrash (d. 1982) are included in the section "Biographies and Hagiographies." Writings about the Fatimi caliph al-Hakim bi-Amr Allah (r. 996–1021), who is central to the Druzes, are also listed here separately in the same section. In addition, the works about the prominent 16th-century leader Fakhr al-Din al-Ma'ni II are also included here.

Since it is almost always impossible to separate works on the Druze religious doctrine from those on Druze history, society, or politics, such books and articles are listed under a section called "History, Faith, and Society." Subcategories list works on Druzes in Syria and Lebanon, Palestine and Israel, and the Druze diaspora. The bibliography ends with a section for general works related to the Druzes, including selected dictionaries and encyclopedias, as well as works on sectarianism, Shi'ism and Isma'ilism, and metempsychosis (*taqamus*).

BIBLIOGRAPHIES

Bleaney, C. H. *Modern Syria: An Introduction to the Literature*. Durham, N.C.: University of Durham, 1979.

Diya'i, Ali Akbar. *Fihris Masadir al-Firaq al-Islamiyyah: Al-Masadir al-Durziyyah* [*A Bibliography of Islamic Sects: The Druze Sources*]. Beirut: Dar al-Rawdah, 1992.

Ivanow, W. *A Guide to Isma'ili Literature*. London, 1933.

———. *Isma'ili Literature: A Bibliographical Survey*. Tehran, 1963.

Karameh, Rufa'il. *Masadir Tarikhiyya li-Hawadith Lubnan wa Suriyya, 1745–1800* [*Historical Sources for the Events in Lebanon and Syria, 1745–1800*]. Beirut, 1929.

Patai, Raphael. *Jordan, Lebanon, Syria: An Annotated Bibliography*. Westport, Conn.: Greenwood Press, 1975.

Poonawala, Ismail K. *Bibliography of Isma'ili Literature*. Malibu, Calif.: Undena Publications, 1977.

Swayd, Samy. *The Druzes: An Annotated Bibliography*. Kirkland, Wash.: Ises Publications, 1998.

PERIODICALS AND NEWSLETTERS

'Amamah, al- (Israel)
Duha, al- (Lebanon)
IDS Update (United States)
'Irfan, al- (Lebanon)
Journal of Druze Studies (United States)
Mithaq, al- (Lebanon)
Safa', al- (Lebanon)

DOCUMENTS

Abu Husayn, Abdul-Rahim. *The View from Istanbul: Lebanon and the Druze Emirate in the Ottoman Chancery Documents, 1546–1711*. London: Centre for Lebanese Studies in Association with I. B. Tauris Publishers, 2004.

Abu Izzeddin, Sulayman. *Masadir al-Tarikh al-Lubnani: Watha'iq min Muntasaf al-Qarn al-Sabi' 'Ashar ila Sanat 1860* [*The Sources of Lebanese History: Documents from the Middle of the 17th Century to 1860*]. Edited by Nejla Abu Izzeddin. Beirut, 1995.

Breasted, James H. *Ancient Records of Egypt, Historical Documents from the Earliest Times to the Persian Conquest*. 5 vols. Chicago: University of Chicago Press, 1906–1907. Reissued in 1962.

Heyd, U. *Ottoman Documents on Palestine 1552–1615*. Oxford: Clarendon Press, 1960.

Hishshi, S. H. *Al-Murasalat al-Ijtima'iyya Wal-Iqtisadiyya Li-Zu'ama' Jabal Lubnan Khilal Thalathat Qurun, 1600–1900* [*The Social and Economic Correspondence of Leaders of Mount Lebanon during Three Centuries, 1600–1900*]. Beirut, 1882–1885.

Isma'il, 'Adel. *Documents Diplomatiques et Consulaires Relatifs à l'Histoire du Liban et des Pays du Proche-Orient du XVII Siècle à Nos Jours*. 20 vols. Beirut, 1975–1981.

Shahak, Israel. *The Non-Jew in the Jewish State: A Collection of Documents*. Jerusalem, 1975.

MANUSCRIPTS

Adab al-Shaykh al-Fadil [*The Manners of al-Shaykh al-Fadil*]
Durar al-Mudi'ah, al- [*The Luminous Pearls*]
Kashf al-Haqa'iq [*Disclosing the Truths*]
Khabaya al-Jawahir [*The Hidden Jewels*]
Mukhtasar al-Bayan fi Majra al-Zaman [*A Concise Summary of Historical Events*]
Munfarid bi-Dhatihi, al- [*In Solitude with Oneself*]
Nuqat wal-Dawa'ir, al- [*The Points and Circles*]
Qisas Mubarakah [*Blessed Stories*]
Rasa'il al-Hikmah [*The Epistles of Wisdom*]
Rasa'il al-Hind [*The Epistles to India*]
Sharh al-Mithaq [*A Commentary on the Covenant*]
Shari'a al-Ruhaniyya, al- [*The Spiritual Path*]
Shuruhat al-Amir al-Sayyid al-Tanukhi [*Commentaries of al-Sayyid al-Tanukhi*]
Sijill al-Arslani, Al- [*The Arslani Genealogical Register*]
'Umdat al-'Arifin [*The Chief Sages*]

MEMOIRS AND TRAVELERS' ACCOUNTS

Andrea, Charles Joseph Edouard. *La Révolte Druze, 1925–1926* [*The Druze Revolt, 1925–1926*]. Paris, 1937.

Arslan, 'Adil. *Mudhakkarat [Memoirs]*. Edited by Yusef Ibish. 3 vols. Beirut, 1983.

Asher, A., ed. *The Itinerary of Rabbi Benjamin of Tudela*. 2 vols. Berlin: A. Asher, 1840.

Atrash, Sultan. *Mudhakkarat [Memoirs]*. Collected by Nabih al-Qasim. 2 vols. Jerusalem, 1979.

Bell, Gertrude. *Syria: The Desert and the Sown*. London, 1985.

Bordeaux, Henry. *Dans la Montagne des Druses [In the Druze Mountain]*. Paris, 1926.

Buckingham, James Silk. *Travels among the Arab Tribes Inhabiting the Countries East of Syria and Palestine*. London, 1825.

Burckhardt, J. L. *Travels in Syria and the Holy Land*. London, 1822.

Burton, Isabel. *The Inner Life of Syria, Palestine and the Holy Land*. London, 1884.

Burton, R. F., C. F. T. Drake, and I. Burton. *Unexplored Syria*. 2 vols. London, 1872.

Castlereagh, Viscount. *Journey to Damascus*. 2 vols. London, 1847.

Champdor, Albert. *Terres et Dieux de Syrie [Lands and Gods of Syria]*. Paris, 1936.

Churchhill, Charles Henry. *Mount Lebanon: Ten Years' Residence, 1842–1852*. 3 vols. London, 1853.

Egmont, J. A., and J. Heyman. *Travels*. 2 vols. London, 1959.

Ewing, William. *Arab and Druze at Home: A Record of Travel and Intercourse with the Peoples East of the Jordan*. London, 1907.

Gordon, Helen Cameron (Lady Russell). *Syria As It Is: The Republic of Lebanon, the Republic of Syria, the Government of Latakia, the Government of the Djebel Druze, the Autonomous Sandjak of Haytay*. London, 1939.

Green, John. *A Journey from Aleppo to Damascus*. London: W. Mears, 1736.

Hakim, H. *Mudhakkarat [Memoirs]*. 2 vols. Beirut, 1965.

Jessup, Henry H. *Fifty-Three Years in Syria*. 2 vols. New York, 1910.

Klippel, Ernst. *Unter Senusy-Brudern, Drusen und Teufelsanbetern; im Sattel zu Orientalischen Geheimsekten [Among the Sanusi Brothers, Druzes, and Devil Worshipers: In the Saddle of the Secret Oriental Sects]*. Braunschweig, 1942.

Maundrell, Henry. *A Journey from Aleppo to Jerusalem in 1697*. Beirut, 1963.

Niebuhr, Karsten. *Travels through Arabia and Other Countries in the East*. 2 vols. Edinburgh, 1792.

Oliphant, Laurence. *The Land of Gilead, with Excursions in the Lebanon*. New York, 1881.

Parfit, Joseph Thomas. *Among the Druzes of Lebanon and Bashan*. London, 1917.

Paton, A. A. *The Modern Syrians or Native Society in Damascus, Aleppo, and the Mountains of the Druzes from Notes Made in Those Parts during the Years 1841–1843*. London, 1844.

Porter, J. L. *Five Years in Damascus*. 2 vols. London, 1917.

———. *The Giant Cities of Bashan and Syria's Holy Places*. London, 1867.

Rey, G. N. E. *Voyage dans le Haouran et aux bords de la Mer Morte, éxecuté pendant les années, 1857–8.* Paris, 1859.

Robinson, E., and E. Smith. *Biblical Researches in Palestine and Adjacent Region: A Journal of Travels in the Years 1838 and 1852.* 3 vols. Jerusalem, 1970.

Sanderson, John. *The Travels of John Sanderson in the Levant 1584–1602.* London, 1931.

Seabrook, W. B. *Adventures in Arabia.* New York, 1927.

Volney, Constantin-Francois. *Travels through Syria and Egypt in the Years 1783, 1784 and 1785.* Farnborough, UK, 1972.

Williams, Samuel H. *Rebecca Williams Hebard of Lebanon, Missionary in Beirut, Syria and to the Druzes of Mount Lebanon, 1835–1840.* Glastonbury, Conn., 1950.

BIOGRAPHIES AND HAGIOGRAPHIES

General

Abu Ghanim, Shafiq. *Muwwahhidun fi Risalat wa-Maqamat [Unitarians in Messages and Shrines].* 'Amattur, Lebanon: Matba'at Duwaik, 1987.

Abu Khallah, Muhammad. "Al-Nabi Shu'ayb 'Alayhi al-Salam Kama Waradat Siratuhu fil-Tawrah wal-Qur'an" [The Prophet Shu'ayb/Jethro (pbuh) according to the Old Testament and the Qur'an]. *Fil-Turath wal-Tarbiya,* October 1990, 64–72.

Abu Muslih, Hafiz. *Adrihat al-'Ubbad al-Muwwahhidin al-Duruz fi Lubnan [The Tombs of the Unitarian Druze Sages in Lebanon].* N.p., n.d.

Abu Shaqra 'Arif. *Thalathat 'Ulama' min Shuyukh Bani Ma'ruf [Three Learned Druze Shaykhs].* Beirut: Dar al-Ghad, 1957.

Abu Shaqra, Sami. *Al-Tawhid al-Durzi fi Madmunihi al-Insani: Al-Sayyid al-Tanukhi, al-Shaykh al-Fadil, and al-Shaykh Muhammad Abu Shaqra [Druze Unitarianism in Its Human Context: Al-Tanukhi, al-Fadil, and Abu Shaqra].* 'Amattur al-Shuf, Lebanon: Maktabat al-Anwar, 1984.

Andary, Nezar. *On Druze Identity: Shakib Arslan, Kamal Junblat, Nadia Tuéni, and Samih al-Qasim.* N.p., 1994.

Basha, Muhammad Khalil al-. *Mu'jam A'lam al-Duruz [Druze Biographical Dictionary].* 2 vols. Beirut: al-Dar al-Taqadumiyya, 1990.

B'ayni, Najib. *Rijal min Biladi [Men from My Homeland].* 2 vols. Beirut: Mu'ssasat Dar al-Rihani, 1984.

———. *Shu'ara' min Jabal Lubnan [Poets from Mount Lebanon].* Beirut: Mu'ssasat Dar al-Rihani, 1987.

Bustani, Karam al-. *Amirat Lubnan [The Princesses of Lebanon].* Beirut: Maktabat Sadir, 1950.

Committee on Religous Affairs, ed. *The Tawhid Faith: Pioneers and Their Shrines.* Knoxville, Tenn.: ADS, 1990.

Hodgson, Marshall G. S. "Al-Darazi and Hamza in the Origin of the Druze Religion." *Journal of the American Oriental Society* 82 (1962): 5–20.

Kamal, Fawwaz, et al. *Al-Muwwahhidun al-Duruz fil-Mahjar: Venezuela* [*The Druze Unitarians in the Diaspora: Venezuela*]. N.p., n.d.

Makarem, Sami Nasib. *Al-Shaykh 'Ali Faris Radiya Allahu 'Anhu* [*The Shaykh 'Ali Faris, May God Be Pleased with Him*]. Beirut: al-Dar al-Taqadumiyya, 1990.

Na'im, Rajih. *Al-Shaykh Halim Taqi al-Din: Sirah wa-Mawqif* [*The Shaykh Halim Taqi al-Din: A Biography and Stance*]. Beirut: Hay'at al-Ta'lim al-'Ali, 1984.

Nasr al-Din, Amal, Salman Falah, and Musbah Halabi, eds. *Entsiklopedyat Shemot, 1800–1995* [*An Encyclopedia of Names*]. Daliyat al-Carmel: Beit Yad la-Banim ha-Druzim, 1995.

Nuwayhid, 'Ajaj. *Sirat al-Amir al-Sayyid Jamal al-Din 'Abdalla al-Tanukhi* [*The Biography of al-Amir al-Sayyid al-Tanukhi*]. Beirut, 1975.

———. *Al-Tanukhi al-Amir al-Sayyid Jamal al-Din 'Abdalla wal-Shaykh Muhammad Abu Hilal (al-Ma'ruf bil-Shaykh al-Fadil)* [*al-Sayyid al-Tanukhi and al-Shaykh al-Fadil*]. Beirut: Dar al-Sahafa, 1963.

Nuwayhid, Nadia al-Jurdi. *Nisa' min Biladi* [*Women from My Homeland*]. Beirut: al-Mu'ssasah al-'Arabiyyah lil-Dirasat wal-Nashr, 1986.

Sa'b, Najib. *Al-Qura al-Durziyah fi-Isra'il wal-Julan* [*Druze Villages in Israel and the Golan Heights*]. Jenin: Matba'at Jenin al-Tijariyah, 1978.

Taqi al-Din, 'Adil Hamdan. *Al-Shaykh Halim Taqi al-Din*. Introduced by Muhammad Khalil al-Basha. Beirut, 1985.

Tarif, 'Abdallah Salim. *Sirat Fadilat al-Shaykh Amin Tarif* [*The Biography of Shaykh Amin Tarif*]. Jerusalem, 1987.

Al-Hakim bi-Amr Allah

Assad, Sadik A. *The Reign of al-Hakim bi-Amr Allah*. Beirut: Arab Institute for Research and Publishing, 1974.

Bouthoul, Betty. *Le Calife Hakim* [*The Caliph al-Hakim*]. Sagitaire, 1950.

Ess, Josef van. *Chiliastische Erwartungen und die Versuchung der Göttlichkeit: d. Kalif al-Hakim (386–411 A.H.)* [*Chiliastic Expectations and the Search for Divinity: The Caliph al-Hakim*]. Heidelberg, 1977.

'Inan, Muhammad 'Abdallah. *Al-Hakim bi-Amr Allah wa-Asrar al-Da'wah al-Fatimiyyah* [*Al-Hakim bi-Amr Allah and the Secrets of the Fatimi Call*]. Cairo, 1937, 1959.

Kirmani, Ahmad al-. *Al-Risala al-Wa'izah* [*The Counseling Letter*]. Edited by Muhammad Kamil Husayn. Cairo: Matba'at Jami'at Fu'ad al-Awwal, 1952.

Majid, 'Abd Al-Mun'im. *Al-Hakim bi-Amr Allah: Al-Khalifa al-Muftara 'Alaihi* [*Al-Hakim bi-Amr Allah: The Defamed Caliph*]. Cairo: Maktabat al-Anglo al-Misriyya, 1982.

Makarim, Sami Nasib. "Al-Hakim bi-Amr Allah's Appointment of His Successors." *Al-Abhath* 23 (1970): 319–325.

Tamir, 'Arif. *Al-Hakim bi-Amr Allah, Khalifah wa-Imam wa-Muslih* [*Al-Hakim bi-Amr Allah: Caliph, Imam, and Reformer*]. Beirut: Dar al-Afaq al-Jadidah, 1982.

Fakhr al-Din al-Ma'ni II

Ahdab, 'Aziz. *Fakhr al-Din Mu'assis Lubnan al-Hadith* [*Fakhr al-Din: The Founder of Modern Lebanon*]. Beirut: Dar al-Kitab al-Lubnani, n.d.

Arcache, Jean. *L'Emir à la Croix, Fakhreddine II Maan* [*The Prince at the Cross, the Ma'ni Prince Fakhr al-Din II*]. Paris: Plon, 1938.

Bustani, Fu'ad Afram al-. *Khawatir wa-'Ibar fi Dhikra Fakhr al-Din al-Kabir* [*Thoughts and Lessons in Memory of the Great Fakhr al-Din*]. Juniyah, Lebanon, 1976.

Chebli, Michel. *Fakhreddine II Maan, Prince du Liban (1572–1635)* [*Fakhr al-Din II, the Ma'ni Prince of Lebanon*]. Beirut, 1946, 1984.

Ghanim, Bulus. "Fakhr al-Din al-Ma'ni al-Thani" [Fakhr al-Din al-Ma'ni II]. *Al-Adib* 8 (August 1965): 2–7.

Khalidi, Ahmad Ibn Muhammad al-Safadi. *Lubnan fi 'Ahd al-Amir Fakhr al-Din al-Ma'ni al-Thani* [*Lebanon during the Reign of Fakhr al-Din al-Ma'ni II*]. Beirut: al-Jami'ah al-Lubnaniyah, 1969.

Khazin, Louis. "Fakhr al-Din al-Thani" [Fakhr al-Din II]. *Al-Mashriq*, April 1937, 256–263.

Ma'luf, 'Isa Iskandar al-. *Tarikh al-Amir Fakhr al-Din al-Ma'ni al-Thani* [*The History of the Prince Fakhr al-Din al-Ma'ni II*]. Juniyah, 1934; Beirut, 1966.

Najati, Ahmad. "Al-Amir Fakhr al-Din al-Thani: Batal Watani Am Hakim Arada al-Baqa'?!" [The Prince Fakhr al-Din II: A National Hero or a Ruler Who Wanted to Stay in Power]. *Majallat Tarikh al-'Arab wal-'Alam*, February 1979, 35–37.

Qara'li, Bulus. "Fakhr al-Din al-Ma'ni al-Thani" [Fakhr al-Din al-Ma'ni II]. *Al-Mashriq*, October-December 1937, 526–534.

———. *Fakhr ad-Din II, Principe del Libano, e la Corte di Toscana, 1605–1635* [*Fakhr al-Din II, the Prince of Lebanon, and the Court of Tuscany, 1605–1635*]. 2 vols. Rome, 1936–1938.

Ra'd, Marun Sum'an. *Maqam al-Amir Fakhr al-Din al-Ma'ni al-Thani fil-Gharb* [*The Shrine of the Prince Fakhr al-Din al-Ma'ni in the Gharb Region*]. Beirut, 1980.

Wustenfeld, Ferdinand. *Fachr ed-Din der Drusenfurst* [*Fakhr al-Din the Druze Prince*]. Göttingen: Dieterich, 1886.

Shakib Arslan

'Affash, Fadl. "Al-Amir Shakib Arslan, 1869–1946" [Prince Shakib Arslan]. *Majallat al-Thaqafa*, April 1985, 9–12.

Arslan, Shakib. *Banu Ma'ruf, Ahl al-'Urubah wal-Islam* [*Sons of Mercy: The People of Arabism and Islam*]. Edited by Sa'ud al-Mawla. Beirut: al-Majlis al-Durzi lil-Buhuth wal-Inma', 1990.

———. *Diwan al-amir Shakib Arslan* [*Collected Poems*]. Edited by Rashid Rida. Cairo, 1935.

———. *Al-Hulal al-Sundusiyyah fil-Akhbar wal-Athar al-Andalusiyyah* [*The Richness of the Remnants of al-Andalus*]. Vol. 1. Beirut, 1936, 1966.

———. *Limadha Ta'khkhara al-Muslimun wa-Limadha Taqaddama Ghayruhum?* [*Why Did Muslims Decline while Others Progress?*]. Cairo, 1939; Lahore, 1962.

———. *Mahasin al-Masa'i fi Manaqib al-Imam al-Awza'i*. Edited by Shakib Arslan. Cairo, 1933.

———. *Al-Nahdah al-'Arabiyyah fil-'Asr al-Hadir* [*The Modern Arab Awakening*]. Cairo, n.d.

———. "Al-Naqd al-Tarikhi wa-'Urubat al-Duruz" [Historical Criticism and the Arabness of Druzes]. *Majallat al-Majma' al-'Ilmi al-'Arabi*, 1931, 449–463.

———. *Al-Rawd al-Shaqiq* [*The Simple Eloquence*]. Damascus, 1925.

———. *Al-Sayyid Rashid Rida aw Ikha' Arba'in Sanah* [*Rashid Rida, or a Friendship of Forty Years*]. Damascus, 1937.

———. *Shawqi aw Sadaqat Arba'in Sanah* [*Shawqi, or a Friendship of Forty Years*]. Cairo, 1936.

———. *Sirah Dhatiyya* [*An Autobiography*]. Beirut: Dar al-Tali'ah lil-Tiba'ah wal-Nashr, 1969.

———. "'Urubat Al Ma'ruf" [The Arabness of Druzes]. *Majallat al-Majma' al-'Ilmi al-'Arabi*, 1931, 449–463.

———. *'Urwat al-Itihad bayna Ahl al-Jihad* [*The Bonds of Unity among the People of Jihad*]. Buenos Aires: al-'Alam al-'Arabi, 1941.

———. *Al-Wahdah al-'Arabiyyah* [*Arab Unity*]. Damascus, 1937.

Cleveland, William L. "Ataturk Viewed by His Arab Contemporaries: The Opinions of Sati' al-Husri and Shakib Arslan." *International Journal of Turkish Studies* 2 (1983): 15–23.

———. *Islam against the West: Shakib Arslan and the Campaign for Islamic Nationalism*. Austin, Tex., 1985.

Dahhan, Sami al-. *Al-Amir Shakib Arslan: Hayatuhu wa-Atharuhu* [*Shakib Arslan: His Life and Work*]. Cairo, 1960.

———. *Muhadarat 'an al-Amir Shakib Arslan* [*Lectures on Shakib Arslan*]. Cairo, 1958.

———. *Qudama' Wa-Mu'asirun* [*Ancients and Contemporaries*]. Cairo, 1961.

Sharabasi, Ahmad al-. *Amir al-Bayan: Shakib Arslan* [*The Prince of Eloquence: Shakib Arslan*]. 2 vols. Cairo, 1963.

———. *Shakib Arslan: Da'iyat al-'Urubah wal-Islam* [*Shakib Arslan: Propagator of Arabism and Islam*]. Cairo, 1963.

———. *Shakib Arslan: Min Ruwwad al-Wihda al-'Arabiyya* [*Shakib Arslan: One of the Pioneers of Arab Unity*]. Cairo, 1963; Beirut, 1978.

Tahir, Muhammad Ali. *Dhikra al-Amir Shakib Arslan* [*In Memory of Shakib Arslan*]. Cairo, 1947; Al-Mukhtara, Lebanon, 1988.

Kamal Junblat

Abu Hamdan, Samir. *Kamal Junblat fi Bu'dihi al-Akhar* [*Kamal Junblat in His Other Dimension*]. Beirut: Manshurat 'Uwaydat, 1991.

Abu Muslih, Kamal. *Kamal Junblat, 1917–1977*. Beirut, 1981.

Atrash, Fu'ad Yusef al-. *Kamal Junblat, Mu'allim al-Risalah al-Khalidah* [*Kamal Junblat: The Teacher of the Eternal Message*]. Beirut, 1981.

Faqih, Fayiz al-. *Ma'a Kamal Junblat* [*With Kamal Junblat*]. Beirut, 1979.

Farraj, Afif. *Kamal Junblat: Jadaliyat al-Mithali wal-Waqi'i* [*Kamal Junblat: The Dialectic of an Idealist and a Realist*]. Beirut, 1977.

Ghandur, Dahir. "Hizb al-Nakhbah Fi Fikr Kamal Junblat" [The Elitist Party in the Thought of Kamal Junblat]. *Dirasat 'Arabiyya*, July–August 1989, 38–47.

Hadi, Nabil. *Kamal Junblat: Al-Tahadi al-Kabir* [*Kamal Junblat: The Great Challenge*]. Beirut, 1985.

Hasan, Rashid, ed. *Kitab al-Anba': Sura bil-Alwan lil-Qa'id Kamal Junblat* [*The Book of News: A Colorful Picture of the Commander Kamal Junblat*]. N.p., 1977.

Junblat, Kamal. *Fima Yata'ada al-Harf* [*What Is beyond the Ordinary*]. N.p., n.d.

———. *Hadhihi Wasiyati* [*This Is My Will*]. Beirut: al-Watan al-'Arabi, 1978.

———. *Haqiqat al-Thawra al-Lubnaniyya* [*The Truth about the Lebanese Strife*]. 4th ed. Beirut, 1987.

———. *Pour de Liban* [*I Speak for Lebanon*]. Paris: Stock, 1978.

———. *Rub' Qarn Min al-Nidal* [*A Quarter Century of Struggle*]. 2nd ed. Al-Mukhtarah, Lebanon: al-Dar al-Taqadumiyyah, 1987.

———. *I Speak for Lebanon*. Translated from the French by Michael Pallis. Recorded by Philippe Lapousterle. London: Zed Press, 1982.

Kamal Junblat, 1917–1977: The Man and His Struggle. Beirut, 1977.

Khalil, Khalil Ahmad. *Kamal Junblat: Thawrat "al-Amir al-Hadith"* [*Kamal Junblat: The Rebellion of "the Modern Prince"*]. Beirut: Dar al-Matbu'at al-Sharqiyah, 1984.

Khazin, Farid al-. "Kamal Junblat: The Uncrowned Druze Prince of the Left." *Middle Eastern Studies*, n.d., 178–205.

Markaz al-Watani lil-Ma'lumat wal-Dirasat, al-. *Kamal Junblat, 1917–1977*. Beirut, 1990.

Mukhtarat: fi Dhikra Miladihi al-Sittin [*Selections: In Memory of His Sixtieth Birthday*]. Introduced by Khalil Ahmad Khalil. Beirut, 1977.

Schenk, Bernadette. *Kamal Gunbulat*. Berlin: Klaus Schwarz Verlag, 1994.

Yunis, Ali Ahmad, ed. *Kamal Junblat: Sirah Fikriyya, 1943–1977* [*Kamal Junblat:*

An Intellectual Biography, 1943–1977]. Introduction by Khalil Ahmad Khalil. Beirut, 1980.

Sultan al-Atrash

Abu Hassun, Ahmad. *Nisr al-Jabal: Min Hayat al-Batal Sultan Basha al-Atrash* [*The Mountain's Eagle: From the Life of the Hero Sultan al-Atrash*]. Damascus, 1985.

B'ayni, Hasan Amin. *Sultan al-Atrash: Masirat Qa'id fi Tarikh Ummah* [*Sultan al-Atrash: The March of a Leader in the History of a Nation*]. Beirut, 1985.

Shufi, Nazih al-. *Sultan al-Atrash: Sayf 'Arabi min Tanukh* [*Sultan al-Atrash: An Arab Sword from Tanukh*]. Damascus, 1993.

Thabit, Karim Khalil. *Al-Duruz wal-Thawra al-Suriyya wa-Sirat Sultan al-Atrash* [*The Druzes, the Syrian Revolt, and the Biography of Sultan al-Atrash*]. Cairo, 1925.

HISTORY, FAITH, AND SOCIETY

General

'Abd al-Khaliq, Nayif. *Shama'il al-Muslimin al-Duruz wa-Dala'il al-Ayat wal-Rumuz* [*Muslim Druzes and the Keys to Verses and Symbols*]. Dayr Qubayl, Lebanon, 1993.

Abu Ghanim, Shafiq. *Al-Tawhid* [*Unitarianism*]. 2nd ed. N.p., 1989.

Abu Hamdan, Taysir. *Al-Duruz, Maslakan wa-Mu'taqadan* [*The Druzes, Path and Faith*]. Amman, 1995.

Abu al-Husn, Sa'id. *Banu Ma'ruf Bayna al-Sayf wal-Qalam* [*Sons of Mercy between the Sword and the Pen*]. Suwayda, n.d.

Abu-Isma'il, Salim. *Al-Duruz: Wujudahum wa-Madhhabahum wa-Tawatunahum* [*The Druzes: Their Existence, Sect, and Settlement*]. Beirut, 1954.

Abu Izzeddin, Nejla M. *The Druzes: A New Study of Their History, Faith, and Society*. Leiden: Brill, 1984, 1993.

Abu Salih, Abbas, and Sami Makarem. *Tarikh al-Muwahhidin al-Duruz al-Siyasi fil-Mashriq al-'Arabi* [*The Political History of the Druzes in the Arab East*]. Beirut, 1981.

'Assrauy, Najib. *Al-Madhhab al-Tawhidi al-Durzi* [*The Druze Unitarian Sect*]. 2nd ed. Brazil, n.d.

———. *O Druzismo* [*The Druzes*]. Belo Horizonte, 1967.

A'war, Saji' Yusuf. *Al-Ahkam Al-Shar'iyyah wal-Qanuniyyah fil-Wasiyyah wal-Zawaj wal-Talaq 'Inda al-Duruz* [*Religious Laws regarding Wells, Marriage, and Divorce among the Druzes*]. Beirut, 1989.

———. *Al-Ahwal al-Shakhziyah al-Durziyah* [*Druze Family Law*]. Beirut, 1983.

Betts, Robert Brenton. *The Druze*. New Haven, Conn.: Yale University Press, 1988.

Bradford, Gamaliel. *The Return of the Druses*. New York, 1897.

Branca, Paolo. "More Details and Typologies of the Druze Manuscripts in European Libraries." *Journal of Druze Studies*, 2001, 1–30.

———. "Origins and Diffusion of the So-Called Druze Manuscripts in European Libraries." *Journal of Druze Studies*, 2000, 95–110.

Bryer, David. "The Origins of the Druze Religion." *Der Islam* 52 (1975): 47–84.

———. "The Origins of the Druze Religion." *Der Islam* 53 (1976): 4–27.

Busch, Moritz. *Drusen und Derwische [Druzes and Dervishes]*. Munich: Arbeitsgemeinschaft für Religions- und Weltanshaungsfragen, n.d.

Committee on Religous Affairs. *The Tawhid Faith*. Knoxville, Tenn.: ADS, 1996.

———. *The Tawhid Faith: Ethics and Morality*. Knoxville, Tenn.: ADS, 1987.

———. *The Tawhid Faith: Stories, Lessons, and Prayers*. Edited by Wahbah A. Sayegh. Knoxville, Tenn.: ADS, 1983.

———. *The Tawhid Faith: Theosophical Foundations*. Knoxville, Tenn.: ADS, 1985.

Dana, Nissim. *The Druze in the Middle East: Their Faith, Leadership, Identity and Status*. Brighton, UK: Sussex Academic Press, 2003.

Dhubyan, Jamil. *Islamiyat al-Muwahhidin al-Duruz: Falsafah, Din, wa-Dunya [The Islamicness of the Druzes: Philosophy, Religion, and Politics]*. N.p., 1992.

Dubaysi, Yusef Salim. *Ahl al-Tawhid: Al-Duruz wa-Khasa'is Madhhabihim al-Diniyah wal-Ijtima'iyah [The People of Unitarianism: The Druzes and the Religious and Social Characteristics of Their Sect]*. 5 vols. Suwayda, Syria, 1992.

Dupont, Marie. *Les Druzes [The Druzes]*. Paris, 1994.

Firro, Kais. *A History of the Druzes*. Leiden: Brill, 1992.

———. "Political Behavior of the Druze as a Minority in the Middle East: A Historical Perspective." *Orients* 27 (September 1986): 463–479.

Florsheim, Paul, and David Gutmann. "Mourning the Loss of Self as Father: A Longitudinal Study of Fatherhood among the Druze." *Psychiatry: Interpersonal and Biological Processes* 55 (May 1992): 160–177.

Ghayth, Shaykh Bahjat. *Fi Ma'arij al-Ruh [In the Ascents of the Soul]*. Beirut, 1997.

Govinda, Dhira dasa. *Krishna, Israel and the Druze: An Interreligious Odyssey*. N.p.: Vedic College Press, 1994.

Guys, Henri. *La Nation Druse [The Druze Nation]*. Paris, 1863; Amsterdam, 1979.

———. *Théogonie des Druzes, ou abrégé de leur système religieux [The Theogony of the Druzes, or a Summary of Their Religious System]*. Paris, 1863.

Habiqa, Butrus. "Tanasur al-Umara' al-Lam'iyyin al-Matniyyin" [The Conversion to Christianity of the Lam' Princes from the Matn Region]. *Al-Mashriq* 19 (1920).

Hakki, Ismail Izmirli. *Durzi Mezhebi [The Druze Sect]*. Istanbul, 1926.

Hasr al-Litham 'an Nakabat al-Sham: Fil-Isma'iliyin wal-Duruz [On Isma'ilis and Druzes]. Beirut: Dar Lahd Khatir, 1985.

Hichchi, Selim Hassan. *La Communauté Druze: Son Origine et son Histoire* [*The Druze Community, Its Origin and History*]. Beirut, 1973.

Hitti, Philip K. *The Origins of the Druze People and Religion, with Extracts from Their Sacred Writings*. New York: Columbia University Press, 1928.

Husayn, Muhammad Kamil. *Ta'ifat al-Duruz: Tarikhuha wa-'Aqa'iduha* [*The Druze Sect: Its History and Beliefs*]. Cairo, 1968.

'Israwi, Najib. *Al-Madhhab al-Tawhidi al-Durzi* [*The Druze Unitarian Sect*]. N.p., n.d.

Karami, Nawwaf. *Safahat Mudi'ah min Tarikh Bani Ma'ruf* [*Highlighted Chapters in the History of the Sons of Mercy*]. Beirut, 1993.

Khatib, M.A. *'Aqidat al-Duruz: 'Ard wa-Naqd* [*The Druze Faith: Exposition and Refutation*]. Amman, 1980.

Layish, Aharon. *Marriage, Divorce and Succession in the Druze Family*. Leiden: Brill, 1982.

Makarem, Sami Nasib. *Adwa' 'ala Maslak al-Tawhid al-Durziyah* [*Lights on the Path of the Druze Faith*]. Introduced by Kamal Junblat. Beirut, 1966.

———. *The Druze Faith*. Delmar, N.Y.: Karavan Books, 1974.

———. *Maslak al-Tawhid* [*The Path of Unitarianism*]. Beirut, 1980.

Misri, Muhammad al-. *Al-Dawlah al-Durziyyah* [*The Druze State*]. Damascus, 1984.

Moukarim, Moustafa F. *Faith of the Druze: Simplified for the Youth*. N.p., n.d.

Najjar, 'Abd Allah al-. *Madhhab al-Duruz wal-Tawhid* [*The Druze Sect and Unitarianism*]. Cairo, 1965.

Nakadi, 'Arif al-, et al. *Al-Waqi' al-Durzi wa-Hatmiyat al-Tatawwur* [*The Druze Condition and the Necessity for Development*]. Beirut, 1962.

Nasr, Mursal. *Al-Muwahhidun al-Duruz fil-Islam* [*The Unitarian Druzes in Islam*]. Beirut, 1996.

Nasr, Mursal, and Halim Taqi al-Din. *Al-Wasiyah wal-Mirath 'Inda al-Muwahhidin al-Duruz* [*Wills and Inheritance among Unitarian Druzes*]. Beirut, 1983.

Nimr, 'Abd al-Mun'im al-. *Al-Shi'ah, al-Mahdi, al-Duruz: Tarikh wa-Watha'iq* [*The Shi'a, the Messiah, and the Druzes: History and Documents*]. Cairo: Dar al-Hurriyah, 1987.

Perillier, Louis. *Les Druzes* [*The Druzes*]. Paris, 1986.

Qanun al-Ahwal al-Shakhsiyah lil-Ta'ifah al-Durziyah fi Isra'il [*Family Law among the Druze Sect in Israel*]. Jerusalem, 1964.

Rose, G. H., Sir. *The Afghans, the Ten Tribes, and the Kings of the East, the Moabites, the Druses, the Early Spread of Circumcision*. London: Hatchards, 1852.

Sa'b, Afifa. *Al-Duruz wa-Hatmiyat al-Tatawwur* [*The Druzes and the Necessity for Development*]. Beirut, n.d.

Sa'di, Nabih Muhammad al-. *Madhhab al-Tawhid (al-Durziyya) fi Maqalat 'Ashr* [*The Unitarian Druze Sect in Ten Articles*]. Damascus, 1994.

———. *Al-Muwahhidun al-Duruz* [*The Druze Unitarians*]. Damascus, 1995.

————. *Sifr al-Takwin al-Falsafi fi Madhhab al-Muwahhidin* [*The Book of Creation in the Tawhid Sect*]. Damascus, 1993.

Sa'igh, Nabil al-Zawahirah. *Mawsu'at al-Ahwal al-Shakhsiyah li-Jami' al-Madhahib wal-Adyan fi Suriyah, al-Urdun, wa-Lubnan* [*Family Law among All the Sects and Religions in Syria, Jordan, and Lebanon*]. Damascus, [1983?].

Salih, Shakib. *Toldot ha-Druzim* [*History of the Druzes*]. Ramat Gan, Israel, 1989.

Salman, Tawfiq. *Adwa' 'ala Tarikh Madhhab al-Tawhid* [*Lights on the History of the Sect of Unitarianism*]. Beirut, 1963.

Sghayar, Sa'id al-. *Banu Ma'ruf fil-Tarikh* [*Sons of Mercy in History*]. Al-Qrayah, Syria, 1984.

Silvestre de Sacy, Antoine Isaac. *Exposé de la Religion des Druzes* [*Exposition of the Religion of the Druzes*]. 2 vols. Paris, 1838, 1964; Amsterdam, 1964.

Swayd, Samy. "Rethinking Druze Historiography." *Journal of Druze Studies* 1 (2000): 111–147.

Tali', Amin. *Asl al-Muwwahhidin al-Duruz wa-Usulahum* [*The Origin of the Druzes and Their Roots*]. Introduced by Maroun 'Abboud. Beirut, 1961.

————. *Mashyakhat al-'Aql wal-Qada' al-Madhhabi al-Durzi 'Abra al-Tarikh* [*The Druze Spiritual Leadership and the Druze Legal Code throughout History*]. Beirut, 1971.

Taqi al-Din, Halim. *Al-Ahwal al-Shakhsiyyah 'inda al-Duruz* [*Druze Family Law*]. Beirut, 1981.

————. *Qada' al-Muwahhidin al-Duruz fi Madihi wa-Hadirihi* [*The Druze Unitarian Legal System in Its Past and Present*]. Beirut, 1979.

Taqi al-Din, Riyad Hamid. *Al-Tajribah al-'Askariyah al-Durziyah wa-Masaruha al-Taqaddumi* [*The Druze Military Experience and Its Progressive Path*]. Beirut, 1987.

Zahr al-Din, Salih. *Tarikh al-Muslimin al-Muwahhidin "al-Duruz"* [*History of the Muslim Unitarian "Druzes"*]. Introduced by Mursal Nasr. Beirut, 1991.

Zayn al-Din, 'Abd Allah Yusef. *Kitab Maftuh: Al-Radd 'ala al-Katib Anis Mansur* [*An Open Letter: A Response to the Writer Anis Mansur*]. Damascus, 1990.

Zenner, Walter, and Maurice Richter. "The Druzes as a Divided Minority Group." *Journal of Asian and African Studies* 7 (Summer 1972).

Zu'bi, Muhammad 'Ali al-. *Al-Duruz: Zahiruhum wa-Batinahum* [*The Druzes: Their Exoteric and Esoteric Dimensions*]. Beirut, 1956, 1972.

Syria and Lebanon

Abi Rashid, Hanna. *Hawran al-Damiyah* [*Bloody Hawran*]. Beirut, 1926, 1961.

————. *Jabal al-Duruz: Bahth 'Amm* [*The Druze Mountain: A General Study*]. Cairo, 1925.

Abkaryus, Iskander ibn Ya'qub. *The Lebanon in Turmoil, Syria and the Power in 1860*. Translated and annotated by J. F. Scheltema. New Haven, Conn., 1920.

————. *The Massacre of Mount Lebanon*. N.p., 1877.

———. *Nawadir al-Zaman fi Waqa'i' Jabal Lubnan* [*Stories from the Past in regard to the Events of Mount Lebanon*]. Edited by 'Abd al-Karim Ibrahim al-Sammak. London, 1987.

Abraham, Antoine J. *Lebanon at Mid-Century: Maronite-Druze Relations in Lebanon, 1840–1860: A Prelude to Arab Nationalism*. Washington, D.C., 1975, 1981.

Abu Izzeddin, Sulayman. *Ibrahim Pasha fi Suriya* [*Ibrahim Pasha in Syria*]. Beirut, 1929.

Abu Khalil, As'ad. "Druze, Sunni and Shiite Political Leadership in Present-Day Lebanon." *American Sociological Quarterly*, Fall 1985, 28–58.

———. "Ottoman Reform and the Politics of Notables." In *The Beginnings of Modernization in the Middle East*, edited by W. R. Polk and R. Chambers, 46–63. Chicago, 1968.

Abu Salih, Abbas. *Al-Azamah al-Lubnaniyya 'Am 1958* [*The Lebanese Crisis of 1958*]. Beirut, 1998.

Abu Salih, Abbas, and Sami Makarem. *Al-Tarikh al-Siyasi lil-Imara al-Shihabiyya fi Jabal Lubnan 1697–1842* [*The Political History of the Shihabi Emirate in Mount Lebanon 1697–1842*]. Beirut, 1984.

Abu Shaqra, Husayn Ghadban. *Al-Harakat fi Lubnan ila 'Ahd al-Mutassarrifiyah* [*The Movements in Lebanon up to the Era of the Mutassarrifiyah*]. Edited by 'Arif Abu Shaqra. Beirut, 1952.

'Alamuddin, Nura S., and Paul D. Starr. *Crucial Bonds: Marriage among the Lebanese Druze*. Delmar, N.Y., 1980.

Ali, Muhamad Kurd. "Jabal al-Duruz wa-Fitanihi" [The Druze Mountain and Its Revolts]. *Al-Muqtabas* 5 (1910): 242–250.

'Ammar, Yahya Husain. *Tarikh Wadi al-Taym wal-Aqalim al-Mujawirah* [*The History of Wadi al-Taym and the Surrounding Regions*]. Yanta, 1985.

Andrea, General. *Thawrat al-Duruz wa-Tamarrud Dimashq* [*The Druze Rebellion and the Revolt in Damascus*]. Translated from the French by Hafiz Abu Muslim. Beirut, 1971.

Andrew, Christopher, and A. S. Kanya-Forstner. *France Overseas: The Great War and the Climax of French Imperial Expansion*. London, 1981.

Armanazi, N. *Suriya min al-Ihtilal Hatta al-Jala'* [*Syria: From Occupation to Independence*]. Beirut, 1973.

'Aysami, Shibli. *Muhafazat al-Suwayda* [*The District of Suwayda*]. Damascus, 1962.

B'ayni, Hasan Amin. *Duruz Suriyah wa-Lubnan fi 'Ahd al-Intidab al-Faransi, 1920–1943* [*The Druzes of Syria and Lebanon during the French Mandate, 1920–1943*]. Beirut, 1993.

———. *Jabal al-'Arab, 1685–1927* [*The Arab Mountain, 1685–1927*]. Beirut, 1985.

Ben Dor, Gabriel. "Levanon: Hitporirotah Shel Medinah" [Lebanon: The Disintegration of a Nation]. In *Lebanon: War And Reconstruction*, edited by Itamar Rabinovich, 35–44. Haifa: Institute of Middle Eastern Studies, Occasional Papers on the Middle East no. 4, 1982.

Bokova, Lenka. *La Confrontation Franco-Syrienne à l'Epoque du Mandat, 1925–1927* [*The French-Syrian Confrontation during the Mandate Era, 1925–1927*]. Paris, 1990.

Chamie, Joseph. "Religious Groups in Lebanon: Descriptive Investigation." *International Journal of Middle Eastern Studies* 11 (April 1980): 175–187.

Chasseaud, George Washington. *The Druzes of the Lebanon: Their Manners, Customs and History, with a Translation of Their Religious Code*. London, 1855.

Churchhill, C. *The Druzes and the Maronites under the Turkish Rule from 1840–1960*. London, 1862.

Cooper, Monica. *Impressions of Syria, Lebanon, Alouite State, and Djebel Druze*. Beirut: Imprimerie Catholique, 1932.

Deeb, Maurice K. "Lebanon: Prospects for National Reconciliation in the Mid-1980s." *Middle East Journal* 38 (Spring 1984): 267–283.

Dimashqi, Mikhael. *Tarikh Hawadith al-Sham wa-Lubnan* [*History of the Events of Syria and Lebanon*]. Edited by Ahmad Sabanu. Damascus, 1981.

Doolittle, George Curtis. *Druzes of Syria: Their Relation to Christianity and Islam*. N.p., n.d.

Drysdale, Alasdair. "The Syrian Political Elite, 1966–1976: A Spatial and Social Analysis." *Middle Eastern Studies* 17 (January 1981): 3–30.

Dubois, T. *Des Populations du Liban, et Principalement des Druses* [*Of the Populations of Lebanon and Mainly of the Druzes*]. Paris, 1860.

Firro, Kais. "Hadruzim be-Levanon: me-'Imda Dominantit le-Ma'vak 'Al Kium" [The Druzes in Lebanon: From a Dominant Stance to a Struggle for Existence]. In *Lebanon: War and Reconstruction*, edited by Itamar Rabinovich, 27–34. Haifa: Institute of Middle Eastern Studies, Occasional Papers on the Middle East no. 4, 1982.

———. "The Druze in and between Syria, Lebanon and Israel." In *Ethnicity, Pluralism and the State in the Middle East*, edited by Milton J. Esman and Itamar Rabinovich, 185–197. Ithaca, N.Y.: Cornell University Press, 1988.

———. "Silk and Agrarian Changes in Lebanon, 1860–1914." *International Journal of Middle Eastern Studies* 22 (May 1990): 151–169.

Hamzeh, Nadim Nayif. *Al-Tanukhiyyun Ajdadu al-Muwahhidin (al-Duruz) wa-Dawrahum fi Jabal Lubnan* [*The Tanukhis, Ancestors of Unitarians (the Druzes) and Their Role in Mount Lebanon*]. Beirut, 1984.

Harik, Iliya. "Iqta' System in Lebanon: A Comparative Political View." *Middle East Journal* 9 (Autumn 1965): 405–421.

Harik, Judith P. "Change and Continuity among the Lebanese Druze Community—The Civil Administration of the Mountains, 1983–90." *Middle Eastern Studies* 29 (July 1993): 377–398.

———. "Perceptions of Community and State among Lebanon Druze Youth." *Middle East Journal* 47 (Winter 1993): 41–62.

————. "Shaykh al-'Aql and the Druze of Mount-Lebanon—Conflict and Accommodation." *Middle East Studies* 30 (July 1994): 461–485.

Hichchi, Salim Hassan. *Duruz Bayrut: Tarikhahum wa-Ma'asihum [The Druzes of Beirut: Their History and Hardships]*. Beirut, 1985.

Hourani, Albert. *Syria and Lebanon: A Political Essay*. London, 1954.

Huxley, Frederick Charles. *Wasita in Lebanese Context: Social Exchange among Villagers and Outsiders*. Ann Arbor, Mich., 1978.

Joseph, Suad, and Barbara Pillsbury, eds. *Muslim-Christian Conflicts: Economic, Political, and Social Origins*. Dawson, Colo.: Westview Press, 1978.

Kennedy, Scott R. "The Druze of the Golan: A Case of Non-Violent Resistance." *Journal of Palestine Studies*, Winter 1984, 48–64.

Khalidi, Ahmad Ibn Muhammad al-Safadi. *Lubnan fi 'Ahd al-Amir Fakhr al-Din al-Ma'ni al-Thani [Lebanon during the Reign of Fakhr al-Din al-Ma'ni II]*. Beirut, 1969.

Khoury, Philip S. *Syria and the French Mandate: The Politics of Arab Nationalism, 1920–1945*. Princeton, N.J., 1989.

Lapp, John A. "Non-Violent Protest in the Golan Heights." *Christian Century*, August 4–11, 1982, 813–814.

Makarem, Sami Nasib. "Al-Tanukhiyyun wa-Dawrahum al-Siyasi fil-Jabal al-Lubnani" [The Tanukhis and their Political Role in Mount Lebanon]. *Al-Duha*, June 1995, 60–63.

Makaryus, Shahin. *Madhbahat al-Jabal [The Mountain's Massacre]*. Beirut, 1987.

Ma'luf, I. "Duruz Hawran wa-Harb Ibrahim Pasha" [The Druzes of Hawran and the War against Ibrahim Pasha]. *Majallat al-Muqtataf* 67 (May 1935): 497–503.

————. "Duruz Hawran wa-Ibrahim Pasha" [The Druzes of Hawran and Ibrahim Basha]. *Majallat al-Muqtataf* 68 (May 1926): 556–558.

————. "Tanasur al-Umara' al-Shihabiyyin wal-Lam'iyin Fi Lubnan" [The Conversion to Christianity of the Princes of Shihab and Lam']. *Al-Mashriq* 18 (1920).

Mar'i, Tayseer, and Usama Halabi. "Life under Occupation in the Golan Heights." *Journal of Palestine Studies* 22 (Autumn 1992): 78–93.

Mundhir, Nawfal. "Al-Julan: Al-Ard wal-Sukkan" [The Golan Heights: Land and Population]. *Al-Duha* (July 1995): 72–75.

————. "Al-Julan: Ard al-Butulat" [The Golan Heights: The Land of Heroism]. *Al-Duha*, March 1995, 60–62.

Murad, Muhammad. "Al-Mu'athir al-'Urubi fil-Tashakul al-Ijtima'i fi Bilad al-Sham" [The Arabist Influence in the Social Formation of Syria]. *Majallat al-Muntalaq* (Beirut) 81–82 (1991): 85–124.

Najjar, 'A'idah. *Al-Taqlid wal-Tajdid fil-Musahamat al-Nisa'iyah al-Durziyah khilal al-Harb al-Ahliyah fi Jabal Lubnan, 1975–1990 [Old and New in Druze Women Participation during the Civil War in Mount Lebanon]*. Beirut: Dar al-Malak, 1997.

Najjar, 'Abd Allah al-. *Banu Ma'ruf fi Jabal Hawran* [*Druzes in the Hawran Mountain*]. Damascus, 1924.

Puget de Saint-Pierre, M. *Histoire des Druses* [*History of the Druzes*]. Paris, 1763.

Qatmah, Muhammad Khalid. *Qisat al-Dawlatayn al-Maruniyyah wal-Durziyyah* [*The Story of the Maronite and Druze States*]. Beirut, 1985.

Richani, Nazih. "The Druze of Mount Lebanon: Class Formation in a Civil War." *Middle East Report*, January–February 1990, 26–30.

Sa'b, Mahmud Khalil. *Qisas wa-Mashahid min Jabal Lubnan* [*Stories and Scenes from the Lebanese Mountain*]. Beirut, 1980.

Sa'id, 'Abd Allah. *Tatawwur al-Malakiyah al-'Aqariyah fi Jabal Lubnan fi 'Ahd al-Mutassarrifiyah* [*The Development of Landed Property Ownership in Mt. Lebanon during the Mutassarrifiyah Rule*]. Beirut, 1986.

Salibi, Kamal. "The Buhturids of the Gharb, Medieval Lords of Beirut and Southern Lebanon." *Arabica* 8 (1961).

Salih, Shakib. "The British-Druze Connection and the Druze Rising of 1896 in the Hawran." *Middle East Studies* 13 (1977): 251–257.

Schmucker, Werner. *Krise und Erneuerung im Libanesischen Drusentum* [*Crisis and Renewal of Lebanese Druzism*]. Bonn, 1979.

Seale, Patrick. *The Struggle for Syria: A Study of Postwar Arab Politics, 1945–1958*. New Haven, Conn., 1986.

Swayd, Yasin. *Al-Tarikh al-'Askari lil-Muqata'at al-Lubnaniyya* [*The Military History of the Lebanese Provinces*]. Beirut, 1980.

Sweet, Louise. "Visiting Patterns and Social Dynamics in a Lebanese Druze Village." *Anthropological Quarterly* 47 (January 1974): 112–119.

Tarabieh, Bashar. "Education, Control and Resistance in the Golan Heights." *Middle East Report*, May–August 1995.

Touma, Toufic. *Paysans et Institutions Féodales chez les Druses et les Maronites du Liban du XVIIe siècle à 1914* [*Peasants and Feudal Institutions of the Druzes and Maronites in Lebanon from the 17th Century to 1914*]. Beirut, 1986.

Ziade, Nicolas. *Lubnaniyat: Tarikh wa-Suwar* [*"Lebaneseness": History and Images*]. London, 1992.

Palestine and Israel

Atashi, Zeidan. *Druze and Jews in Israel*. Brighton, UK, 1995.

Ben-Dor, Gabriel. *The Druzes in Israel, a Political Study: Political Innovation and Integration in a Middle Eastern Minority*. Jerusalem, 1979.

———. "Intellectuals in Israeli Druze Society." In *Palestine and Israel in the 19th and 20th Century*, edited by Elie Kedourie and Sylvia Haim, 229–254. London: Frank Cass and Comp. Ltd, 1982.

———. "The Military in the Politics of Integration and Innovation: The Case of the Druze Minority in Israel." *African and Asian Studies*, 1973, 339–369.

Ben-Zvi, Itzhak. *The Druze Community in Israel*. Jerusalem, 1954.

Blanc, Haim. *Ha-Druzim* [*The Druzes*]. Jerusalem, 1938.

———. *Studies in North Palestinian Arabic: Linguistic Inquiries among the Druzes of Western Galilee and Mount Carmel*. Jerusalem, 1953.

Doron, Pninah. *Ha-'Aravim, ha-Druzim, veha-Bedvim bi-Medinat Yisra'el* [*The Arabs, the Druzes, and the Bedouins in the State of Israel*]. Merhaviah, 1977.

Edelman, Martin. "The Druze Courts in the Political System of Israel." *Middle East Review* 19 (Summer 1987): 54–61.

Falah, Salman Hammud. *Toldot Hadruzim bi-Yisra'el* [*The History of the Druzes in Israel*]. Jerusalem, 1974.

Faraj, Raja Sa'id. *Duruz Falastin fi Fatrat al-Intidab al-Baritani* [*The Druzes of Palestine during the British Mandate*]. Daliyat al-Carmel, Israel, 1991.

Faraj, Salman. *Al-Rabitah al-Durziyah al-Isra'iliyah* [*The Israeli Druze Association*]. Acre, 1967.

Firro, Kais. *The Druzes in the Jewish State*. Leiden: Brill, 1999.

Friendly, Alfred, and Eric Silver. *Israel's Oriental Immigrants and Druzes*. London, 1972, 1981.

Frisch, Hillel. "The Druze Minority in the Israeli Millitary: Traditionalizing an Ethnic Policing Role." *Armed Forces and Society* 20 (Fall 1993): 51–67.

Gelber, Yoav. "Antecedents of the Jewish-Druze Alliance in Palestine." *Middle East Studies* 28 (April 1992): 352–373.

———. "Druze and Jews in the War of 1948." *Middle East Studies* 31 (April 1995): 229–252.

Gharizi, Wafiq. *Mu'anat al-Muwahhidin al-Duruz fil-Aradi al-Muhtallah* [*The Suffering of Druzes in the Occupied Lands*]. Beirut, 1984.

Granot, Yigal. *Ha-Druzim* [*The Druzes*]. Tel-Aviv, 1982.

Haberfeld, Ednah. *Sajur: Seker Demografi, Hevrati, Kalkali* [*Sajur: A Demographic, Social, and Economic Survey*]. Haifa, 1973.

Hajjar, Lisa. "Israel's Interventions among the Druze." *Middle East Report*, July–September 1996, 2–6, 10.

Halabi, Rafiq. "Israel Minority in the Middle." *New York Times Magazine*, December 27, 1981, 14–17, 30.

———. *The West Bank Story: An Israeli Arab's View of Both Sides of the Tangled Conflict*. Translated from the Hebrew by Ina Friedman. New York, 1985.

———. *Yesh Gvul: Sipur ha-Gadah ha-Ma'ravit* [*There Is a Limit: The West Bank Story*]. Translated by Ya'el Hen. Jerusalem: Keter, 1983.

Halabi, Usama. *Al-Duruz fi Isra'il: Min Ta'ifa ila Sha'b* [*The Druzes in Israel: From a Sect to a People*]. N.p., 1989.

Har-El, Menashe. *Yanuh: Kfar Druzi ba-Galil* [*Yanuh: A Druze Village in Galilee*]. Jerusalem, 1959.

Hayik, Tsvi, et al. *Ha-Chaverim ha-'Aravim veha-Druzim ba-Histadrut* [*The Arab and Druze Members in the Histadrut*]. Tel Aviv: al-Niqabah al-'Ammah lil-'Ummal fi Israel, 1989.

Mayer, Egon. "Becoming Modern in Bayt al-Shabab." *Middle East Journal* 29 (Summer 1975): 279–294.

———. "The Druze of Bet Jann: Modernization and the Activation of Minorities In Israel." *Middle East Review*, Winter 1976/1977, 16–29.

Natur, Salman. *Ta'ifa fi Bayt al-Nar* [*A Sect in the House of Fire*]. Shafa 'Amr: al-Mashriq, 1995.

Parsons, Laila. *The Druze between Palestine and Israel, 1947–49*. New York: St. Martin's Press, 2000.

———. "The Palestinian Druze in the 1947–1949 Arab-Israeli War." In *Nationalism, Minorities and Diasporas: Identities and Rights in the Middle East*, edited by Kirsten E. Schulze, Martin Stokes, and Colm Campbell, 144–157. London: I. B. Tauris Publishers, 1996.

Qasim, Nabih. *Al-Duruz fi Isra'il* [*The Druzes in Israel*]. Haifa: al-Wadi, 1995.

Sherman, Arnold. *The Druse*. Tel Aviv, 1975.

Shidlowsky, Benjamin. *Ha-Yishuvim ha-'Arviyim veha-Druziyim bi-Yisra'el* [*Arab and Druze Settlements in Israel*]. Jerusalem, 1969.

Stendel, Uri. *Ha-'Aravim veha-Druzim bi-Yisra'el* [*The Arabs and the Druzes in Israel*]. Jerusalem, 1980.

———. *The Minorities in Israel: Trends in the Development of the Arab and Druze Communities 1948–1973*. Jerusalem, 1973.

Teitelbaum, Joshua. "Ideology and Conflict in a Middle Eastern Minority: The Case of the Druze Initiative Committee in Israel." *Orient* 26 (September 1985): 341–359.

Vilnay, Zev. *Minorities in Israel: Moslems, Christians, Druzes, Baha'is*. Jerusalem, 1959.

Wasserstein, David. *The Druzes and Circassians of Israel*. London, 1976.

Yanai, Amnon. *Ha'idah Ha-Druzit* [*The Druze Sect*]. Haifa, 1955, 1972.

Zgaier, 'Ali. *Kfar Yerka ve-Svivato* [*The Village of Yerka and Its Surroundings*]. Haifa, 1993.

Diaspora

Adeney, Miriam, and Kathryn DeMaster. "Muslims In Seattle." In *Muslim Communities in North America*, edited by Yvonne Yazbeck Haddad and Jane Idelman Smith, 195–205. Albany: State University of New York Press, 1994.

Azzam, Intisar J. *Change for Continuity: The Druze in America*. Beirut: M.A.J.D., 1997.

Beynon, E. D. "The Near East in Flint, Michagan: Assyrians and Druze and their Antecedents." *Geographical Review* 24 (January 1944): 234–274.

Hadad, Y. Y., and J. I. Smith. "The Druze in North America." *Muslim World* 81 (April 1991): 111–132.

Hamady, Walter. *The Quartz Crystal History of Perry Township since the Earliest*

Creation of Life: Being an Eye Witness Account of the First Druze Settler to Show Up in Driftless Wisconsin. Mt. Horeb, Wis.: Perishable Press, 1979.

LANGUAGE, ART, AND LITERATURE

Abu 'Asali, Najib. "Al-Ughniya al-Sha'biyya fi Muhafazat al-Suwayda" [The Folk Song in the Suwayda District]. *Al-Duha*, 1994, 56–59.

Atrash, Shibli al-. *Diwan fi al-Shuruqi wal-Zajal [A Poetry Collection of Shuruqi and Zajal]*. Damascus, 1950.

Barakat, Leila. *Sous les Vignes du Pays Druze [Under the Vineyards of the Druzes]*. Paris, 1993.

Gharizi, Wafiq. "Al-Sha'ir Husain Muhana Min al-Jalil" [The Poet Husain Muhanna of Galilee]. *Al-Duha*, 1994, 60–61.

Jarrah, Nuri al-. "Samih al-Qasim: Hadhihi al-Qisah al-Kamilah le-Rihlati Ila Dimashq" [Samih al-Qasim: This Is the Complete Story of My Trip to Damascus]. *Al-Mushahid al-Siyasi*, August 1997, 16–18.

Tueni, Nadia. *Nadia Tueni: la prose (oeuvres complètes)*. Beirut, 1986.

OTHER RELATED WORKS

Dictionaries

Abu Khalil, As'ad. *Historical Dictionary of Lebanon*. Lanham, Md.: Scarecrow Press, 1998.

Commins, David. *Historical Dictionary of Syria*. Lanham, Md.: Scarecrow Press, 1996.

Gubser, Peter. *Historical Dictionary of Jordan*. Lanham, Md.: Scarecrow Press, 1991.

Reich, Bernard. *Historical Dictionary of Israel*. Lanham, Md.: Scarecrow Press, 1992.

Encyclopedias

Abbas, Ihsan. *Tarikh Bilad al-Sham min ma Qabla al-Islam hatta Bidayat al-'Asr al-Umawi, 600–661 [The History of Syria from before Islam to the Beginning of the Umayyad Era, 600–661]*. 'Amman: al-Jami'ah al-Urduniyah, 1990.

'Abd Allah, Halim. *Al-Wajh al-Akhar lil-Harb fi Lubnan: ma lam Yuktab Ba'd 'an al-Harb fi Lubnan [The Other Dimension of the War in Lebanon: What Has Not Been Written]*. N.p., 1993.

Abu 'Abd Allah, 'Abd Allah Ibrahim. *Mawsu'at Tarikh Lubnan 'Abra al-Ajyal:*

Mundhu Fajr al-Tarikh hatta al-Istiqlal [*History of Lebanon throughout the Ages: From the Beginning of History to Independence*]. N.p., 1991.

Sectarianism

Badawi, A. *Madhahib al-Islamiyyin* [*The Islamic Sects*]. 2 vols. Beirut, 1973.

Baghdadi, Abu Mansur Abd al-Qahir b. Tahir. *Al-Farq Bayna al-Firaq* [*The Difference among the Sects*]. Edited by M. Badr. Cairo, 1910.

Baydawi, Abdallah ibn Umar al-. *Anwar al-Tanzil wa-Asrar al-Ta'wil* [*The Lights of Revelation and the Secrets of Esoteric Interpretation*]. Edited by H. L. Fleisher. Leipzig, 1846–1848.

Crow, Ralph E. "Religious Sectarianism in Lebanon: Descriptive Investigation." *International Journal of Middle East Studies* 11 (April 1980): 175–187.

Makarem, Sami. "Fil-Ta'ifiyya wal-Musawat" [About Sectarianism and Equality]. *Al-Duha*, July 1995, 34–37.

Nawbakhti. *Firaq al-Shi'a* [*The Shi'i Sects*]. Edited by H. Ritter. Istanbul, 1931.

Naysaburi. *Istitar al-Imam*. Edited by W. Ivanow. Cairo, 1936.

Nu'man b. Muhammad b. Hayyun. *Da'a'im al-Islam*. Edited by A. A. Fyzee. 2 vols. Cairo, 1951.

———. *Iftitah al-Da'wa*. Edited by Wadad al-Qadi. Beirut, 1970.

———. *Ta'wil Da'a'im al-Islam*. 2 vols. Cairo, 1969.

Shahrastani, Abi al-Fath Muhammad al-. *Al-Milal wal-Nihal* [*Religions and Sects*]. Beirut, 1995.

Shak'ah, Mustafa al-. *Islam bila Madhahib* [*Islam without Sects*]. Cairo, 1961.

Yamani, Muhammad. *Kashf Asrar al-Batiniyya* [*Uncovering the Secrets of the Batiniyya*]. Baghdad, 1955.

Shi'ism and Isma'ilism

Daftary, Farhad. *The Isma'ilis: Their History and Doctrines*. Cambridge: Cambridge University Press, 1990.

Ghalib, Mustafa. *Tarikh al-Da'wa al-Isma'iliyya* [*The History of the Isma'ili Call*]. Beirut: Dar al-Andalus, 1979.

Halm, Heinz. *The Fatimids and Their Traditions of Learning*. London: I. B. Tauris and the Institute of Isma'ili Studies, 1997.

Hamdani, Abbas H. *The Beginning of the Isma'ili Da'wa in Northern India*. Cairo, 1956.

Ivanow, W. *The Alleged Founder of Isma'ilism*. Bombay, 1964.

———. *Isma'ili Traditions concerning the Rise of the Fatimids*. Oxford, 1942.

Kirmani, Ahmad Hamid al-Din al-. *Majmu'at Rasa'il al-Kirmani* [*The Collection of al-Kirmani's Letters*]. Edited by Mustafa Ghalib. Beirut: al-Mu'assassah al-Jami'iyyah lil-Dirasat wal-Nashr, 1987.

———. *Rahat al-'Aql*. Edited by M. Ghalib. Beirut, 1983.

Kurd, 'Ali. *Khitat al-Sham*. 3rd ed. 6 vols. Damascus, 1983.

Lewis, Bernard. *The Origins of Isma'ilism*. Cambridge: Heffer and Sons, 1940.

———. *The Origins of Isma'ilism: A Study of the Historical Background of the Fatimid Caliphate*. Cambridge: Heffer and Sons, 1940.

Makarem, Sami Nasib. *The Doctrine of the Isma'ilis*. Beirut, 1972.

———. "Isma'ili and Druze Cosmology in Relation to Plotinus and Aristotle." In *Islamic Theology and Philosophy: Studies in Honor of George Hourani*, edited by Michael Marmura, 81–91. Albany: State University of New York Press, 1984.

———. *The Political Doctrine of the Isma'ilis: The Imamate*. Delmar, N.Y., 1977.

———. *Al-Taqiyya fil-Islam* [*Dissimulation in Islam*]. London: Druze Heritage Foundation, 2004.

Vatikiotis, P. J. *The Fatimid Theory of State*. Lahore, 1957.

Walker, Paul E. *Early Philosophical Shi'ism: The Isma'ili Neoplatonism of Abu Ya'qub al-Sijistani*. Cambridge: Cambridge University Press, 1993.

———. "The Isma'ili Da'wa in the Reign of the Fatimid Caliph al-Hakim." *Journal of the American Research Center in Egypt* 30 (1993): 161–182.

Yamani, Muhammad. *Kashf Asrar al-Batiniyya*. Baghdad, 1955.

Taqamus (Metempsychosis, Reincarnation)

Abu Shaqra, Samir. "Hakadha Fahima Suqrat Falsafat al-Taqamus wal-Tawhid" [This Is How Socrates Understood the Philosophy of Metempsychosis and Unitarianism]. *Al-Duha*, May 1997, 65–71.

'Ammar, Shawqi. "Al-Taqamus fil-Anajil" [Metempsychosis In The Gospels]. *Al-Duha*, June 1995, 83–85

A'war, Sami Salman al-. "Al-Taqamus" [Metempsychosis]. *Al-Duha*, June 1997, 67–68.

Daie, N. E., M. Mark Witztum, and S. Rabinowitz. "The Belief in the Transmigration of Souls—Psychotherapy of a Druze Patient with Severe Anxiety Reaction." *British Journal of Medical Psychology* 65 (June 1992): 119–130.

Ghush, Qays. *Al-Taqammus: Ahuwa Haqiqa am Khayal?* [*Metempsychosis: Is It Reality or Imagination?*]. Tripoli, Lebanon, 1991.

Head, Joseph, and S. L. Cranston, eds. *Reincarnation: An East-West Anthology*. Wheaton, Ill., 1961.

Jamal, Ibrahim Muhammad al-. *Al-Hayah Ba'da al-Mawt* [*Life after Death*]. Beirut, 1988.

Rafi', Shawqi. "Al-Hayah Ba'da al-Mawt" [Life after Death]. *Al-'Arabi*, May 1994, 78–84.

Tali', Amin. *Al-Taqammus* [*Metempsychosis*]. Paris and Beirut, 1980.

Other Sources

Akarli, Engin. *The Long Peace: Ottoman Lebanon, 1861–1920*. Berkeley: University of California Press, 1993.

Alin, Erika G. *The United States and the 1958 Lebanon Crisis: American Intervention in the Middle East*. Lanham, Md., 1994.

Antaki, Yahya ibn Sa'id al-. *Tarikh* [*History*]. Edited by L. Cheikho et al. Beirut, 1909.

Antonius, George. *The Arab Awakening: The History of the Arab Nationalist Movement*. London, 1939.

Avi-Ran, R. *The Syrian Involvement in Lebanon since 1975*. Translated from the Hebrew by David Maisel. Boulder, Colo., 1991.

Awad Abd al-Aziz, M. *Al-Idara al-'Uthmaniyya fi Wilayat Suriya 1864–1914* [*The Ottoman Administration in Syria, 1864–1914*]. Cairo, 1969.

Badawi, 'Abd al-Rahman. *Al-Aflatuniyya al-Muhdatha 'ind al-'Arab*. Cairo, 1955.

Baydun, Ahmad. *Al-Sira' 'ala Tarikh Lubnan* [*The Struggle over the History of Lebanon*]. Beirut, 1989.

Baydun, Ibrahim. *Tarikh Bilad al-Sham* [*The History of Syria*]. Beirut, 1997.

Binder, Leonard, ed. *Politics in Lebanon*. New York, 1966.

Bulloch, John. *The Death of a Country: The Civil War in Lebanon*. London, 1977.

Bustani, Butrus ibn Bulus, al-. *Nafir Suriyah* [*Syrian Inhabitants*]. Beirut, 1990.

Chamie, Joseph. *Religion and Fertility: Arab Christian-Muslim Differentials*. Cambridge, 1981.

Cobban, Helena. *The Making of Modern Lebanon*. London, 1985.

Corm, Georges. *Géopolitique du Conflict Libanaise* [*The Geopolitics of the Lebanese Conflict*]. Paris, 1987.

Davison, Roderic H. *Reform in the Ottoman Empire: 1856–1876*. Princeton, N.J., 1963.

Dawisha, Adeed I. *Syria and the Lebanese Crisis*. London, 1980.

Duwayhi, Istifan. *Tarikh al-Azmina* [*History of the Ages*]. Edited by F. Taoutel. Beirut, 1951.

Entelis, John P. *Pluralism and Party Transformation in Lebanon: Al-Kata'ib 1936–1970*. Leiden, 1974.

Esman, M. J., and Itamar Rabinovich. *Ethnicity, Pluralism, and the State in the Middle East*. Ithaca, N.Y.: Cornell University Press, 1988.

Farabi, Abu Nasr. *Ara' Ahl al-Madina al-Fadila* [*The Opinions of the Pious City*]. Edited by F. Dieterici. Leiden, 1895.

Farah, Caesar E. *The Road To Intervention: Fiscal Politics In Ottoman Lebanon*. Oxford, 1992.

Fawaz, Leila Tarazi. *Merchants and Migrants in Nineteenth Century Beirut*. Cambridge, Mass.: Harvard University Press, 1983.

———. *An Occasion for War: Civil Conflict in Lebanon and Damascus in 1860*. Berkeley: University of California Press, 1994.

Friedman, Thomas L. *From Beirut to Jerusalem*. New York, 1989.

Fyzee, 'Asaf A. A. *Compendium of Fatimid Law*. Simla, 1969.

Ghalyun, Burhan. *Hiwarat min 'Asr al-Harb al-Ahliyah [Dialogues during the Civil War]*. Beirut, 1995.

Gordon, David C. *The Republic of Lebanon: Nation in Jeopardy*. Boulder, Colo., 1983.

Haddad, George. *Fifty Years of Modern Syria and Lebanon*. Beirut, 1950.

Hanf, Theodor. *Coexistence in Wartime Lebanon: Decline of a State and Rise of a Nation*. London, 1993.

Haqqi, Isma'il. *Lubnan, Mabahith 'Ilmiyya [Lebanon, Scientific Studies]*. 2nd ed. 2 vols. Beirut, 1913, 1969–1970.

Harik, Ilya. *Lebanon: Anatomy of Conflict*. Hanover, 1981.

———. *Man Yahkumu Lubnan [Who Governs Lebanon]*. Beirut, 1972.

Hill, Gray. *With the Bedouins: A Narrative of Journeys and Adventures in Unfrequented Parts of Syria*. London, 1891.

Hitti, Philip K. *The History of the Arabs from the Earliest Times to the Present*. 9th ed. New York, 1967.

———. *History of Syria Including Lebanon and Palestine*. New York, 1961.

———. *Lebanon in History: From the Earliest Times to the Present*. London, 1957.

Hourani, Albert. *A History of the Arabs*. New York, 1991.

———. *Minorities in the Arab World*. London, 1947.

———. *Syria and Lebanon: A Political Essay*. London, 1946.

Hudson, Michael C. *The Precarious Republic: Political Modernization in Lebanon*. New York, 1968.

Ibn al-Qalanisi. *Dhayl Tarikh Dimashk*. Edited by H. F. Amedroz. Beirut, 1908.

Ibn Taghri-Birdi. *Al-Nujum al-Zahira [The Luminous Stars]*. 16 vols. Cairo, 1929–1972.

Ibn al-Walid. *A Creed of the Fatimids*. Translated by W. Ivanow. Bombay, 1936.

Ibn Yahya, Salih. *Tarikh Beirut [The History of Beirut]*. Edited by Francis Hourse and Kamal Salibi. Beirut, 1969.

Ikhwan al-Safa'. *Rasa'il [Epistles]*. Edited by Kh. Zirikli. 4 vols. Cairo, 1928.

Kerr, Malcom H., ed. and trans. *Lebanon in the Last Years of Feudalism, 1840–1868: A Contemporary Account by Antun Dahir al-'Aqiqi and Other Documents*. Beirut, 1959.

Khalaf, Samir. *Lebanon's Predicament*. New York, 1987.

———. *Persistence and Change in 19th Century Lebanon*. Beirut, 1979.

Khuri, Fuad I. *Imams and Emirs: State, Religion, and Sects in Islam*. London: Saqi Books, 1990.

Ma'arri, Abu al-'Ala. *The Letters of Abu al-'Ala of Ma'arrat al-Nu'man*. Edited and translated by D. S. Margoliouth. Oxford, 1898.

Mamour, Prince P. H. *Polemics on the Origins of the Fatimi Caliphs*. London, 1934.

Ma'oz, Moshe. *Ottoman Reform in Syria and in Palestine 1840–1861: The Impact of the Tanzimat on Politics and Society*. Oxford, 1968.

Maqrizi. *Khitat*. 4 vols. Cairo, 1906–1908.

Mishaqa, Mikha'il. *Kitab Mashhad al-A'yan bi-Hawadith Suriya wa-Lubnan [The Book of Eye-Witness of the Events in Lebanon and Syria]*. Edited by Milham Khalis Abduh and Andrawus Hanna Shakhashiri. Cairo, 1908.

————. *Murder, Mayhem, Pillage and Plunder: The History of the Lebanon in the 18th and 19th Centuries*. Translated by Wheeler M. Thackston Jr. Albany, N.Y., 1988.

Norton, Augustus Richard. *Amal and the Shi'a: Struggle for the Soul of Lebanon*. Austin, Tex., 1987.

Rabinovich, Itamar. *The War for Lebanon, 1970–1983*. Ithaca, N.Y., 1984.

Salibi, Kamal. *Crossroads to Civil War: Lebanon, 1958–1976*. Delmar, N.Y., 1976.

————. *A House of Many Mansions: The History of Lebanon Reconsidered*. Berkeley: University of California Press, 1988.

————. *A Modern History of Lebanon*. London, 1965.

Schiff, Ze'ev, and Ehud Ya'ri. *Israel's Lebanon War*. London, 1984.

Shahbander, 'Abd al-Rahman. *Al-Thawra al-Suriyya al-Wataniyya [The Syrian Nationalist Revolt]*. Damascus, 1933.

Shatzmiller, Maya, ed. *Crusaders and Muslims in Twelfth Century Syria*. Leiden, 1993.

Shehadi, Nadim, and Dana H. Mills, eds. *Lebanon: A History of Conflict and Consensus*. London, 1988.

Shidyaq, Shaykh Tannus al-. *Kitab Akhbar al-A'yan fi Jabal Lubnan [The Book of Stories in the Lebanese Mountain]*. Edited by Fouad E. Boustany. 2 vols. Beirut, 1970.

Shihabi, Amir Haydar Ahmad al-. *Lubnan fi 'Ahd al-Umara' al-Shihabiyyin [Lebanon in the Era of the Shihabi Emirs]*. Edited by Asad Rustum and Fouad E. al-Boustani. 3 vols. Beirut, 1969.

Smilianskaia, I. M. *Al-Harakat al-Fallahiyya fi Lubnan 1800–1850 [The Peasants' Movements in Lebanon, 1800–1850]*. Beirut, 1972.

Strothmann, R., ed. *Gnosis Text der Ismailiten [Gnostic Text of the Isma'ilis]*. Gottingen, 1943.

Suleiman, Michael W. *Political Parties in Lebanon: The Challenge of a Fragmented Political Culture*. Ithaca, N.Y., 1967.

Tibawi, A. L. *American Interests in Syria, 1800–1901: A Study of Educational, Literary, and Religious Work*. Oxford, 1966.

Zamir, Meir. *The Formation of Modern Lebanon*. London, 1985.

About the Author

Samy Swayd holds bachelor's degrees in business administration and political science (1981–1985) and a master's degree in international studies (1985–1987), all of which were earned at the University of Washington, Seattle. His Ph.D. is in Islamic studies (1988–1993) from the University of California, Los Angeles. His research includes a reference book titled *The Druzes: An Annotated Bibliography* (1998) and a forthcoming volume on Druze scriptural identity. In 1998, he established the Institute of Druze Studies as an academic nonprofit organization and two years later inaugurated an occasional scholarly publication, the *Journal of Druze Studies*. Swayd teaches world religions, religious diversity, and comparative mysticism at San Diego State University.